To Kno *and* To Give

Rear of the Girls' School

'The best teachers are those with a twinkle in their eye.
The memorable ones have some degree of eccentricity'

Walter Higgins
Teacher at South Wigston Secondary Modern Boys' School
1938 - 1940 and 1946 - 1951

Derek Seaton and Pamela Ward

First published in England in 2011 by South Wigston High School and Arts College.

Copyright © Derek Seaton and Pamela Ward

A CIP catalogue record for this book is available from the British Library.

ISBN 978-0-9569759-0-4

The funding for this publication has been provided by the Heritage Lottery Fund whose support and generosity is greatfully acknowledged.

Designed by Birdhouse Design Limited, Leicestershire
Telephone 01530 837333

Printed by George Street Press Limited, Stafford
Telephone 01785 258226

The schools nearing completion, August 1938
note the workmen's jackets still hanging on the railings!
(Leicester Mercury)

This book is dedicated to all pupils and teachers, past and present, of the South Wigston Secondary Modern Schools, with Intermediate Departments, and the South Wigston High School and Arts College.

Side view of the School, 2008

Acknowledgements

The authors, Pamela Ward and Derek Seaton wish to thank the following people for their invaluable help with memories, information and photographs. Certain photographs have been used from the Duncan Lucas collection which includes items from the work of the late Peter Mastin.

The authors regret that it was not possible to include many photographs relating to the latter chapters due to the relevant pictures not being available.

It has not been possible in every instant to place names to faces. We hope that the reader may identify themselves not only in the pictures but as they relate to events within the history.

Without the help of the following people this history could not have been written.

Mrs Stanley Allen
Anthony Allton
Barry Allton
Marion Baker
Anthony Ballard
Linda Bartholomew
Marion Bartholomew
Shirley Baxendale
Maurice Belben
Jean Betts
Dipan Bhagalia
Ann Bigger
David Blankley
William Blankley
Michael Booth
Eric Bothamley
Amanda Bradbury
Janet Bradley
John Breen
Dorothy Brown
June Bull
Aubrey Burl
Judith Burl
David Burley
Stephen Butt*
*Radio Leicester**
David Buswell
Nick Carter*
*Leicester Mercury**
David Cawthorn
Alan Chapman
Jean Chapman
Pauline Chapman
Doris Clements
Christine Colebourne
Jane Collins
Jack Cooper
Peter Davie
Lance Davis
Elsie Dawson
Cynthia Deakin
Samuel de Soto
Valerie de Soto
Colin Dougherty
David Dryden

Louis Duncan
Neville Duncan
Norman Durham
Susan East
John Elders
Colin Elliott
Hillary Fairbairn
Joan Falkner
Avis Fawcitt
Karen Fitchett*
*Leics County Council**
Roy Fowkes
Geoffrey Garlick
Kenneth Ginns
Adam Goodwin*
*County Record Office**
Donald E. Green
Jean Green
Jean Griffith*
*Leics County Council**
Sheila Hackett
Sidney Hales
Ann Hammonds
George Harratt
Clare Harris
Robert Hattersley
Jeremy Herbert
Mary Herbert
Peter Herbert
Valerie Herbert
Ian Higgins
David Hillsdon
Frederick Hipwell
Margaret Hipwell
Joan Hogarth
Dorothy Hollis
Peter Hollis
Lee Hoos* *Leicester City Football Club**
Derek Hubbard
Roy Hughes
Patrick Hunt
Colleen Jefford
Sylvia Jervis
Beryl Johnson

Sarah Jones*
*Leicester Mercury**
Anthony Kellett
Shirley Kendall
Christine Kenney
Mr J Kenney
Deborah Kent*
*Leics County Council**
Alan Kind MBE
Brenda Kind
Christopher Lingard
Duncan Lucas
Christopher Marsland
Colonel R. C. J. Martin OBE
Judith Matharu
Sheila Mckenley
Ann Mellor
Louis Moore
Ellen Morris
John Morse
Jean Neesham
Richard Nelson
Jenny Nixon
Graham Norris
David Nutt
Derek Ogden
Joan Pechey
John Penlington
Keith Perch*
*Leicester Mercury**
Judith Pettitt
Brenda Phillips
Rosemary Pratt
Jennifer Purkiss
John Purkiss
Dennis Rawlinson
Mr Rayner
Mrs Rayner
Charles Reeve
Joan Reeve
John Reeve
Joyce Richardson
Mary Sharman
Henrietta Schultka
Christine Sharpe

Clifford Sheppard
Roy Sherwin
Carole Shuter
Lynda Smart*
*Leicester Mercury**
Derek Smith
Shirley Smith
Frank Spencer
Sheila Strong
Anne Swierczek
Leon Taylor
Rose Taylor
Shirley Tebbs
Ann Tester
Edward Thomas
Margaret Thompson
Stephen Thompson
Stanley Tibbles
John Tipper
Gary Toward
Margaret Triggs
Meryl Wain
Sylvia Walton
Violet Ward
Carol Warrad
Ruth Warren
Sheila Bailey Watts
Joan Welsh
Peter Wheeler*
*Leicester Tigers**
Carole Williams
Isobel White* *House Of Commons Library**
Leslie Wild
Gerald Wilson
Leslie Wilson
Jean Whitehead
Beverley Whiting
Beryl Whitmore
John Whitmore
Terrence Whittaker
Ralph Willcox
Margaret Wooley
Ronald Wright
Lorraine Yates

Asterisks denote people with organisation

Contents

Front Cover: Main Pictures
South Wigston Secondary Modern Schools 1938
'Spanning the Generations'. Back Row. L to R Megan Footman, Tommy Ginns and Jessica Newland.
Front Row L to R Leslie Wild, former Deputy Headmaster, Gary L Toward, Head Teacher
and Avis Fawcitt, former Music Teacher
Foreground: Hurdler, Christine Riley

Back Cover:
The girls of South Wigston Intermediate School, 1924
The Great Bell of Burley, 1953
Dame Kelly Holmes
Kris Akabusi MBE

Foreword

South Wigston High School has been part of my life since 1993. From the moment I walked through the front door, I knew I wanted to work in the school. After two days of interviews I had earned that prize, as I was lucky enough to be chosen to be the new Deputy Head.

I was replacing Ted Thomas, who had been at the school for ages. He bequeathed to me a huge set of keys, (which I still have) to allow me into even the Caretaker's secret cupboards! Seven years later luck was on my side again, as I was also chosen to replace Eric Bothamley, who had been Head for eighteen years. I can honestly say that I have enjoyed every day that I have been here.

Everyone who visits South Wigston High School talks about the 'feel' of the place. Walk around it in the middle of the day when lessons are in full swing or during break or lunch times, and you'll know what they mean. It just feels right. Purposeful, orderly and above all, a place that feels like it's where good things happen. That's what I felt when I first walked in, and it's never left me.

What I've learned since is that it's never left most of the people who have spent time here either. Seventy years is a ripe old age for a school, and I'm proud to be the leader of an establishment with great traditions, heritage and memories.

Pamela and Derek have delved deep to put this book together, and in it they provide remarkable detail of the development of this wonderful school, from conception to 'old age'. All schools have tales to tell, secrets known only to certain staff and pupils, and this story certainly lets a few of those slip.

This year we celebrate our seventieth birthday and to accompany this book we plan to publish on our website a series of videos, documenting life at school. Our school production entitled, 'Those Were The Days' celebrates the dance, music and drama that spans those years, and our 'Hall of Fame' has begun to showcase some of the many successful people, from all walks of life, who graced our corridors over the years. Hopefully, we'll find more to add over the coming years.

It's people who make schools, the pupils, the staff, the Governors and parents. All add to the rich tapestry of life here. Memories from a wide variety of sources are recorded here, some sad, but mostly happy, because it seems that the school over the years has indeed been a happy place for so many.

Indeed, since the book was started, we've moved on past the school's 70th birthday and reached new heights. In 2010 we were re-designated as an Arts College and achieved the grade of 'Outstanding' in our Ofsted Inspection. What made that special was that it wasn't just about staff; Governors and pupils alike were graded outstanding for their contribution to the school's success. Her Majesty's Inspector said, "There is something very special going on at this school." He's very right!

So read and enjoy, you might even find yourself in here somewhere, either in the text, or in a photograph. If not, you'll surely recognise others, and of course you will forever be part of the school's fabric.

My thanks to you and everyone else who has left a part of their soul here, helping to create such a fantastic school. Future generations will surely feel the same and bring, as our new school motto says; 'Success for All'.

GARY L. TOWARD
Head Teacher (2000-present)

Chapter One
Laying The Foundations
(1903 - 1938)

As the twentieth century dawned, the local School Boards, created by Forster's Elementary Education Act of 1870, had clearly served their purpose and a whole new future beckoned.

With the passing of the Balfour Education Act of 1902, the School Board system was replaced by Local Education Authorities, thus the provision of education became, for the first time, a Local Government responsibility - effectively from 1 July 1903.

Leicestershire was in the vanguard of the educational revolution and this was, in no small measure, as a result of the appointment of the authority's first Director of Education, William Allport Brockington. Born in Birmingham on 18 June 1871, he was the son of a gold beater, Thomas Alfred Brockington and his wife, Fanny Allport. He was educated at King Edward VI Grammar School, Birmingham and the local Mason University College. Brockington obtained a BA as a London University external candidate, with first-class honours in 1890 and an MA three years later.

Following a period of seven years as a lecturer at Mason University College, he was the principal of Victoria College, Worcester from 1898 for the next five years. In 1903 he applied for the post of Director of Education for the Leicestershire County Council.

Sixty applications were received for the position and the council wisely chose a man who was to serve the authority, with distinction, for the next forty-four years. His commencing salary was £500 per annum with £50 for travelling expenses and no pension rights.

William Brockington was to emerge as an influential figure, both locally and nationally, in the development of what was to become the Secondary Modern School. The task of this great pioneer began in July 1903 as he assumed responsibility for the educational needs of Leicestershire children.

Between 1903 and the outbreak of the Great War, Brockington centralised the administration of education in Leicestershire and successfully placed the new Education Department on a firm footing.

The office of William Allport Brockington at 33 Bowling Green Street, Leicester

In 1917 he began to restructure the county's elementary schools. The Education Act 1918 raised the school-leaving age to fourteen years, effectively from 1921. During 1919, Brockington introduced a general secondary school selection examination for admission to grammar schools. The "Scholarship", as it became known, was required to be taken by all pupils when aged eleven and, if they were successful, they were enabled to have the opportunity of a grammar school education. A significant number of children received high marks in the examinations, but fell short of the pass marks required and were thus, "border-liners" for admission to a grammar school. Brockington became convinced that all children, upon reaching eleven years of age should receive a secondary education and that the word "secondary" should be widened to encompass all children in Leicestershire.

A vital component of Brockington's revolution was the establishment of a system of secondary modern schools throughout the county to enable all elementary school children to transfer to separate senior schools at eleven years. This he achieved over a number of years by means of persuasion, diplomacy and leadership of the highest calibre.

In November 1922 the Director of Education reported to the County Education School Staffing Committee that in company with H M Inspector of Schools, Mr A.T. Kerslake, he was inspecting senior classes organised in Public Elementary Schools. He went on to report upon: "The prospect of establishing a County Intermediate School for South Leicestershire where there was from 200 to 300 places available". A month later, the Managers of the Wigston Council Schools offered their full co-operation in the working of the scheme. On 23 June 1923, Brockington submitted his proposals for the establishment of an Intermediate Department: "By adapting part of the premises of the South Wigston Boys' and Girls' Schools". He received committee approval and the first Intermediate Department in Leicestershire became a reality on 27 August 1923.

By September 1923 the Director was able to report: "There were now 76 boys in attendance in the County Intermediate Department, South Wigston. Of this number, 52 were from South Wigston, the remaining 24 from twelve surrounding villages. In the Girls' Department, 59 had been admitted, 46 from South Wigston and 13 girls from surrounding villages". The new Intermediate Girls' Department was established in two classrooms at the Bassett Street school.

By virtue of William Brockington's experimental model at South Wigston, the new type of school, with an Intermediate Department, known as a "Central School", was a first-class educational establishment and provided an alternative secondary education for the above-average children who had narrowly failed to qualify for a grammar school.

Kelly's Directory of Leicestershire and Rutland 1925 shows the village schools at South Wigston as follows:

South Wigston (Boys) erected in 1886 and enlarged in 1892 for 390 children:
John Herbert Butler, *Master*
South Wigston (Girls) erected in 1903 for 380 children:
Miss Emma Gertrude Smith, *Mistress*
South Wigston (Infants) erected in 1892 for 450 children:
Miss Florence Knight, *Mistress*

All three schools were situated in Bassett Street in close proximity to a slaughterhouse owned by the local butcher, John Rawlinson. Only the former Girls' School remains today.

Girls' School, South Wigston

Bassett Street Girls' School 1925
(Now the South Wigston Bassett Centre for use, by the community, as a centre and public library)

Bassett Street Boys' School (Demolished in 1984)

South Wigston was represented on the Leicestershire County Council at this time by Alderman John Wycliffe Black, a local businessman and Liberal politician. "J.W." as he was known to his colleagues, and as he referred to himself, was a boot and shoe manufacturer in

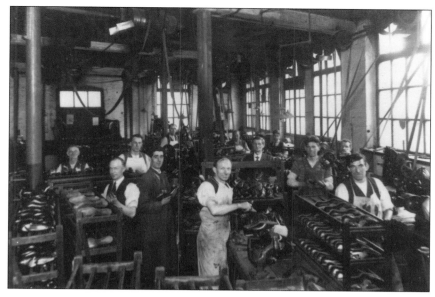

Workers at the factory of J.W Black and Co. Limited

South Wigston. Initially, his firm was known as Toone and Black, with premises on Saffron Road and later became J.W. Black and Co. Limited.

A committed Liberal, "J.W." was first elected to the Leicestershire County Council in 1903. By 1935, with a break of three years, he had been a member for 29 years. He had also served as a councillor on Wigston Urban District Council and was Chairman of that local authority on two occasions. In 1923, John Wycliffe Black was elected to Parliament as the representative for the Harborough constituency for Leicestershire. He served as a Member of Parliament for a brief period between the General Elections held in December 1923 and October 1924.

As a member of the Leicestershire County Council, Alderman Black served on numerous committees including the Education Committee where he was a powerful voice. He was widely known to all in South Wigston, including the schoolchildren. Mrs Violet Ward, nee Kitchen, who attended South Wigston Intermediate School from 1922 to 1926 recalls that, at election time, the children of the Bassett Street schools would sing:

Vote, vote, vote for Johnny Black,
You can't vote for a better man,
We'll have him back if we can;
Vote, vote, vote for Johnny Black.

The successful development of the Intermediate Department at South Wigston, encouraged Brockington to establish a similar scheme at Coalville in north-west Leicestershire. On 26 June 1926 a meeting of the County Education Building and Site Committee received a report from William

The girls of South Wigston Intermediate School 1924 (The photograph shows the first pupils in their new uniforms) Nancy Lucas is standing extreme left on the back row, Violet Kitchen sixth left back row, Irene Willis tenth left, back row and Olive Thornton, later Chapman, extreme right, middle row

South Wigston School Rugby Team 1929-1930
(Clifford Cave is seated on the second row, third from the left next to the captain)

Brockington following his discussions with the Coalville Council Schools regarding school accommodation in the town.

It was agreed to the: "Grouping together of selected seniors - to extend the greatest measure of good from their last two or three years at school - it will be possible to form a Central School somewhat on the lines of the Intermediate School at South Wigston to provide an alternative education of secondary type for those children who cannot be kept under bond at school until the age of 16 years".

The building chosen to house the new school was Broom Leys House, a nineteenth century mansion, built in open countryside by the Whetstone family formerly of Leicester. During the

Broom Leys Secondary Modern School with Intermediate Department

First World War the house was utilised to provide accommodation for wounded soldiers, from the Western Front, requiring convalescence.

The new co-educational Central School, which was formerly opened in 1929, was created to serve Coalville and the neighbouring villages.

The South Wigston Schools gained a reputation for their sporting excellence and began to achieve considerable success, particularly on the rugby field. Clifford Cave, the father of Susan East, attended the Boys' School from 1926 to 1930. He was a member of the School Rugby Team 1929-30 which successfully won the Leicester Schools' Senior Football Shield when they defeated Belgrave Road Boys' School, Leicester, in the final at the Leicester Tigers' ground on Monday 21 April 1930. The result was 12-0 and the report of the game (*Leicester Mercury* 21 April 1930) contained the following: "Cave who had been prominent all through, gave Wigston the lead with an unconverted try".

He continued to play Rugby after leaving school and played for the Aylestonians Rugby Club until 1950. Having benefited from the school's emphasis on technical subjects, he went on to obtain an apprenticeship and a career as a pattern maker.

Mrs East proudly possesses three medals awarded by the Leicester Schools' Rugby Union to her father for the years, 1928, 1929 and 1930.

In his report to the Leicestershire County

The Retirement of Mr John Henry Butler 1936
The retirement photograph shows the visiting dignitaries and members of staff.
Back row, left to right: Nichola Picozzi, A.N. Other, Norman Harrison, Billy Mew, Harold Billson,
Miss Evans, Ernest Powdrill, John Moorhouse, 'Paddy' Plimmer. Walter Higgins, Kenneth Harris,
Lucy Tingle, Orson Kind, A.N. Other.
Seated, left to right: Mr Perkins, Manager, Arthur Holmes Manager,
Arthur Payne, Chairman of the Managers, Mrs Edith Butler, Miss Grudgings, Mr John Henry Butler,
Mr William Allport Brockington, Director of Education, John Henry Holmes, Manager
and Mr Main, Manager

Council, presented in July 1928 and entitled "The Organisation of Public Elementary Schools", William Brockington gave a detailed explanation of the *Hadow Report* of 1926, which advocated that all children over the age of eleven should receive a secondary education as a matter of national policy and the level of reorganisation reached within the county. He went on to explain that there were only two schools in Leicestershire, known as Selective Central Schools, which gave advanced instruction with a practical bias. They were the Central Schools at South Wigston and Coalville Broom Leys who: "Admit scholars who are 'placed' in the Annual Schools' Examination List but who are not offered scholarships or whose parents although unable to keep them at school to the age of sixteen have given an undertaking to allow them to remain to fifteen-plus".

By this time, fifty-four all age elementary schools had been "beheaded" by the Director who, in the process, never lost sight of the challenge to stimulate and motivate pupils as evidenced by his support for the teaching of cookery, gardening and woodwork in the secondary modern schools.

One young pupil-teacher, who was to experience life at South Wigston Intermediate Boys' School was Walter Higgins. He was born at Markfield, Leicestershire in 1915. Both of his parents were teachers at Markfield Church of England School and it was there where he commenced his education, at the age of five, as a pupil in his mother's class known as "the babies". Much later, having passed "the scholarship", he gained a place at Wyggeston Grammar School in Leicester in 1927.

Six years later, Walter's father arranged for him to become a student-teacher at South Wigston at the princely salary of £40 per annum. In his autobiography, *Well Wunted: A Leicestershire Lifetime*, he gives a vivid description of the Headmaster at the time. He was John Herbert Butler an old-fashioned schoolmaster known to all as 'Percy'. A Methodist local preacher, he was a non-smoker and teetotaller who abhorred all forms of gambling. A man who, Walter noted: "Subscribed firmly to the dictum that to spare the rod was to spoil the child!".

During his three years at the school, Walter worked with, and greatly admired, a group of experienced teachers who were to have an influence upon his career both during his time as a student-teacher and later when he qualified as a full-blown teacher himself. The teachers, whose names were well-known throughout South Wigston, were Harold Billson, Orson Kind, Billy Mew and Ernest Powdrill.

Walter Higgins also benefited from having entered a hotbed of rugby football where he gained useful experience in the coaching of the game. At the end of his first season at the school, Leslie Rainbow, from Blaby, who was the captain of the First XV, won his international schoolboy cap when he skippered England v Wales in the 1933-34 season. In doing so, he became the eighth boy from South Wigston to play for the England Under 15 Schoolboys and the school's second England captain. The school had provided England with more schoolboy internationals than any other Midlands school. A truly remarkable record.

Walter felt, very strongly, that during his time at Bassett Street he learned **how** to teach and this stood him in good stead when he left South Wigston in 1936 to become a student at Chester College. Chester was the first teacher-training college to be established in the country when it opened in 1839.

1936 was also the year which marked the retirement of John Henry Butler.

Following his retirement 'Percy' Butler was appointed as the Day School Lecturer by the Leicestershire and Rutland Band of Hope Union. He lectured at the local schools on hygiene, food and Temperance for which an annual grant of £25 was paid by the County Education Committee to the Union.

By the mid 1930s, the South Wigston Schools were too small to accommodate the numbers of pupils requiring places in an expanding local community added to which children were coming to the senior schools from twenty-four villages within a wide catchment area as Brockington's reorganisation plans gathered momentum. Additional accommodation was required as a matter of some urgency and the matter had to be seriously addressed.

The question of overcrowding was considered by the Leicestershire County Council and the decision was taken to acquire an available area of land locally as a site for the building of replacement schools. At its meeting, on 14 December 1934, the County Council, received a report from its Education Committee. The report read as follows:

Wigston School Accommodation

"Your Committee, after conferring with the Managers of the Wigston Schools, have agreed to negotiate for the purchase of about 18.5 acres in South Wigston for the purposes of erecting a Modern School for Boys, the provision of playing fields and, ultimately, the erection of a Modern School for Girls".

In the meantime, the Education Committee had arranged the following temporary accommodation: "The Trustees of the South Wigston Methodist Church Sunday School had agreed to the hire of two schoolrooms for two classes from the Intermediate Boys' School for a sum of £130 per annum inclusive of heating, lighting and caretaking. A similar arrangement had been entered into with the Trustees of the St Thomas' Church Sunday School to provide accommodation for two classes from South Wigston Girls' School."

Events moved forward rapidly when, on 13 February 1935, the County Council received a further report from the Education Committee which stated that: "Your Committee has resolved to purchase from the Executors of W.J.R. Pochin, for a sum of £1,900 a site of about 18.5 acres for the South Wigston Modern Boys' and Girls' Schools".

The late owner was William John Reynolds Pochin, MA of the Manor House, Newgate End, Wigston Magna. He had been a landowner with large holdings in Wigston Magna and South Wigston, in addition to being a Barrister at Law and a Master of the Bench of Gray's Inn. Described as both "a lawyer and a country gentleman", William Pochin had had a distinguished career both in classics and law and had a London residence at 6, New Square, Lincoln's Inn. He died suddenly in his Chambers at 11 Gray's Inn Square on 17 May 1930, aged 80 years.

Warm tributes were paid to William Pochin, following his death, in the Gray's Inn Magazine (Michaelmas 1930) and locally in the *Leicester Evening Mail* and the *Leicester Mercury*. He is still remembered today by the close named after him situated near to the Manor House.

The Manor House, Newgate End, Wigston Magna

Pochin's Close, Wigston Magna

Site of the South Wigston Schools
Beyond the trees to the right of the picture

Details of the Pochin land available for sale was, initially described in the Auctioneer's brochure (July 1930):

"Four enclosures of pasture land with derelict building affronting Blaby Road, (previously known as Blaby Lane) South Wigston let to Mr William Thornton, embracing an area of 18 acres, 2 roods and 21 perches. Long frontage of 246 yards."

William Thornton was a local dairyman and the land was known as "Old Mowy Thornton's fields". The description of the land area in acres, roods and perches still conjures up nightmares for many who were school children in that era!

It was no doubt rather fortunate that, during the depression years of the early 1930s, the Pochin estate had not been sold by auction and was, therefore, available for purchase by the Education Committee for the sum of £1900 in early 1935.

The path was now clear for the new South Wigston Schools to be built and, on 13 February 1935, the Leicestershire County Council also took the decision: "That South Wigston shall become the centre of a new Modern School district, this will necessitate the immediate provision of a Modern School for Boys with accommodation for about 450 pupils at a cost of £18,000. The Girls' School can be adapted by the provision of an extra block to accommodate a similar number (cost about £5000). A continued increase of school population could later be met by the building of a Modern School for Girls, and the expansion of the Primary School into the present Girls' Building." (Leicestershire County Council Education Department minutes 13 February 1935).

The following year the Director of Education reported to his committee that, following an interview with the Board of Education, he had been informed that the Board would give favourable consideration to the building of both of the Boys' and Girls' Modern Schools at the same time.

The County Council then took the sensible decision to authorise the Director to proceed with the planning and building of the two schools as a joint enterprise. The resultant plans were for the creation of the schools to accommodate 480 boys and 480 girls with a central kitchen, dining halls and gymnasia.

The proposed construction of the South Wigston

Schools represented an enormous leap forward by the Leicestershire County Council, both in terms of the sheer size of the project and the considerable catchment area the schools would serve. During the thirty-two years in which the Authority, through its Education Committee, had carried out its responsibilities under the Education Act 1902 nothing on this scale had been attempted locally. This was to be a flagship development in the provision of Secondary Modern Schools, where the children would reap the benefits of being educated in purpose-built surroundings, coupled with "advanced" instruction in the Intermediate Departments.

In a localised 'revolution' such as was being witnessed in the field of Education in Leicestershire, in the 1930s, the principal architect of the scheme, William Brockington, required the unqualified support of the political leader of the Local Authority. In all of this, he could not have had a more supportive and influential master than Lieutenant-Colonel Robert Edmund Martin, who was both the Chairman of the Leicestershire County Council and its powerful Education Committee. He was educated at Eton and King's College, Cambridge and became a civil engineer. In the First World War he commanded the 4th Battalion of the Leicestershire Regiment and was severely wounded in the assault on the Hohenzollern Redoubt on 13 October 1915, an action in which every one of his fellow officers was killed or wounded.

He was mentioned in despatches and was awarded the CMG (Companion of the Order of St Michael and St George) for his wartime services.

Having become a County Councillor in 1909, Lieutenant-Colonel Martin returned to his work at the council after the war had ended. He was elected Chairman of the Leicestershire County Council in 1924 and, such was the esteem in which he was held, he was re-elected to the office, annually, for the next thirty-five years.

Robert Martin's greatest concern, as a local politician, was the field of education and the chairmanship of the Education Committee proved to be his abiding passion. His admiration for William Brockington was legendary. He once described his eminent chief officer as: "The most distinguished of England's Directors of

Lieutenant-Colonel Robert Edmund Martin CMG, TD, MA. DL, JP

Education". With the backing of two such formidable figures, the realisation of the proposed new schools at South Wigston was assured.

The responsibility for the entire school-building programme, throughout the county, rested with Captain Ernest George Fowler, FRIBA, Architect and Surveyor to Leicestershire County Council. A native of Loughborough, Captain Fowler had been in the service of the Education Committee since it was constituted in 1903 and was appointed Architect to the Committee in 1908. Before and after the First World War, Ernest Fowler served with the Territorial Army. During the war he was commissioned into the Army Service Corps (became the Royal Army Service Corps in 1918) and was always proud of his military connections.

In addition to directing the building programme, during the period of school reorganisation, Captain Fowler designed many of the new schools including the Secondary Modern Schools and the expansion of Loughborough College. The design and erection of the South Wigston Modern Boys' and Girls' Schools together with a Health Centre, was to be one of the major projects of this talented architect.

Tenders were invited in the spring of 1937 and seven tenders were considered by the Building and Sites Committee, the result being that the Education Committee accepted the tender of Messrs J.C. Kellett and Son in the sum of £68,850 for the building of the South Wigston Schools and

Captain Ernest George Fowler, FRIBA (Leicester Mercury)

firm was Messrs Constone Limited, artificial stone manufacturers on Blaby Road whose works faced the site of the school buildings. On 8 May 1937 a tender by Constone Limited was accepted for carrying out the following work:

Reconstructed stone dressings £1833-3s-4d

Staircases and landings   £232-2s-0d

Health Centre. Ultimately, the Health Centre was known locally as The Clinic.

The firm of J.C. Kellett & Son was founded in 1830 by John Cornelius Kellett and was one of the oldest firms of building contractors in Leicester. Initially, the firm operated from modest premises at 24½ Asylum Street. John Cornelius' son, John Henry Kellett, succeeded to the business in the late 1880s and, in 1892, the firm moved to a three-storey building at 40 Southgate Street, Leicester.

J.C. Kellett and Son became involved in the building of schools on behalf of the Leicester School Board which functioned from 1871 to 1903. The firm erected and fitted out many of the Board Schools in Leicester. In addition to the building of schools, the firm specialised in the manufacture of school furniture which they designed and supplied in huge quantities and included desks for the headteachers, assistant teachers and pupils, blackboards, easels, cupboards and bookcases.

The building of schools, on behalf of both the Leicestershire County Council and the Leicester City Council, became a significant part of the business of J.C. Kellett and Son. The records of the Leicestershire County Council Education Committee show that between 1930 and the outbreak of the Second World War, the firm built twenty one new schools, ranging in price from £1000 to £70,000. In addition, this prestigious firm secured contracts for the furnishing of a number of schools in London,

Construction of the new South Wigston Schools commenced in the summer of 1937 and other local firms were involved as sub-contractors. One such

The Works of Messrs Constone Limited

One of the craftsmen from Constone Limited, who was engaged in the stonework, was Samuel Payne who lived in Railway Street, South Wigston. He worked on the staircases, an aspect of his trade in which he specialised, and also left his mark on the schools by helping to make the four huge stone acorns which proudly surmount the central facade above the stained glass windows bearing the coat of arms of the Leicestershire County Council. Presumably the acorns were to signify the well known line, "Great oaks from little acorns grow" - unattributed proverb (circa 14c).

A major problem encountered by the building contractors, from the onset, was the water level on the low-lying site. During a storm, in July 1937, the basement floor 'blew up' quite literally when flood water built up a force of pressure. The story goes that 'a local', advised the foreman that this would happen if the floor was not reinforced since the overflow from the brickyard pit ran through the fields. Fortunately this occurred when there was no one working on site.

It was necessary for a pump to be installed in order to cope with the problem in the long-term. The pump was housed in a small brick built pump-

The Pump-House

house erected on the frontage adjacent to the Girls' School.

The problem of the water level, on the site, has now been overcome by a more adequate drainage system.

By June 1938 the Schools' Staffing Committee was in a position to consider the staffing of the new schools. The first sixteen teachers to be appointed (eight for the Boys' School and eight for the Girls' School) were, in fact, existing teachers due to be transferred from the Bassett Street Schools, as the following minute reveals:

25 June 1938
The following arrangements for the staffing of the South Wigston Schools after the reorganisation were approved:

Modern Boys' School	**Modern Girls' School**
Mr W.M. Mew	Miss C.M. Wright
Mr E.O. Powdrill	Miss C.D. Draper
Mr O.J. Kind	Mrs S. Beaton
Mr N. Picozzi	Miss F.L. Davis
Mr H. Billson	Miss M.E. Vann
Mr J. Moorhouse	Miss N.G. White
Mr E.H.J. Churches	Mrs J.J. Tindall
Mr K.H. Harris	Miss C.M. Baskett
Plus one additional teacher	Plus one additional teacher

Headship	**Headship**
11 teachers invited to apply for the headship. Special meeting for interviews to be held on 8 July 1938.	To transfer Miss E.G. Smith from the present Girls' Intermediate School.

In the event, six teachers applied for the position of Headmaster and it was: "Unanimously resolved that Mr Howard Kenneth Harrison, BSc (Bristol) First Assistant Master at Broom Leys Central School, Coalville be appointed to the Headship as from 29 August 1938." It was also noted in the minutes of the Schools' Staffing Committee: "That in view of the advanced instruction given in the Intermediate Department, an additional salary be paid".

'HKH.' as he was known to his colleagues, was born in The Manse at Uley, Gloucestershire on 22 March 1904. He was the son of the Reverend Francis George Harrison, a Baptist minister and his wife Minnie Agnes. A graduate of Bristol University, H K Harrison was appointed to the staff of Broom Leys Central School, South Wigston's sister school on 1 March 1929. At thirty four years of age he was the county's youngest senior school head.

Howard Kenneth Harrison, BSc pictured centre at a school presentation

Howard K. Harrison, in his first appointment as a Headmaster, assumed responsibility not only for the formidable task of opening a huge new school but, at the same time, having to face the possibility of Britain becoming involved, once more, in the horrors of a world war. He would prove to be more than equal to the challenges he faced.

The new schools and health centre were duly completed and handed over to the Leicestershire County Council in June 1938.

The School Clinic

The clinic was used for the immunisation and provision of dental treatment for the pupils, also for meeting the welfare needs of local mothers and babies.

One of the first tasks in order to prepare the buildings and to arrange for their ongoing usage was to appoint the caretaking and cleaning staff. At a meeting of the Building and Site Committee, on 20 August 1938, Captain Fowler reported that 184 applications had been received for the position of Caretaker of which he had interviewed 23 of the candidates. Nine of the applicants were duly interviewed by the committee which resulted in the appointment of Mr John T. Gisborn of 8 Kate Street, Leicester to commence on 29 August 1938, at a salary of £150 per annum. The huge number of applicants for the post gives an indication of the high level of unemployment which existed in the 1930s. An Assistant Caretaker, Mr J.G. Smith was appointed at a salary of £125 per annum. Six women cleaners to work for one or two hours each evening was also authorised.

The iconic building was ready, Head Teachers and teaching staff were in place, the caretakers and cleaners were dusting and polishing, all that remained was for the mass influx of hundreds of boys and girls through the portals of their wonderful new seat of learning.

Chapter Two
Bells and Sirens
(1938 - 1948)

The opening of the new schools took place on 31 August 1938 when 366 pupils were admitted to the Boys' School and 385 attended the Girls' School. To enter these impressive new buildings, which dominated the skyline of South Wigston, was both an exciting and daunting experience for the 751 children as they commenced the first term of the 1938-39 academic year.

An article in the *Leicester Mercury* (31 August 1938) under the heading 'New luxury school opens at South Wigston' described the school as follows: "It is the finest of its kind in the county which must have appeared vastly different to the old-fashioned and somewhat drab surroundings to which many of the new scholars had been accustomed in their old schools". Certainly this was in stark contrast to the Bassett Street Boys' School where the largest room had housed two first year classes separated by only a flimsy, dark green curtain.

The local newspaper reporter also commented upon: "One of the main features of the school was the palatial accommodation for mid-day meals and it will be possible to provide 350 scholars each with a really good dinner at 4d a head".

The amenities included two separate gymnasiums (which were also used for assemblies) changing rooms and showers, a spacious library, workrooms for the boys and a cookery section for the girls. Probably the greatest attraction of all, for many of the boys, was the basement where the boilers were heated by furnaces fed by three robot stokers but the area was strictly out of bounds and woe betide any boy venturing into this prohibited wonderland.

The catchment area, served by the new schools, was widened which enabled children who lived some considerable distance from South Wigston to receive their secondary education in wonderfully modern surroundings.

The following list of junior schools, known as contributory schools, indicated the spread of villages involved when the schools opened in 1938:

Blaby	Kirby Muxloe
Braunstone	Leire
Broughton Astley	Leicester Forest East
Cosby	Narborough
Countesthorpe	Oadby
Croft	Saddington
Enderby	South Wigston
Fleckney	Theddingworth
Frolesworth	Whetstone
Glen Hills	Wigston Magna
Huncote	Willoughby Waterleys
Kilby	

Other villages, included in the scheme, as contributory schools, who sent boys and girls included:

Ashby Magna	Kibworth Harcourt
Birstall	Littlethorpe
Earl Shilton	Lubbenham
Elmsthorpe	Ratby
Great Glen	Smeeton Westerby
Humberstone	Stoney Stanton

HM School Log Books had to be completed by the Head Teacher on a daily basis, the requirement being 'Every school must have a diary or log book which should be a bare record of the events which constitute the history of the school'. The initial entries, by the respective Head Teachers, gave details of the staff and their duties:

Boys' School

Howard Kenneth Harrison BSc (Bristol)	Headmaster	English with all forms
Harold Billson, BSc (London)	Form Master of 1B (39 boys)	French and Geography
Edward Henry John Churches	Form Master of 1C (38 boys)	Physical Training in Upper School
Kenneth Holmes Harris	Form Master 1A	Music throughout school and Maths in 2A and 2B

Boys' School *Continued*

Orson James Kind	Form Master 3B	Science and History
William Merrifield Mew	Form Master 2A	Art and Maths
John Moorhouse, BSc (Leeds)	Form Master 4	Science & Gardening
Nicola Picozzi, MA (Glasgow)	Form Master 2B	Maths and Physical Training
Ernest Oscar Powdrill	Form Master 3A	English and Geography
Cyril Charles Tweed		Woodwork

Girls' School

Miss E.G. Smith	Headmistress	
Miss C.M. Wright	First Assistant Form 1A (40)	Art and Needlework
Miss C.D. Draper	Form III (33)	French and English
Mrs S. Beaton	Form III Sc (32)	History & Geography
Miss C.M. Baskett	Second Year A (47)	Needlework and Handwork
Miss N.G. White	Second Year B (43)	Physical Training
Mrs J.J. Tindall	Retarded Class (31)	
Miss F.L. Davis	Form II (41)	Physical Training

Plus supply teachers, Mrs Winder and Mrs Jewell, who taught forms First Year A and First Year B respectively.

Many pupils of that era retain vivid memories of the teachers they encountered at the new schools. Some of the staff quickly acquired nicknames, especially in the Boys' School and a number were viewed as having distinctive characteristics and personalities. The senior masters were 'Scrounger' Kind and 'Dinky' Powdrill.

Mr Orson James Kind, who went on to become Deputy Headmaster, was born in Whetstone, Leicestershire on 4 September 1889. His family relocated to South Wigston in 1904. He trained as a teacher at Exeter Training College 1913-15 prior to joining the Devonshire Regiment as an officer cadet during 1915. He was wounded at Kut-el-Amarah, Mesopotamia and subsequently invalided out to India. There he joined the Somerset Light Infantry as a Lieutenant and was involved in the Third Afghan War in 1919.

Upon demobilisation, he took up a teaching post as Science and History master at Bassett Street Boys' School. He married Margaret Phipps

Metcalf at Burton on Trent in 1920. They had two sons, John, born at 'Oxford House'. Blaby Road and Alan, born at 30 Leopold Street, South Wigston. The family moved to 106 Saffron Road, South Wigston in 1930, where he remained for the rest of his life.

A keen participant and supporter of rugby football, he was President of Wigston Rugby Football Club. He also served as an Independent councillor for Bassett Ward of Wigston Urban District Council, for nine years and was Chairman in 1943-44.

The mystery of O J Kind's nickname has been kindly unravelled by his son, Alan: "His school nickname of 'Scrounger' emanates from his acquisition of any material or objects that could be recycled. He would often make his own demonstration material, a magic lantern comes to mind, along with crystal radio sets".

One of the best-loved and most respected teachers, was Billy Mew. Born in Portsmouth, on

2236 Lieutenant Orson James Kind

"Billy Mew

William Merrifield Mew
by courtesy of Donald E. Green

10 June 1875, he was educated at Winchester College and came to South Wigston as a teacher in 1896.

Walter Higgins in his autobiography *Well Wunted: A Leicestershire Lifetime*, gives a superb description of Billy Mew: "A diminutive man but the best disciplinarian I have ever known, famous for his gargantuan consumption of Park Drive (cigarettes), his mathematical expertise and his exquisitely neat blackboard sketches".

Colin Dougherty of South Wigston, who attended the Intermediate School at Bassett Street in 1937 and moved to the new school in 1938 to complete his final two years of education, provides a fascinating insight into the redoubtable Billy Mew: "One of his many subjects was mathematics. He was an excellent teacher with many years of experience. What a wealth of experience that little man had. I call him 'little' because he was only a very small man but he was also a man of great stature when it came to his knowledge and his ability to pass it on to all who were fortunate enough to be in his class." This veteran master also taught Colin's brother, Roy, who passed through Bassett Street Boys' School four years earlier and, amazingly, their father Dennis, who was a pupil of Billy Mew in the early 1900s.

Charles Reeve, who lived at Blaby and commenced at the new school on the opening day, recollects that Billy Mew was a crack shot with a piece of chalk and invariably scored a direct hit "when he had you in his sights".

Another teacher from the Bassett Street era was Ernest Powdrill, known as 'Dinky'. Tall and gangling, he too was a veteran of the Great War. He had a reputation for being 'a stormy petrel' when attending meetings of the National Union of Teachers, nevertheless, he was popular with the boys when teaching English Literature and

Ernest Powdrill

Ernest Oscar Powdrilll
by courtesy of Donald E. Green

geography. He also taught scripture using the 'Little Bible' which had been specifically written for use in schools.

Harold Billson, who taught French and geography, was a high flyer academically. Having obtained a BSc (London) he went on to gain a PhD. Stan Tibbles, who attended Bassett Street and Blaby Road Schools between 1935 and 1939, recalls that Harold Billson would stand in front of the class with a huge map, denoting countries of the British Empire coloured in red, mounted on the wall behind him. On one occasion he predicted that the British Empire would eventually fall as this had happened to all empires throughout history. This predicted view of history landed him "in a spot of bother" as he received a nasty letter from a parent accusing him of unpatriotic teaching.

The nickname by which Mr Billson was known was 'Caliban' the significance of which was not always apparent to his pupils. Caliban was a Shakespearean character described as a savage and deformed slave in *The Tempest*. There must have been occasions when Harold Billson felt distinctly uncomfortable both in the classroom and staffroom!

Walter Higgins recalled another former Bassett Street master, who transferred to the Blaby Road School in 1938, Nicola Picozzi MA (Glasgow) who taught mathematics as his specialised subject. An accomplished soccer player, he was a Scottish schoolboy international and had been on the books of Celtic Football Club as an amateur.

Colin Dougherty's description of Nicola Piccozi will be familiar to many old boys from that period: "We referred to him as 'Old Nick' because he had a very short fuse and often threw chalk, blackboard dusters (wooden backed ones) or anything that came to hand at anyone he thought was not paying attention".

One of the younger teachers from Bassett Street was Kenneth Holmes Harris, an inspirational Music Teacher who also taught mathematics. His love of music was infectious and resulted in many boys acquiring an appreciation of and an interest in classical works. He was also disposed to administering a surprise clout on inattentive and unsuspecting pupils.

The girls were perhaps a little more respectful towards their teachers or could it be that they were

Kenneth Holmes Harris
by courtesy of Donald E. Green

somewhat more apprehensive about the use of nicknames? A description by one of the first entrants reads: "From day one the discipline was built-in. The staff were remote, or at least that is how they seemed to me. You could not even imagine what their Christian names were. To use them would be a hanging offence. I do not even recall anyone giving them nicknames".

Nevertheless, some rather less dramatic nicknames did emerge. Miss Emma Gertrude Smith, the Headmistress, was a stern, remote figure who walked with a limp and was referred to, in whispered tones, as "Gertie". The Needlework and Art Mistress, Miss Constance Madeline Wright, had auburn coloured hair, was a noted disciplinarian and was not widely popular. She had vast teaching experience and some remember her for her pearls of wisdom. One girl remembers her counselling her class thus:

"There are not many people in the world today who are doing a job they really want. Most end up tolerating the job they had to take for one reason or another. You are not all going to be hairdressers, fashion designers or top executives. What you can be are well-rounded, well-balanced, confident individuals. That is most important." Thus spoke the red-headed philosopher, known behind her back to those who dare utter the word: "Connie".

For those girls who enjoyed physical training and sports, Miss Norah White, P.T. Mistress, was particularly liked. Described by one of her admiring pupils as: "Our enthusiastic sports

Donald Green incurs the wrath of Mr Picozzi
by courtesy of Donald E. Green

mistress was a compact figure in her green pinafore dress and white blouse". A number of the girls went on to be members of the County Netball Team for which they were full of gratitude for Miss White for her skilful coaching and encouragement.

Undoubtedly the favourite teacher of many of the girls, at that time, was Miss Constance Dorothy Draper who taught French and English and was Mistress of Form 3. Her teaching of English Literature was quite stimulating and this, coupled with a warm personality, resulted in her pupils describing her as lovely, kind and gentle, adjectives not freely attributed to members of staff generally.

Miss Draper married a German national, Arthur Holm at Holborn, London in the autumn of 1938. He was interned after the outbreak of the Second World War in September 1939.

For the pupils who attended the Bassett Street schools, the transfer from one school to another involved a journey 'around the corner' or 'up the road'.

Among those moving from the old school to the pristine new version was John Tipper whose time at the schools spanned four years from 1936 to 1940. John was a great rugby football enthusiast, having acquired his love of the game at Bassett Street. After leaving school in 1940 he worked for the local firm of Reid and Sigrist Limited, electrical engineers before his wartime service with the Fleet Air Arm of the Royal Navy from 1942 to 1946. He managed to fit in a game of rugby whenever circumstances permitted and played occasionally for Bath Rugby Football Club. Whilst in the Royal Navy, he played as hooker a position which he had played during the early development of his game at South Wigston.

Another local boy who arrived on day one of the 'New School' was Donald E. Green, formerly of Kirkdale Road, South Wigston, who attended the Intermediate School at Bassett Street. Whilst there he was responsible for the launch of the school magazine which he personally illustrated and printed.

He vividly remembers his school days where he first displayed his artistic talents by copying pictures of popular cartoon characters – Donald Duck, Popeye, etc. given to him by some of the teachers. However, the unpredictable Nicola Picozzi took an instant dislike to Donald and, in front of the entire class, declared: "The only difference between you, Green, and the rest of the class, is that you copy better than they do".

The effect of this 'putting down' of the young Donald Green caused him to reflect, on his way home from school that day, that Mr Picozzi was right and thus he became determined to create his own images and to become an artist.

During his time at the school, Donald developed into a good rugby player and later played for South Wigston Rugby Football Club and went on to be the Club President.

He can recall the incomparable Billy Mew pushing a pram along, from his home on Saffron Road, to call upon Frank Collet, the local grocer and outdoor beer licensee at 12 Kirkdale Road, in order to replenish his stock of bottled beer!

Donald left school in 1939 and his career commenced in the printing industry with the *Leicester Evening Mail*. During the Second World War he served in the Queen's Royal Regiment which was part of the 7th Armoured Division (The Desert Rats) of which he remains justifiably proud. Whilst on active service he made drawings of action on the front lines as his regiment fought its way across Europe. His drawings were placed on file at the Imperial War Museum.

During the 1950s Donald Green became a professional artist, most of his work was London-based and published internationally. He became an accomplished illustrator and cartoonist and his drawings featured in a number of prestigious national magazines including *The Field, Mayfair Magazine, Shooting Gazette and The Tatler*.

Donald has drawn most of the famous actors and actresses of the 1960s and 1970s on stage at Stratford and in the London theatres. A 1982 pencil drawing of Sir Oswald Mosley, which he drew in the Café Royal, was accepted for permanent display at the National Portrait Gallery. In later years he received commissions to produce caricatures of the Officers and NCOs of 150 regiments of the British Army. His pictures hang in houses throughout Leicestershire as well as in London and New York and his work continues to be in demand.

Donald E. Green, a self-portrait

Among the girls turning up for school on that momentous day, 31 August 1938, was Joyce Richardson, nee Kirby, who lived in Waterloo Crescent, Countesthorpe. As an eleven year old she was: "One of the first to go to the school and was very proud to be going there". Joyce recalls that the Countesthorpe children came by bus and they often had to get off the vehicle at the humpback bridge at Crow Mills because the bottom of the bus was scraping the bridge; the dramatic lessening of the weight did the trick and everyone clambered back on board to complete the journey.

For many girls an introduction to the school kitchen was a memorable event. A contemporary photograph showed three of the girls ladling out soup in the kitchen. This illustration was carefully cut out and pasted into the Headmistress' Log Book.

Girls at South Wigston Secondary Modern School take turns in serving the mid-day meal. Here they are ladling out soup

Interestingly, the next entry in Miss Smith's Log Book after the photograph appeared, read:
"17 November 1938 – Miss N G White (teacher) who has been suffering from food poisoning, returned today."

The fine tradition of rugby continued to flourish at the Boys' School and the development of individual players to reach high standards was maintained. Peter Herbert, who lived in Wigston Fields, also moved from Bassett Street in August 1938 and attended the new school until 1941. The game of rugby has been a lifelong passion for Peter who was taken as a young boy to Welford Road, Leicester to see his uncle, Don Herbert, play for the Tigers. Peter became a fine player and played for South Wigston Intermediate School against Moat Road Intermediate School, Leicester in the Sir Jonathan North (Under14s) Trophy on the Tigers ground in 1937. He also played in an England Schoolboys trial match.

After the war, Peter went on to play for Leicester Tigers (1946-47) then for Aylestone St. James, 'The Jimmies', where he was the player coach and captain, followed by a second spell with the Tigers (1952-53). He played on 68 occasions for the Tigers First XV and scored eight tries. Peter's favoured position was open side wing forward but he was versatile and could play virtually anywhere, which he often did when injuries occurred.

During his career with the Leicester Tigers, Peter actually played in every position in the Extra First XV. His involvement with the Tigers led him to become the Secretary of the Juniors and Club President in 1984, he remains in touch with the club to this day.

Roy Murgatroyd was another boy from that period who developed into a fine rugby player. He went on to spend two seasons with the Leicester Tigers 1949-50 and 1950-51 during which time he made five appearances in the first team.

Discipline was very much the order of the day at South Wigston. In the Boys' School all of the masters would administer the cane which consisted of a short piece of wood which they used to hit the boys across each hand; it was a painful experience. The Headmaster had both a short stick and a long cane which he used on a regular basis whenever he spotted acts of disobedience or when boys were sent to his office for the ultimate chastisement.

The ruler was the main weapon of punishment used in the Girls' School where discipline was also rigidly observed. Miss Connie Wright who, in addition to teaching needlework and art, was the First Assistant Teacher, effectively the Deputy Headmistress, was a liberal exponent of the ruler, which was used to smack the girls across their hands.

The reports in the local press were entirely accurate in describing the wide-eyed wonder with which the first intake of boys and girls took place. Pupils continuing their secondary education and those moving from junior to secondary status arrived from far and wide to commence a new chapter in their young lives in Leicestershire's pristine and unrivalled new schools.

On 2 November 1938 the Boys' School was open to parents and friends during the afternoon. All were welcomed with tea and biscuits served in the dining hall for which a charge of 3d was made.

Three weeks later came the day of the official opening of the schools by Mr Kenneth Martin Lindsay MP., Parliamentary Secretary to the Board of Education. He was a man of considerable achievement, having been educated at St Olave's Grammar School close to Tower Bridge. In 1916 he went straight from school, at the age of 18 years, to join the Honourable Artillery Company and was wounded at Passchendaele – the Third Battle of Ypres when his Battery received a direct hit. It is a great coincidence that much later in the school's history, this famous battleground was to become a major feature in school life. After recovering from his wounds and completing his war service, he had a distinguished career at Worcester College, Oxford, where he was President of the Union in 1922-23 and gained a Blue for Association Football. He obtained a degree in modern history and went on to serve on Stepney Borough Council before entering Parliament as a National Labour candidate at a by-election in November 1933 for the Kilmarnock Burghs, a seat he was to hold for the next twelve years.

During this time, Kenneth Lindsay was Civil Lord of the Admiralty 1935-37 before becoming Parliamentary Secretary to the Board of Education, a post he was to hold for four years. He had a deep interest in education and wrote and spoke on secondary education with authority and foresight.

The official opening of the South Wigston Modern Schools on Friday 25 November 1938 was widely reported in the local press, the *Leicester Mercury* of the same date gave due prominence to the speech by the Minister. Lieutenant-Colonel Robert Martin, as Chairman of Leicestershire County Council presided at the formal opening, he was to receive a Knighthood the following year.

In his opening speech, Mr Lindsay said: "Owing to their keenness and the able guidance of their Chairman, Lieutenant-Colonel Martin and the Director, Mr W A Brockington, Leicestershire Education Committee had already reorganised

Leicester Mercury PHOTO NEWS

their elementary schools to the extent of over seventy per cent – one of the highest in the county areas throughout the country.

The *Leicester Mercury* article reported on the remarkable statistics relating to the schools:

"A front elevation of 476 feet, it stood on a site of over 18 acres and could accommodate over 900 pupils." It emphasised the fact that it was the largest school erected by the County Council at that time.

One of the most amazing facilities at the new schools, were the showers. Many of the pupils lived in small, terraced houses, where bathrooms were unknown and the weekly cleansing process consisted of bathing in a tin bath in front of a coal fire in the living room, with kettles of hot water, towels and huge quantities of steam much in evidence. To actually take a shower came as a 'culture shock' as we would say today. Certainly going into the showers with other pupils was a real shock to many of the boys and girls, some of whom, initially, hated the experience but the majority soon came to appreciate this new-found luxury.

The member of staff responsible for the constant supply of hot water for the showers and the school in general was John Gisborn, the Head Caretaker. He moved from Leicester to live in Leopold Street, South Wigston and was well known to Colin Dougherty and his family who resided in the street. 'Jack' Gisborn had served in the Royal Navy as a Chief Petty Officer Stoker and had years of experience of life in the stokehole. His stories of life at sea enthralled the young Colin who developed an ambition to join the Royal Navy when he was old enough but was eventually conscripted into the Army.

During the first term at the Boys' School, two new masters were appointed, both of whom were to exert a profound influence on the life of the school and to go on to have distinguished careers.

Firstly, on 19 September 1938, Leslie Wild joined the staff. Born in Gainsborough, Lincolnshire on 25 February 1915 he had trained at Leeds College but had undergone some years of experience, having previously taught at the Benjamin Adlard Boys' School, Gainsborough and at the village school in Kirmington, North Lincolnshire. He was appointed to take charge of Form II and to specialise in art and crafts throughout the school.

Leslie Wild was a fine all-round sportsman and went on to play for Leicestershire Nomads, the county's premier amateur association football club. As a bowler batsman, his cricket, which he played for Leicester Nomads, was up to Minor Counties standard.

Leslie Wild
by courtesy of Donald E. Green

He was followed on 1 December 1938 by Walter Higgins who, having obtained his teaching qualification at Chester College, was delighted to take up a post at South Wigston where he assumed responsibility for the teaching of history to first through to fourth year pupils and also for rugby football. As he recorded at the time: "It would be an honour to be in charge of rugby at a school with such a fine tradition in the game". The appointment also enabled him to renew his acquaintance with a number of teachers who had influenced his early career.

Walter Higgins had a cheerful countenance and wore a permanent grin; he quickly became known, affectionately, to all and sundry among the pupils

Walter Higgins
by courtesy of Donald E. Green

as 'Smiler' Higgins. He and Leslie Wild became very good friends.

Two additional appointments were made to the staff of the Girls' School during the first term. Their appointments were recorded in the Log Book, by the Headmistress as follows:

3 October 1938	Miss M.E. Jones, BA
10 October 1938	Miss B. Williams, BSc

Miss Jones, who specialised in music, became responsible for the First Year A (40 girls) and Miss Williams, whose specialised subjects were science and geography, became the teacher for First Year B (39 girls). They replaced the two supply teachers, Mrs Jewel and Mrs Winder.

Another of the bus routes to present problems was the one along Coalpit Lane in Leicester (now Braunstone Lane) where the school bus was routed from Kingsway, Braunstone. Once again a humpback bridge had to be negotiated, in this instance, the canal bridge by Aylestone boathouse. Here, similar problems to those encountered at Crow Mills, South Wigston, had to be overcome which necessitated everyone having to alight in order to reduce the overall weight before the journey could continue.

One of the boys who travelled on the Kingsway bus was Leslie Wilson of Braunstone. Les attended the Intermediate School from 1939 to 1943 (Forms 1A to 4A). He has vivid recollections of the teachers and his description of the much maligned Harold (Caliban) Billson makes fascinating reading:

"On entering the classroom he would sniff the air and retreat into the corridor whereupon he would shout instructions 'Murgatroyd open the windows' followed by 'Open your books at page 32'. He would then conduct the first part of the lesson from the corridor. Eventually he would re-enter the classroom, sniff the air once more and, finding it more acceptable, would resume the lesson normally."

The great joy for Les was to play rugby for his house, Burnaby, and for the school on Saturday mornings against schools in Leicester such as Moat Road, Ellesmere Road and King Richard's Road schools. Les recalls: "We had a great team and almost always won". Ever the romantic, Les would serenade the girls on the Midland Red bus from Kingsway, Braunstone, by playing his banjo. One of the girls relates that she received a love letter from Les, who was considered to be 'quite dishy', however hopes were soon dashed when it was discovered that Les had written love letters to every girl in that particular class.

Les Wilson was a born entertainer whose talents led him to achieve success on the professional stage. He commenced his theatrical career in Combined Services Entertainments, during his service with the Royal Air Force and toured the Far East for two years in a show called 'At your service' alongside such illustrious names as Kenneth Williams and Stanley Baxter.

After a period as a garment manufacturer, Les achieved success on television in the 1970s edition of "New Faces", "Seaside Special" and "The Ronnie Corbett Special". In the eighties Les added another string to his bow by playing a straight part in the series, "Muck and Brass" with Mel Smith, followed by further success on television. He has appeared as principal comedian at most of Britain's seaside resorts, including the Grand Theatre, Blackpool and the now cult Pavilion Theatre,

Les Wilson

Cromer, where he appeared in four summer season shows.

He was awarded the accolade of 'Midland Comedian of the Year' following in the footsteps of Jasper Carrott and Don MacLean.

Les continues to be actively involved in the theatre world. He appears at the Little Theatre, Leicester once a year with Jimmy Cricket in his own show and has, for some years, entertained on cruise ships for Page and Moy and is looking forward to appearing on the Ocean Majestic in 2008. A former Leicestershire and Midland Counties 400 metres champion, Les still likes to keep fit but now it is a case of "Anyone for tennis?"

Saffron Road in South Wigston was a road to be avoided by all boys, whenever possible as six of the masters lived on the road, in close proximity to each other:

'Smiler' Higgins	92
H.K. Harrison	94a
'Scrounger' Kind	106
Billy Mew	130
Leslie Wild	72 (in lodgings)
John Moorhouse	81 (in lodgings)

Saffron Road, South Wigston

Leslie Wild recalls that the road was nicknamed 'Teachers' Road' by the boys who gave that section of the road a wide berth, both in term time and during school holidays, as they quickly realised that six pairs of beady eyes could be focused on their every movement.

1939: WHAT GOODIES ARE BEING HANDED OUT TO PUPILS?

THIS photograph was recently found by Mrs Mary Freestone, of Wigston, and sent to me by Mr Alan Pearson, of Newbury. The back of the photograph has the stamp "Leicester Even-ing Mail Copyright Photo-graph" and is dated August 1, 1939. Apart from this, there are no more details.

The picture seems to have been taken at a boys school with something being handed out by the teachers. It looks as though the boys are taking the items from the baskets and boxes, so it probably isn't a school prize day. It could be preparations for the Second World War, which was only just over a month away.

Mr Pearson asks: "Does any reader know what the occasion was and do any readers recog-nise themselves?"

Pictured are the pupils receiving refreshments from the Headmaster, Mr HK Harrison and teachers Mr Kenneth Harris and Mr Ernest Powdrill. Watching the exercise are Mr WA Brockington, Director of Education, Mr Salter Davies, His Majesty's Inspector and various A.R.P. officials. (Leicester Mercury)

Leslie also has recollections of the House System, which was devised for the Boys' School by 'Scrounger' Kind and 'Dinky' Powdrill, shortly after the school was opened.

The Houses, named after local historical figures and colours were as follows:

Beaumont	Blue
Burnaby	Green
Montfort	Yellow
Wycliffe	Red

The Girls' School also created a House system and chose the names of nationally known heroines with accompanying colours:

Charlotte Bronte	Yellow
Elizabeth Fry	Green
Lady Jane Grey	Red
Florence Nightingale	Blue

During the first year in the life of the new schools there was a deep anxiety, shared by pupils and staff alike, that the outbreak of war in Europe was becoming unavoidable and was rapidly approaching. In readiness for the anticipated declaration of war, arrangements were put in hand for eight air raid shelters to be constructed immediately behind the Boys' School. They were located on the right-hand side of the playing fields, alongside the hedge and parallel with Windsor Avenue, Glen Parva. The shelters were built during the August break of 1939 to serve both the Boys' and Girls' Schools.

During the afternoon of 1 August 1939 a 'trial' evacuation procedure was practised by the teachers and pupils; this was to prepare the school to receive and assist in distributing evacuee children from the big cities, to families in Wigston and nearby villages. Children from the Boys' School and others assembled at Wigston Magna railway station and later 630 of them proceeded to the school where they were 'distributed' amongst several

Glen Parva Barracks. The sole remaining barrack block, later used by the Department of Education and Science

villages in the district. A 'token' medical examination was provided for the children. The exercise was concluded at 4.30pm.

On 3 September 1939 the British Prime Minister, Neville Chamberlain sombrely announced to the Nation at 11.00 o'clock that morning that: "A state of war exists between ourselves and Germany". For the first seven months there was what became known as the 'Phoney War' in which little happened except that a blackout was enforced, in the event of enemy air raids and food rationing was introduced. Evacuation procedures were carried out, at frequent intervals, at both schools. Time was of the essence in case of an air raid and the Headmaster's Log Book showed that the entire Boys' School could be evacuated within three and a half minutes.

A nearby hive of activity at this time was Glen Parva Barracks situated on Saffron Road. The Regimental Depot of the Leicestershire Regiment (became the Royal Leicestershire Regiment in 1946) was built in 1881 by the firm of Thomas Bland and Sons, Joiners and Builders of Harvey Lane, Leicester. It was here that the fathers of many of the pupils reported for their basic training following receipt of their call-up papers.

Jean Whitehead, who attended the Intermediate School from 1944 to 1948 was born at the barracks as her father, who served in the Great War and was wounded at Passchendaele, was a civilian caterer in the Sergeants' Mess. As a young girl, Jean can recall that Christmas time at Glen Parva Barracks was wonderful. Father Christmas actually came down the huge chimney in the Sergeants' Mess to deliver toys to the children living at the Depot. He

was none other than Regimental Sergeant Major John Meredith who joined the 1st Battalion of the Leicestershire Regiment in 1923 and was promoted to RSM at the Depot in 1941. He went on to serve with the Battalion in Malaya where he was taken prisoner, with his comrades, after the fall of Singapore. RSM Meredith was awarded the Distinguished Conduct Medal which he received from His Majesty, King George VI at Buckingham Palace after the war.

Jean's family had to vacate their home, at the barracks, along with other families and were moved out when war was declared to make room for the intake of new recruits. She recalls that her family had a marvellous social life at the barracks and they were very reluctant to leave but were obliged to do so and went to live at 10 Blaby Road, South Wigston. After leaving school Jean became a legal secretary with the Leicester firm of Bray and Bray Solicitors.

One 'Barrack Boy' whose family had to leave the depot, at the outbreak of the war, was John Purkiss. His father was Sergeant Bernard Purkiss, of the Leicestershire Regiment who was a master cook and had responsibility for all catering at the barracks. John had lived in married quarters all of his life and recalls his family living in barracks at Catterick, Colchester and Londonderry in addition to Glen Parva. He, too, recalls the sadness when his family had to leave the depot to move into a rented house in Kirkdale Road, South Wigston.

John attended the Intermediate School from 1942 to 1946. He married Jennifer Payne who was a pupil in the Intermediate School from 1945 to 1949 she being the daughter of Samuel Payne whose skills helped to create the stone acorns and the staircases which they ran up and down continuously during their time at the South Wigston Schools.

Following the outbreak of war, reservists were quickly recalled in all three services. Colin Dougherty remembers that John Gisborn, the Head Caretaker, was recalled for active service in 1939. His place at the schools was taken by Walter Sutton, one of Colin's old Sunday School teachers at South Wigston Methodist Church.

Another essential duty for which the caretaker Jack Gisborn is fondly remembered was his running of the tuck shop, in the Boys' School, which was located underneath the main staircase. Following the call-up of the caretaker, the running of the tuck shop passed to his successor Walter Sutton. He was ably assisted in the tuck shop, a coveted position, by Sidney Hales another boy who moved from Bassett Street in 1938 for the final period of his secondary education which he completed in 1939.

Sidney, nicknamed 'Titch', enjoyed his brief spell in the tuck shop and accepted sole responsibility for the shop when the caretaker was required to carry out his other duties. He recalls that sweets, chocolate, crisps and biscuits were all popular items amongst the boys. Sadly, the tuck shop became a casualty of the wartime years as rationing of commodities such as sweets and chocolate became necessary as food supplies diminished.

Three of the Hales family attended the Blaby Road Schools. Firstly, Sidney's elder sister Irene, (later Jackson) and Sidney was eventually followed by his sister Doris (married name Clements).

Sidney went on to work for the Leicester firm of British United Shoe Machinery Company Limited, boot and shoe machinery manufacturers, Union Works, 160 Belgrave Road, Leicester. His engineering ability enabled him to become the Apprentice of the Year and he worked for this prestigious company for forty eight years. He worked in both the planning and plant aspects of the firm's business and could operate all of the machinery on the shop floor. During his time with the company some three to four thousand employees worked for the firm which had a worldwide reputation.

During the winter of 1939-40, Leicestershire experienced a severe snow storm. The South Wigston Schools were closed, except to a few local pupils who were deployed in digging out pathways through the snowdrifts, some of which were four feet deep, to gain access to the air raid shelters. This was not the type of work that Colin and his friend Haydn Stevens were very keen on and they soon became very cold. During one of the breaks they decided to 'pop down to the boiler house' (strictly out of bounds) to see Walter Sutton and to

have a warm. They finished up assisting Walter to move a newly delivered supply of special coal for loading into the hoppers which supplied the auto-feed boilers. As Colin explains; "The boiler house had three boilers which were Ashwell and Nesbit (Leicester) auto feed boilers each with a large hopper to contain the specially graded coal. The automatic screw feed would then feed coal into the furnace to maintain the desired temperature in the schools. The special coal was in pieces of about one inch cubes."

Colin's description of what happened next makes interesting reading: "Just imagine us. Two fourteen year old boys dressed in droopy old shirts (Walter had provided them with two of his old shirts to keep their clothes clean) with hands and faces looking as if we had just come up from a coal mine. It was at that point that Miss Smith, the Headmistress of the Girls' School appeared at the door, looking for the caretaker. "Good Heavens!" she explained, "what are you two boys doing down here?" A short explanation satisfied her but she still looked horrified as she mounted the stairs on her way out."

Colin Dougherty, photographed at his home at 44 Leopold Street whilst attending South Wigston Boys' School

The moral of the story is that this particular escapade had an educational value for Colin. During his time in the boiler room he learned a good deal about auto-feed boilers and the importance of using the correct sized pieces of coal for the screw feed to work properly. Some forty years later, in the 1970s, in the course of his work as a service engineer he came across a precision measuring problem at one of the Rolls Royce factories where the wrong size of coal was being used for their auto-feed boilers due to the miners' strike. As a result of his knowledge, gained at school, Colin was able to solve the problem. A case of what was learnt in the boiler-room rather than the classroom!

Colin worked for the firm of Taylor, Taylor and Hobson for over fifty years and relates that one of Billy Mew's general knowledge sessions was of enormous assistance to him when he attended his initial interview with the firm. Billy had explained to the boys how the vacuum brakes worked on railway trains and this was one of the questions Colin was asked at his interview. To be taught by Billy Mew was an invaluable experience.

Another former pupil who attended the school between 1939 and 1943 was Roy Vivian Fowkes, who also greatly enjoyed rugby football. Upon leaving school he was offered a five year engineering apprenticeship at the then new factory Power Jets Limited of Whetstone. In Roy's words: "The fact that I received my education at South Wigston undoubtedly resulted in my selection as an engineer apprentice as opposed to the alternative of a craft apprenticeship". It was during his time as an apprentice, one of the forty apprentices among a workforce of 1200 employees, that he met, for the first time the great English aeronautical engineer, Sir Frank Whittle, who won worldwide acclaim as the inventor of the jet engine.

Roy Fowkes, having completed his apprenticeship in 1949 with qualifications in mechanical and aeronautical engineering and also having attended Loughborough College of Technology to obtain professional qualifications, was offered employment as a designer draughtsman with the National Gas Turbine Establishment (Power Jets Limited having been nationalised by the Government and was now

Sir Frank and Lady Whittle (centre) with Roy and Eileen Fowkes

Mrs Eveline Marjorie Higgins

NGTE). In 1953 he joined the aircraft industry at Weybridge and in 1956 he moved to work for a major oil company in which he served in a number of management positions before retiring in 1983.

In 1979 before retirement he, and a former colleague, encouraged Sir Frank Whittle, who was then living in the United States of America, to make a visit to the United Kingdom. The visit took place in 1980 and Sir Frank and Lady Whittle became firm friends of Roy Fowkes and his wife, Eileen. On their subsequent visits to the U.K. they would stay with Roy and his wife and Roy became Sir Frank Whittle's PR man in the United

Kingdom. In turn Roy and his wife spent all of their summer holidays at the Whittle's home in the U.S.A. for some 16 years until Sir Frank's death on 9 August 1996.

Since Sir Frank Whittle's death, Roy Fowkes has lectured about the life and work of the great aeronautical pioneer in some ninety locations in the United Kingdom, together with a number of lectures in America and other countries. Roy Fowkes was recently interviewed on BBC television following the unveiling of the statue to Sir Frank Whittle in his home city of Coventry.

On 1 March 1940 Mrs Marjorie Higgins, nee Dandy, the wife of Walter Higgins, was appointed to the staff of the Girls' School to be responsible for the teaching of domestic science. Despite the fact that husband and wife were working and teaching within the same complex, the Headmistress, Miss Gertrude Smith, firmly believed in a doctrine of never-the-twain-shall-meet which applied equally to pupils and staff. Thus in Walter's words: "We might as well have been on separate planets".

During 1940, as the war intensified, the effects of the conflict upon school life became increasingly evident. On 30 April 1940 the Boys' School assembled in the hall to say goodbye to Mr Henry William Davies, Form Master of Form II, who taught English and had joined the staff in September 1939, upon being called up for military service. He was the first of many.

Not only were the pupils experiencing the loss of teachers to H.M. Forces, at this juncture, they were also faced with having to say tearful farewells to their own fathers as many were gradually called up into the three services. This was quite an ordeal for the children concerned, with all the uncertainties and fears involved, as their fathers left to go overseas to fight in the various theatres of war.

One casualty of the war was the Metalwork Department in the Boys' School. Obviously, no metal could be made available and the existing machinery was required for wartime production purposes. The metalwork room was closed for the duration of hostilities and was utilised for the storage of bedding, mattresses and emergency supplies.

Many people believed that the school was designed for instant conversion into a hospital in the event of going to war. No evidence has been found to support this theory. Obviously new public buildings being erected in the late 1930s, were subject to a degree of secrecy at that time in relation to multi purpose usage.

In September 1940, two new teachers joined the staff of the Girls' School. Jean Green, nee Palmer, 1940-44, who lived off Narborough Road South recalls the appointment of the teachers in question. They were the sisters Miss Margaret Amy Peel and Miss Marjorie Ena Peel.

The Headmistress's Log Book shows that Miss Margaret Peel, who commenced on 1 September 1940, was trained at Goldsmith's College, London (1936-8) was to specialise in art and crafts and would take responsibility for Form 2B (41 girls). Her sister, Miss Marjorie Peel, who also trained at Goldsmith's College (1938-40), specialised in physical education in the Intermediate School, having completed a month long course at Loughborough College Summer School. She was allocated to Form 1A (42 girls).
Jean remembers that the girls quickly found a way to identify between the two sisters.

Miss Margaret Peel became "Orange Peel"

Miss Marjorie Peel became "Lemon Peel"

Her Form Mistress was Mrs V. Pegg, who had commenced on 1 September 1939 as a supply

The Ritz Cinema

teacher with Form 1B and specialised in geography. Jean recalls that Mrs Pegg introduced herself to her class with the memorable pronouncement: "Now girls, I can either be a policeman or your friend and I'd rather be a friend!"

Mrs Pegg was described as being 'firm, strict but very good'. She remained on the staff of the Girls' School until April 1945. Like many other girls, Jean Green was taught shorthand and typewriting which enabled her to obtain a Pitman's certificate in typewriting whilst studying at school.

The teacher who specialised in the instruction of Pitman's shorthand, typewriting and book-keeping in the newly formed Form IV, was Miss Evelyn Davies who commenced at the school in October 1941. The teaching of commercial subjects appealed to many of the girls who often referred to the "upper school" as the Technical School rather than the Intermediate School. Under the tuition of Miss Davies, pupils developed in these subjects which they were then able to take as part of the Central School's Examination of the East Midlands Educational Union and were ably prepared for entry into the commercial world.

Jean became a librarian upon leaving school in 1944 and went on to be a consultant with Boots Limited.

The sounding of the air raid warnings - the siren was situated on the roof of the Ritz Cinema, Blaby Road, South Wigston - gradually increased, resulting in lessons being disrupted as pupils proceeded to and from the air raid shelters.

Life in the schools, revolved around bells and sirens at this time. With such large numbers of pupils moving around the site, from classroom to playground to gymnasium etc, the ringing of the bells was all-important and had to be rigidly adhered to. Equally, rapid evacuation to the shelters, when an air raid was imminent, called for an urgent and speedy response from pupils and staff alike.

The air raid shelters were constructed in such a manner that they were partly, if only slightly, underground. This often resulted in water collecting on the floors of the shelters and pupils sitting with their feet on the wooden benches throughout the duration of an air raid. Girls were instructed to cover their white blouses, when outside, in case they were seen and subsequently

SS Otranto

machine-gunned by German fighter pilots as they made their way to the shelter.

Gas masks were issued to everyone and had to be carried, religiously, to and from school. Woe betide any pupil spotted without their gas mask! Every school was issued with a stirrup-pump (a hand-operated water pump used to extinguish small fires) at a cost of £1 each and teaching staff were trained in the methods of dealing with fires caused by incendiary bombs.

Another pupil who commenced at the Boys' School in 1940 was Lance Davis, one of three Australian-born brothers who had arrived with their mother, in the United Kingdom in 1938. Lance's parents had emigrated to Australia in the 1920s where he was born at Lismore, New South Wales on 6 October 1930, he was the youngest in a large family of twelve children.

Lance's mother Frances had decided to return to visit her mother in South Wigston who was ill at the time. Together with her sons Lance, Roy (13) and Keith (12) the family endured a seven week voyage on the SS *Otranto* (20,000 tons) a passenger ship of the Orient Line. During the sea journey, Lance worked away at a text book *Examples in Arithmatic* (First Year) for Secondary Schools published in Lismore.

Sadly, on the day the ship docked at Tilbury, news was received that Lance's grandmother had died that day. He, together with his mother and brothers remained in England whilst his father Charles Reynolds Davis managed to get back to the United Kingdom on the last ship to leave Australia before the Second World War commenced, he was a self-employed baker by trade. The rest of the family, being older than Lance and his brothers, remained in Australia.

Initially, the family lived at 33 Station Street, South Wigston, the former home of Lance's

Private Roy Davis King's Shropshire Light Infantry

Private Keith Davis King's Own Scottish Borderers

grandmother. Lance attended Bassett Street Junior School whilst Roy and Keith went straight to the new Modern School. Unsurprisingly, in view of their distinctive accents the three brothers were called 'Aussies' by their contemporaries. A major problem for them was getting used to wearing shoes something they were unaccustomed to doing other than on formal occasions back in New South Wales where the climate was such that children seldom wore footwear. During his two years at Bassett Street, Lance recalls that he, along with other children, took food to school in tins to "stock-up" in case of air raids.

In 1940 Lance followed his brothers to the Modern School and spent the next four years there. He vividly recalls being out with his brother Keith, on 9 July 1941, cycling from Countesthorpe to Willoughby Waterleys when suddenly they spotted a low flying fighter aircraft coming towards them. They instinctively waved to the pilot but suddenly realized, by the markings, that it was a German plane whereupon they "dived into the ditch" before cycling back home at breakneck speed.

Both Roy and Keith Davis were duly called up into the Army during the war. Roy served in the King's Shropshire Light Infantry and Keith was conscripted into the King's Own Scottish Borderers. The brothers served in Egypt with their respective units during their military service.

Lance remembers that one of his form teachers was Mrs Brownjohn and like everyone, of his generation, he recalls the unforgettable Billy Mew. Having served in the Royal Air Force during his National Service Lance remained in England and became a tailor by trade. He had his own business, together with his wife Ellen, firstly at premises in Wigston Magna and later in South Wigston.

By the end of 1940 Ken Harris, Walter Higgins and Leslie Wild had each, in turn, been called-up for military service. Special assemblies were called in order that the boys and fellow teachers could say goodbye to three popular masters. When Walter Higgins left South Wigston to report for military service on 16 May 1940, his wife's Headmistress, the redoubtable and seemingly unromantic Gertie Smith, refused permission for Marjorie Higgins to miss morning assembly in order to see her husband off from the railway station. In true Higgins' spirit, the Head's order was disobeyed.

Following the call-up of 'Smiler' Higgins, responsibility for rugby at the Boys' School passed to Edward Henry 'Johnny' Churches.

School dinners, particularly during wartime, remain an abiding memory for many former pupils. Most of the boys had insatiable appetites and the boy at the head of the table, usually a prefect, together with his trusted lieutenants who brought the food in bowls from the kitchen, always made certain that their portions matched their seniority. First Year boys, at the bottom of the table, ranked low in the pecking (or eating) order and this was reflected in the miniscule amounts which appeared on their plates.

In the Girls' School, Colleen Jefford nee Moore who attended the school between 1941 and 1946 recalls that if pupils ever asked what the school dinner consisted of they were told 'things in stuff!' Colleen who lived in Fleckney and travelled to and fro on the school bus learned shorthand and typing which equipped her for her future career. She has vivid memories of being taught English, French, history, geography, painting, cookery, physical education and music lessons. As with all pupils she also remembers the bicycle sheds, the playground and the playing field. Mrs Holm and the redoubtable Miss Constance Wright live on in her memories.

Cynthia Deakin, nee Terry, 1940-1944 from Great Glen recalls that cheese pie was a favourite but fish pies and stews were not popular. As for the sweets, she recalls: "No one will have forgotten semolina pudding. It was served in a bowl with a spoonful of jam at the bottom. The girls sitting at the bottom of the table were lucky if they saw any of the jam as it wasn't revealed until half of the bowl had been emptied."

Beryl Johnson, nee Bolton, 1940-1944, discovered upon arrival at the Intermediate School that it was a dramatic upheaval from her 'cosy roots' at Whetstone Church of England Primary School. Strict dress code in the form of school uniform and unquestionable discipline, imposed by Miss Wright, who rapped many an unsuspecting pupil on their head with her thimbled finger, are vividly recalled!

As the bombing of British cities by the German Air Force (the Luftwaffe) intensified, large parties of children from London, Birmingham and Sheffield arrived in Leicester under the Government Evacuation Scheme, which had been introduced at the outbreak of the war. When the trains, laden with evacuees, arrived in Wigston, via Spion Kop Station, girls were required to go to the school occasionally on Saturdays to serve tea to the evacuee children prior to their being allocated placements with families in the vicinity. Beryl remembers that she and others would have to remain at the school throughout the day, whether the trains arrived or not.

The only wartime outing Beryl could recall was the Intermediate sections walking up to the 'Pork Pie' Library on Saffron Lane to see a special exhibition of Russian photographs. Her abiding memory of school dinners was the early wartime 'starter' of a piece of raw vegetable, this could be in the form of a piece of turnip or a fragment cut from the heart of a cabbage. This was no doubt of nutritional value but certainly was not universally popular.

On 11 November 1940, Miss Margaret

Elizabeth Robinson commenced work as a junior clerk in the Girls' School.

An interesting entry in the Headmistress's Log Book, dated 14 May 1941 recorded: "This morning one half of the class in Domestic Science Room I saw the washing and dressing of the baby of Mrs Higgins, former Domestic Science Mistress. The remaining half of the class will receive a similar lesson next Wednesday morning". Mrs Higgins had terminated her employment at the school on 5 November 1940 and her son, Ian, was born on 6 April 1941. Thus, Ian Higgins was the third member of his family 'to appear in front of the class' at the new schools.

The reality of war was dramatically brought home during the summer of 1941 when a stick of five bombs was dropped by a German aircraft, in a line, at 300 yard intervals on Saffron Road to Forryan's Farm. Huge craters appeared in the gardens of 134 and 136 Saffron Road and were viewed in horror by the local community. Mr William Mew's home (130 Saffron Road) was just yards away from the incident, and the vulnerability of the school, to an air attack became a frightening possibility.

A great deal of attention was paid to the school uniform in the Girls' School. Many recall that the uniform consisted of a navy pleated tunic and white blouse, a navy and yellow striped tie, black stockings and a navy blazer emblazoned with the school badge. In the summer months, the girls would wear a blue and white gingham dress complete with a 'Peter Pan' collar. The least popular item of the school uniform, for most of the girls, was the navy beret and to be seen not wearing this mark of identity was considered to be a criminal offence. However, once the school buses left the bus-park, the berets would be "whipped off" in defiant profusion.

There was no obligation on the boys to wear a school uniform although for those in the Intermediate School there was a school blazer, complete with badge, which some boys wore on a regular basis but the many wartime strains, on a family budget, was a determining factor. Most boys wore the school cap, an item of apparel which was often snatched and thrown over hedges, into snowdrifts or utilised as a makeshift football.

With the arrival of evacuee children into the

locality, provision had to be made for them to be allocated places in nearby schools. The Headmaster's Log Book shows that, on 2 September 1941, at the commencement of the academic year 1941-42, the total number of boys on the registers had risen to 584. It became necessary for the library and dining hall to be used as additional classrooms, together with the gymnasium and woodwork room which were also utilised for teaching purposes. Extra staff were appointed to cope with the influx. Similar problems were encountered in the Girls' School where the average attendance, during the first week of the autumn term was recorded as 524.7 pupils.

The respective Log Books also recorded details of numerous accidents involving pupils on school premises and the playing fields. This often necessitated the attendance of a doctor for the boy or girl concerned to be taken to the local doctor's surgery for medical treatment. The General Practioner concerned was Dr John Rushworth Lund, Physician and Surgeon whose surgery was nearby at 52 Blaby Road, South Wigston.

With so many of the male teachers being called up for military service, it became necessary for the County Education Committee to fill the gaps by appointing lady supply teachers and, in 1942, the Log Book for the Boys' School records the following teachers in post:

Mrs Vera Henry, BA (Wales)
Mrs Edith Brownjohn
Mrs Lottie Hall
Mrs Martha Outridge
Mrs Violet Partridge
Mrs Grace Saxton
Mrs Edith Harrison (wife of the Headmaster)

By 1942 a national labour shortage was causing severe problems to local farmers and the need for assistance at harvest time was partly resolved by the use of schoolchildren. When the new academic year commenced on 17 August 1942 the Headmaster of the Boys' School, Mr H.K. Harrison, recorded in his Log Book:

"Owing to wartime and the need for boy-labour on the farms for the potato harvest, the summer holiday was divided this year into two parts, one part having just been taken, of a fortnight's duration, the other part to follow in the autumn." The second part commenced on 2 October when the Boys' School closed for a three week break, to allow boys to assist with potato harvesting. The Headmaster revealed:

"Before closing, arrangements were made for the immediate 'call-up' for farm work, if required, of the 298 boys who had volunteered for work during the holidays. This number did not include 46 boys who had made their own arrangements to assist farmers." The Girls' School closed for the same period and many of the girls also volunteered to assist with the potato harvesting on local farms.

The Chairman of the Managers of the two schools, at this time, was Mr Arthur William Holmes, a local dentist with a surgery at 14 Saffron Road, South Wigston. He regularly visited to present various trophies and to examine and sign the Log Books.

Sheila Hackett, nee Brewin, was appointed secretary of the Boys' School in 1942 at the age of 16 years. She had been trained in copper plate writing and was required to carry out a variety of tasks including the keeping of pupils' records, collecting dinner monies, balancing the books and dealing with minor telephone calls. Sheila

occupied a small office which led directly through to the Headmaster's office. She vividly recalls boys standing outside of her office waiting their turn to go through to be caned by Mr Harrison. The pain inflicted was lessened by a glimpse of the beauty of Sheila!

Sheila Brewin

Roy Anthony Allton, Intermediate School 1939-1943, was caned on two occasions by the Headmaster. Firstly, for going into a small ante-room within the music room one lunchtime whereupon he re-tuned the school radio-set in order to put on "Workers' Playtime" which could have resulted in the radio being unavailable for use by the Headmaster, in the event of an air raid warning. The second instance was for complaining when, for one week, the price of the school dinners was increased by six pence from two shillings to two shillings and six pence and, to add insult to injury, the puddings were cut in half. Anthony thought this was most unjust but his protestations only resulted in a second dose of the cane.

Despite his earlier misdemeanours, Anthony became a model of behaviour and progressed to be a prefect and joint Head Boy with Peter Clowes in his final year. Two Head Boys were required during 1942-43 owing to the large intake of evacuee children into the school. One of the responsibilities of the Head Boy was to ring the bell, at the required times, throughout the day. The bell-push was situated in the Secretary's office and the Head Boys would press the bell to sound the change of lessons and at the commencement and the conclusion of break time.

Anthony had a great love of science during his schooldays, and after completing his National Service in the Royal Air Force, he became an electrical engineer with a company in Huddersfield where he still lives.

Later, Anthony's brother Barry attended the school and was captain of the cricket team in his final year. Upon leaving in 1949 he joined the local firm Fox and Company, Incorporated Accountants, 14 King Street, Leicester prior to going to work for

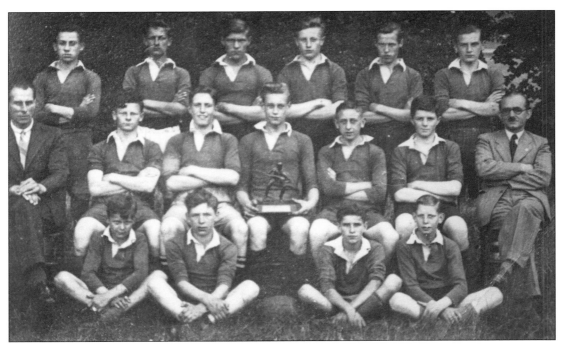

South Wigston Boys' School 7 A Side. Colin is second left, back row. The Headmaster, Mr H.K. Harrison, is seated left with Mr Johnny Churches seated right.

the West Bromwich Building Society. Barry now lives in Stourbridge, Worcestershire.

On 30 April 1942 Mr Nicola Picozzi left the staff of the Boys' School having been appointed Head Teacher at Desford County Junior School in Leicestershire. He took up his appointment the following day and was the first in a long line of teachers, from South Wigston, to progress to Headships.

A distinct advantage of the physical location of the two schools providing different levels of education, within the same building, was the opportunity for some boys and girls to progress from the Secondary Modern School to the Intermediate School. One such pupil was Colin Elliott 1941-45. His School Record Card, completed by the Headmaster, noted that Colin had been transferred "on merit" to the Intermediate School where he went on to obtain his East Midlands Educational Union Schools' Certificate. Colin, who was a fine rugby player, was selected for the school's Sevens A Side and was a member of the school side which won the Leicestershire Schools' Sevens Trophy in 1943-1944 by defeating Moat Road Intermediate School in the final.

After leaving school Colin played for the South Wigston Old Boys until being called up for his National Service (1950-52) where he served in the Royal Army Medical Corps and reached the rank of Corporal.

During the morning of 19 August 1943, the Boys' School was visited by a member of staff on military service, Kenneth Harris, the popular Music teacher, who was serving with the Royal Army Medical Corps. He had been taken prisoner, with others of his unit, by the Italian Army on 21 November 1941 when his unit, the 2nd Light Field Ambulance, was involved in the relief of Tobruk in the Western Desert. He was held in captivity in various Italian Prisoner of War camps in North Africa and Italy until he was repatriated back to England in June 1943.

7385140 Private Kenneth Holmes Harris

Visiting the school enabled Kenneth Harris to personally thank his fellow teachers and the pupils for their kindness in sending him regular parcels of cigarettes and pipe tobacco for which he was enormously grateful. During his time as a prisoner of war, he had effectively contributed to the maintaining of morale among his comrades by forming choirs and concert parties, in addition to teaching English, French and music in a series of classes held within the camps.

The first change of Headship at the South Wigston Schools occurred when Miss Florence Gertrude Smith retired on 15 August 1943.

The candlesticks and trinket box made by Louis Moore

The teaching staff at South Wigston Girls' School on the occasion of the retirement of Miss Smith

Miss Smith's place as Headmistress was taken by Miss Edna Walker, the Headmistress of Melton Mowbray Junior Girls' School, Leicestershire. Miss Walker took up her duties on 30 August 1943.

One pupil who attended the school, during the wartime years, and left as the war continued to rage across the world was Louis Moore from Enderby. He was a pupil at the Intermediate School from 1940 to 1943 and retains vivid memories of the teachers who made a profound impression upon him. The 'brilliance' of Billy Mew whose lessons were unforgettable and Cyril Tweed, the woodwork master, under whose guidance Louis created a pair of candlesticks from African mahogany and a trinket box using Australian wood for the box and Japanese oak to complete the lid. He has treasured these precious artefacts for the past sixty five years.

He also recalls being enthralled by the science lessons taken by 'Scrounger' Kind who taught the boys the mystery of the splitting of the atom.

After leaving school, Louis secured an apprenticeship at Empire Stone, Narborough and served in the Royal Marines during his period of National Service 1947-1949. Senior NCO's in the Royal Marines were not renowned for being the most approachable of mankind but in Sergeant 'Titch' Thirlby, Louis found someone to whom he could relate as he too was a former pupil of South Wigston Boys' School!

CHX 118733 Marine Louis Moore 1948

Louis became a foreman carpenter at Harrow Technical College before spending three years in South Africa in the 1960s. Finally he became Clerk of Works at Decorum, Hemel Hempstead until he retired. He now lives with his wife Olive in Bournemouth where they will celebrate their sixtieth wedding anniversary in September 2009.

On 29 October 1943, Mr Ernest Oscar Powdrill ceased his duties at the Boys' School upon taking up the post of Headmaster of the South Wigston Junior Boys' School. The minutes of the Leicestershire County Council Education Committee (1 November 1943) confirmed his appointment and revealed that twenty teachers had been invited to apply for the Headship under the Committee's Promotion Scheme.

At a farewell assembly, the Head Boy presented Mr Powdrill with £1.5s.0d as a parting gift from the boys of the Fourth Form and the Headmaster presented him with a cheque for £6 being a gift from the staff. 'Dinky' had been a popular teacher and as George Harratt recalled: "He liked to talk about his First World War exploits and was encouraged to do so by the boys!"

Wartime shortages often created problems in the classroom and some teachers were more adept than others in seeing this as a challenge. Maurice Belben who entered the school in 1943 recalls that: 'Scrounger' Kind could get materials brought in by pupils to supplement the needs of his laboratory like no other could. But it also meant we could carry on with our experiments".

Orson James Kind
by courtesy of Donald E. Green

Despite the problems and challenges of educating some 900 pupils, during the wartime years, high levels of attainment were maintained at both schools. On 4 August 1944 the Headmaster, Mr H.K. Harrison, recorded in the Log Book: "Eleven boys left for transfer to Kibworth Beauchamp Grammar School and four to Loughborough College School".

Although the Government was essentially preoccupied with the demands of the war, the Minister of Education, Richard Austen Butler was convinced that a comprehensive reform of the educational system was required. There had been no major reform since 1902 and he was firmly of the view that every child should be given the right to free secondary education. 'Rab' Butler, as he became known to everyone, was responsible for the Education Act 1944 which was considered to be his greatest legislative success and has been frequently referred to as the Butler Education Act. One of the fundamental aspects of the act was the provision to increase the school leaving age to 15 years "as soon as the Minister is satisfied that it has been practical". Amazingly, with the war reaching a critical stage, optimism abounded that victory would be secured thus the planning of post-war education was under way.

The success rate, achieved by many of the girls in commercial subjects continued under the expert tuition of Miss Evelyn Davies. Cynthia Deakin recalls that Miss Davies was an excellent teacher. In 1944, when in her final year in Form 4, she experienced along with other girls, the benefits of commercial training.

In Cynthia's words: "We were very fortunate to have this opportunity as most school leavers had to pay to go to a commercial college". In addition the school made arrangements for the girls to attend interviews to obtain work upon leaving. Cynthia duly obtained a position with the Leicestershire County Council Education Department.

Another girl who studied the commercial subjects for a time was Doris Clements, nee Hales, from Croft who attended the Girls' School from 1943 to 1947. She had hoped to obtain a place at Hinckley Grammar School but her father could only pay for the uniform and books for her brother. In the 1940s girls often had to take second place to

Form 4, Intermediate School. Girls undergoing their training. Back row: Mary Wilson, Sheila Lucas, Margaret Baker, Pamela Hands, Jean Brothwell, Muriel Tams, Audrey Banks, Muriel Herbert, Pearl Lomas. Front row: Miss Evelyn Davies (Form Teacher) Cynthia Terry, Janet Jarrom, Audrey Harris, Audrey Garner, Miss Edna Walker (Headmistress)

their brothers when families decided which of their siblings should have the chance of a grammar school placement.

Nevertheless, Doris enjoyed her time at the school, she made the most of her opportunities and retains happy and positive memories. Remarkably she can still recall the names of the thirty plus girls in her A class, in alphabetical order, as they were read from the register.

She had a fond regard for Miss Davies and clearly she benefited from her tuition. Upon leaving school she worked in a factory but later obtained a position, as a telephonist/receptionist, with Blaby Rural District Council where she was employed for thirteen years. Doris attended school reunions until the 1970s and often met up with former pupils at get-togethers in their own homes. She remains in touch with quite a number of her school friends from over sixty years ago.

On 22 November 1944, a meeting was held at the Girls' School to form an Old Pupils' Association. There were approximately 150 old pupils present. It was agreed to launch the association with the election of the following officers:

President:	Miss Edna Walker
Vice Presidents:	Mrs Constance D. Holm
	Miss Emma G. Smith
	Miss Constance M. Wright
Treasurer:	Miss Constance Wright
Secretary:	Miss Sykes

On 21 December 1944 the Boys' School closed for the Christmas holidays. That day was marked by a special assembly held to say farewell to Billy Mew who was retiring at the age of 69. Speeches and presentations were the order of the day and among the guests were a number of old boys who had come along to say goodbye to a remarkable and much-loved teacher. He was always known as "W.M." to his fellow members of staff and "Billy" to the boys.

All of the boys taught by Billy Mew would have their favourite stories of him. Probably the most memorable related to when, at the commencement of an art lesson, he would transform the huge blackboard into a wonderful picture depicting a seascape or a country scene. Billy would then carefully replace his set of crayons and instruct the boys to copy his artistic work whilst he left the classroom for a short break, adding that he would return in ten minutes to examine the results of their efforts. He then disappeared along the corridor and into a storeroom where he would enjoy a much needed cigarette – his beloved Park Drive!

Speeches of tribute led by the Headmaster culminated with the Head Boy presenting Mr Mew with a cheque for £16, the result of a collection from past and present pupils. References were made to his amazingly long career of 48 years at the South Wigston Schools and 56 years in total as a teacher plus his tremendous loyalty to the school.

A picture of Mr Mew appeared in the *Illustrated*

56 Years A Teacher

William Merrifield Mew (Leicester Mercury)

Leicester Chronicle (16 December 1944) under the heading "56 years a teacher" and showed him in the classroom with some of his scholars.

By the end of the academic year 1943/1944 more girls were moving on to careers in the commercial world as a result of the training they had received from Miss Davies. Beryl Johnson, nee Bolton, stayed on at school to take the commercial course: "under the pleasant tutelage of Miss Davies".

Beryl can recall the names of all of her classmates in her final year in 1944

Having received a good grounding in the commercial subjects, Beryl eventually worked at the London and North Eastern Railway Company's Passenger Station in Great Central Street, Leicester and later at the Leicester Polytechnic for twenty-three years.

Beryl's husband Allan Johnson, also from Whetstone, attended the Intermediate School for three years from 1940 to 1943 and left to become an apprentice model-maker and pattern-maker at Power Jets Limited in his home village. He went on to become the best craft apprentice and spent some time at the Royal Aircraft Establishment at Farnborough.

Allan became one of Sir Frank Whittle's personal model-makers and his work appeared on Sir Frank's mantelpiece when he was interviewed on BBC Television. Allan and Beryl received a letter, personally written by Sir Frank, saying how he always appreciated the work of his model-makers in producing scale aircraft.

As the Second World War entered its sixth year the need for schoolchildren to help with harvesting continued. During October 1944 both the Boys' and Girls' Schools closed for a week in order that pupils could assist local farmers with the potato harvest.

At long last, on 8 May 1945, the war ended in Europe. V.E. Day (Victory in Europe) had arrived and to mark the cessation of hostilities, two days the 8th and 9th May were declared National Holidays. The Headmistress recorded in her Log Book "A very historic occasion". Great

Fourth Form, Intermediate Girls' School 1944. Back row: Margaret Wheeler, Mavis Grimes, Mrs V. Pegg, (Form Teacher) Cynthia Gould, Jean Cherry, Doreen Hodson, Miss Edna Walker (Headmistress), Jean Roberts and Ida Root. Front row: Mary Clarke, Beryl Bolton, Jean Mothersale, Peggy Cross, Carol Saunders and Barbara Foster

celebrations were held in the towns and villages and many boys and girls turned their thoughts to the returning home of their fathers. Sadly for some this was not to be and for others, whose fathers were still involved in the war in the Far East, a further three months of conflict and anxiety awaited.

Gradually, teachers who had served in H.M. Forces were demobbed and returned to their respective schools. One of the first to return was Mr Kenneth Raymond Wilson who was welcomed back to the Boys' School by the Headmaster, on 9 January 1946, having served in the Forces for five years. He took over responsibility for English in the school. As the male teachers returned from active service, it became necessary for the women supply teachers to leave and, on such occasions, the Headmaster paid tribute at assemblies for: "The splendid service given by the ladies during the very difficult period of the war years". The tributes were richly deserved.

Maurice Belben, who became a pupil at the Intermediate School in 1943 was one of three boys whose curiosity got the better of them and resulted in their group expulsion on 1 April 1946 which happened to be the date of Maurice's 14th birthday. Access to the roof space at the schools, was strictly forbidden but the boys in question scaled the loft ladder in order to gain access into the interior of the roof to reconnoitre the area above the girls' changing rooms next to the showers. This caused them to be late for the next lesson and they were: "Eventually traced by the Gymnastics teacher spread-eagled around the girls loft cover like petals on a flower".

Maurice related how they were: "Obviously endeavouring to improve their knowledge in the anatomy of the human female form". Such an explanation cut no ice with the Headmaster and they were promptly expelled from school. When meeting up at the school gates one day with their contemporaries, they were asked the obvious question "Was it worth being expelled for?" Their reply was complete with eyes rolling: "Damned right it was".

During 1946 more teachers were demobilised and returned to take up their former posts at the Boys' School, including the popular trio of Kenneth Harris, Walter Higgins and Leslie Wild.

After six years of wartime service 'Smiler' Higgins recommenced his teaching career on 1 April 1946. Having initially served in the Royal Army Medical Corps, he was transferred to the Army Educational Corps in 1941 where he was immediately promoted to Sergeant-Instructor.

7379293 Sergeant Walter Higgins

He reached the rank of Warrant Office Class II in May 1943 and was promoted to Warrant Officer Class I in January 1946. (The Corps became the Royal Army Education Corps in 1946).

The saying 'Boys will be Boys' comes to mind when one reflects upon the exploits of Bill Blankley and eight of his rugby playing school friends, from Form 3A, in the spring of 1946. Bill, who attended the Intermediate School between 1943 and 1947 recalled that the nine boys in question were assembled and waiting in the gymnasium for Mr Churches, the P.E. master, in order to go through an exercise routine. As Mr Churches had failed to arrive the boys decided to spend their time constructively, Fred Grimes went under the stage where the sports kit was stored and appeared with the rugby ball. Initially, the boys were content with running up and down the gym passing the ball and indulging in a spot of loose kicking. However, the adventurous spirit of Fred and Terry Whittaker then took over when they decided to display their skill in executing a long kick. Fred lay on the floor holding the ball in a

'Direct hit 1946'
by courtesy of David Blankley

vertical position with two fingers. Terry proceeded to run up and produced a magnificent kick which, disastrously, resulted in the ball going straight through the stained glass window bearing the Leicestershire County Council Coat of Arms.

Stained glass window in the Boys' gymnasium

The horrified boys quickly pulled the blackout curtain across the shattered window and decided to keep quiet about the incident. Immediately afterwards Mr Churches appeared, the exercise routine was then carried out and the boys duly beat a hasty retreat.

That evening Terry Whittaker owned up his misdeed to his father who promptly ordered him to confess his crime to the Headmaster the next day. In fear and trepidation, Terry informed Mr Harrison of the incident and at assembly, that morning, the Headmaster read out his usual list of events and finally said: "the following boys will line up outside of my office - Whittaker, Grimes, Blankley, Pawley, Finn, Waterfield (plus three others)."

Terry was the first to enter the Head's office

where he received nine strokes of the cane followed by the second protagonist Fred Grimes who also received nine strokes. The remaining seven boys received six strokes each. Mr Harrison then called the nine boys into his office, whereupon he informed them that the stained glass windows for the school had been specially made at Loughborough College. As part of their punishment each of them would have to pay in excess of £3 for a replacement window to be made.

During the afternoon, the nine disgraced rugby enthusiasts pondered on how they would break the news, of their costly misdemeanour to their parents when Fred Grimes was sent to the Headmaster's office for further punishment for misbehaviour. He received an additional six strokes to make his total for the day fifteen strokes in all. Does this, one wonders, constitute an unenviable personal record which has stood the test of time?

The following academic year saw Terry Whittaker, the confessor of this sorry affair, completely redeemed when he was appointed as school captain by the Headmaster which is ample proof of H K Harrison's sense of fair play and lack of malice.

The wartime efforts of the Girls' School was recognised on 6 June 1946 when the Deputy Headmistress, Miss Constance Wright, attended the Royal Garden Party at Buckingham Palace in recognition of the contribution made by the school in connection with War Savings. This was to be the first of two visits by Miss Wright to a Buckingham Palace Garden Party.

June 1946 witnessed an event to be treasured by every schoolchild, throughout the country, who received a certificate from His Majesty King George VI. The dates of the major conflicts of the Second World War were recorded on the back of

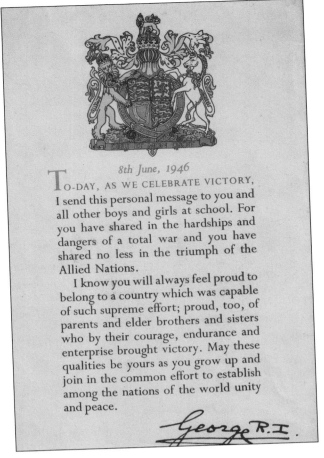

8th June, 1946

TO-DAY, AS WE CELEBRATE VICTORY, I send this personal message to you and all other boys and girls at school. For you have shared in the hardships and dangers of a total war and you have shared no less in the triumph of the Allied Nations.

I know you will always feel proud to belong to a country which was capable of such supreme effort; proud, too, of parents and elder brothers and sisters who by their courage, endurance and enterprise brought victory. May these qualities be yours as you grow up and join in the common effort to establish among the nations of the world unity and peace.

George R.I.

Certificate from His Majesty The King

the certificate and many pupils obtained the autographs of their teachers on the important and treasured 'Gift from the King.'

On 26 June 1946 to conclude an eventful month, in the history of South Wigston schools, the East Midlands Educational Union Schools' Certificate (Part II) was taken for the first time. The examination papers, in the various subjects, were taken throughout the following two weeks.

Kenneth Harris was soon integrated into the developing range of activities in the Boys' School. In addition to his inspirational teaching of music, he introduced boys to out of school challenges and pursuits. Ralph Willcox, 1943-48, recalls that Ken Harris introduced him and other boys to Youth Hostelling. On one occasion in 1946 they cycled up to Derbyshire and stayed at Islam Hall Youth Hostel where they had their first swim in a lake.

Ralph also enjoyed his rugby taught and coached by Johnny Churches. At that time the Leicester Tigers encouraged local schoolboys to watch their home matches at Welford Road, Leicester. Occasionally complimentary tickets were distributed and those lucky enough to obtain tickets, for a home game, would later be asked questions by Mr Churches on different aspects of

the game they had seen, i.e. scrums and line-outs.

In the 1946 examinations, eight of the girls took and passed the higher grade of the E.M.E.U. Certificate and a number of them felt they owed much to Mrs Constance Dorothy Holm from whom, respect and genuine fondness remained undiminished.

One ex-pupil who feels that Mrs Holm was an enormous influence in her life is Jean Chapman, nee Clowes, 1941-1946. She attended the Intermediate School and thoroughly enjoyed English and English Literature, she recalls: "I remember our love of words and literature being fostered by reading aloud in groups, outside if the weather was fine". Mrs Holm lent her a copy of *All Quiet on the Western Front* by the German novelist and former soldier, Eric Maria Remarque and: "Put me in touch with realism in writing". Jean was to go on to achieve literary success.

She was also an excellent Netball player and represented Leicestershire schools in 1946.

Leicestershire County Schools' Netball Team 1946
Left to right: Sheila Greening, Jean Chapman, Peggy Doidge, Dorothy Limb, Betty Holman, A.N.Other, A.N. Other. The team photograph was taken at Wyggeston Girls' School

Remarkably, five of the seven girls came from South Wigston Girls' School. Jean feels that the credit for this achievement must go to Miss Norah White, the Physical Training, Games and Dancing teacher.

Jean was encouraged to stay on at school in order to take the East Midlands Educational Union School Certificate (Part II). Having successfully passed the examination, she initially worked in a solicitor's office then at the *Leicester Mercury* before taking an Open University BA (Hons) Degree which she obtained after marrying Alan Chapman, who also attended the school. Jean went on to teach creative writing and to have fourteen historical novels published. Her most successful novel, *A New Beginning* appeared as two paperback books and also on tape, her first and eighth novels were short listed for the Romantic Novelists' Association (worldwide) major award. Jean feels that her success stems from the teaching and encouragement she received from Mrs Holm.

Jean's husband, Alan, left South Wigston Modern School in 1944 and obtained work as a switchboard operator at the Leicestershire County Police Headquarters, 420 London Road, Leicester. After three years he moved to the new Police Station at Station Road, Wigston Magna. He was called up for National Service and served in the Scots Guards, his unit served in Malaya. After demobilisation he joined the Leicestershire Constabulary and was stationed at Market Harborough and later Oakham. He served for nine years before setting up his own business as a newsagent in Countesthorpe. Alan contributed significantly to Jean's literary success in his role as her researcher.

Sheila McKenlay, nee Dunkley, 1941-45 remembers Mrs Holm as: "My favourite teacher" who taught the third year pupils in English and French. Sheila enjoyed and did well in both subjects and recalls Mrs Holm as being: "Very kind and I think we all liked her very much".

Another girl who was persuaded to stay on at school for an extra year was Anne Tester, nee Donne, who entered the Modern School in 1942. Although having encountered the Headmistress, Miss Walker, on a number of occasions due to her 'bad behaviour', she was finally encouraged by her Headmistress to remain at school and tackle certain subjects at a higher level. It proved to be a real turning point for Anne when she moved up to the Intermediate School at the age of fourteen years. She found the experience to be both challenging and stimulating and went on to obtain her E.M.E.U. Schools' Certificate in the commercial subjects – bookkeeping, typewriting and shorthand plus English, geography and domestic science, having reached her sixteenth birthday.

Anne went on to obtain 'O' Levels at Leicester Technical College and gained admittance to a Teacher Training College followed by a career in teaching in Leicester, York and Cleethorpes. Ultimately she obtained a post as a Community Tutor at Countesthorpe College, moving on to run the Department of Community Education as Vice-Principal.

South Wigston Girls' School gave Anne a good grounding in basic subjects and, most importantly, 'a second chance' at the precise moment she needed it. In her view: "That was the most valuable contribution that a school can offer and for that I am eternally grateful".

On 30 July 1946, the Director of Education presented a Development Plan for Primary and Secondary Schools in Leicestershire, in accordance with the requirements of the Education Act 1944, to a meeting of the Education Committee.

The report contained the following extracts which were to have a profound effect on the long-term futures of the South Wigston schools:

Secondary Technical Schools
Admission to the County Grammar Schools is to be continued on the present scale.

There are two other schools which hitherto provided a form of secondary technical education - Coalville Broom Leys and the Intermediate Departments of the South Wigston Modern Schools for Boys and Girls respectively. It has already been found that the number of qualified children is insufficient to support them and it is proposed that they be discontinued. The South Wigston Schools will continue as Modern Schools, the Secondary Technical Departments merging with the new Secondary Schools referred to below. Coalville Broom Leys will be merged in the Coalville Grammar School.

Grammar Schools
It is proposed that a new Grammar/Technical School be established at Wigston. This school would take, as well as some of the pupils from the district who now travel to Kibworth, the Secondary

South Wigston Old Boys' R.F.C. Photographed during their first season 1946-47
Back row: Alan Chapman, Alan Davies, John Tipper, A.N. Other, Colin Elliott, Gordon Mawby
Centre row: Glyn Measures, Roy Brightwell, Ken Ginns, Arthur Murgatroyd
Front row: Norman Causier, Basil Watkiss, Derrick Herbert, Roy Shepherd, Malcolm Noakes
Founder Members Kenn Ginns, Derrick Herbert and John Tipper all feature in this first photograph

Technical forms from South Wigston Modern School.

The commencement of the Academic Year 1946-47, in September 1946 witnessed a number of changes in the teaching staff as the Log Books show:

Boys' School
Mr Harold Billson, BSc.
left to take up an appointment at Loughborough College

Mr H W Davies
left to take up an appointment at Gateway School, Leicester

Mr J Pringle, BA
appointed to replace Mr Billson

Mr J Beddoes, BA.
appointed to replace Mr Davies

Girls' School
Mrs Grace Saxton *commenced duty as Maths Mistress*

The year 1946 marked another milestone in the history of rugby football at the Boys' School with the formation of the South Wigston Old Boys' Rugby Football Club.

John Tipper, who had been demobilized from the Fleet Air Arm, had joined the firm of Messrs Groby Granite Co. Ltd. He quickly resumed playing rugby and was instrumental in helping to form the South Wigston Old Boys' R.F.C. in 1946. He recalls that Ken Ginns was the first Captain and Derrick Herbert was appointed Club Treasurer. John was the first Secretary and went on to become the club's Chairman and President.

The first game played by the Old Boys was against Belgrave Rugby Football Club at Belgrave Pastures, Leicester on 28 September 1946 and the Old Boys suffered defeat by 22-3. John Tipper recalls that one week later they triumphed by an almost exact reversal of the score, in the previous match, as they achieved their first victory when they overcame King Richard's Road Old Boys in an away match by 23-3. Their first home game on the school playing fields, where the Old Boys were allowed to play their home fixtures by permission of the School Governors, resulted in a 20-0 win against King Richard's Old Boys, John changed his position to full back in 1946 and went on to play for the Leicester Tigers Extra First XV.

John Tipper went on to be employed by a number of local companies before joining En-Tout-Cas Limited, Syston, as the firm's Sales Manager for the U.K. He was promoted to Marketing Director of the International Division, specialising in the provision of all-weather track and field athletic facilities and synthetic grass playing surfaces which enabled him to travel to eighty two countries whilst representing his firm.

John was the President of the Leicestershire Rugby Union 1995-97.

The winter of 1946-47 was the most severe since weather records were commenced with heavy snowfalls often of blizzard proportions. This resulted, on occasions, in the school buses not running or arriving at the schools and on their homeward journeys, very late. Terry Whittaker, the Boys' School Captain, recorded an horrendous homeward journey to Enderby on one of two school buses bound for the village.

The first stoppage occurred just outside of Whetstone where the snow had piled up almost waist high across the road, this necessitated both vehicles having to reverse out of the drifts. The drivers decided to attempt to reach Enderby by way of Littlethorpe. On arriving at Littlethorpe they found that their alternative route was blocked by drifting snow. They then proceeded on to Cosby where they turned down a lane which they hoped would lead them home. Both buses became trapped in the ever-mounting drifts. Shovels were borrowed from a nearby farmhouse and several of the pupils dug "for what seemed like hours" in blinding, blizzard-like conditions.

A sketch of one of the trapped school buses which appeared in The Wasp

It proved impossible to dig the lead bus out, thus all efforts were concentrated on the second bus and after the valiant efforts of the drivers, a number of men on their way home from work together with the boys managed to get the second bus back on to the main road. After travelling round, via Leicester, they eventually reached home at 8.00pm "after a really exciting adventure". The abandoned bus had to be left in the snowdrifts for several days before it could be recovered.

On 12 February 1947, six girls played truant in order to go into Leicester to see the visiting film star, Margaret Lockwood. Their punishment for this misdemeanour, was recorded in the Log Book by the Headmistress as follows: "The six girls were reprimanded. Punishment – suspended from games and house matches for the rest of term and to attend school on Monday 17 February, half-term holiday to make up for lost time". Had boys also been involved in this escapade, there is little doubt that the cane would have been very much in evidence.

1947 witnessed the first publication of the post-war magazines in respect of both the Boys' and Girls' Schools. The Girls' School magazine was edited by Jean Sansome and the first edition was published in January 1947. Jean was assisted in the production of the magazine by a Committee comprising of: Mrs Holm, Miss Vann, Marlene Silcock, Betty Gibbs, Joyce Kirkland, Margaret Smith and Betty Gough.

The first edition of *The Magazine of the South Wigston Modern School for Girls* contained twenty four pages and mention was made of visits to local factories in connection with the teaching of geography. Education visits were made by Form V girls to local factories: J.D. Broughton and Sons, hosiery manufacturers Wigston Magna, Diana Shoe Works Leicester, Parmeko Electric Sound Works, Leicester, Portland Shoe Works, Leicester, W. Holmes and Son, hosiery manufacturers, Wigston Magna. Girls from Form I visited the works of Constone Limited, South Wigston. The visits were considered to be interesting and informative whilst, "Tea in the works canteen was a very welcome and novel feature".

Appreciation was also expressed, in the first edition of the magazine, to Mr John Henry Holmes, a School Governor, for the gift of a handsome Sports Trophy.

The Boys' School Magazine, *The Wasp*, was issued in July 1947 and the editor was the School Captain, Terry Whittaker (4A). The author of two articles in the first edition of *The Wasp* was Michael Chapman 1942-46. One of the articles entitled 'Warning' outlined his first impressions upon entering the great, wide world of work. Michael's concluding piece of advice to pupils leaving the Boy's School was: "Nobody thinks much of a boy who has no ambition. Let that be a warning!".

One boy who clearly agreed with this edict was Norman Durham who attended the school between 1946 and 1950. Norman enjoyed his rugby and was also an accomplished athlete in field events. In the National Schools Athletics Finals, held at Port Sunlight in the summer of 1949, he was placed second in the final of the Discus event, a very creditable achievement.

He recalls two teachers in particular, George Davis who was short in stature whereas Norman was tall which resulted in Mr Davis standing on a stool to "whack" Norman. Mr Penny was a noted chalk thrower as he strove to maintain discipline in the classroom.

Norman was a Police Cadet in the Leicestershire Constabulary from 1950 to 1954 and took part in the East Coast Flood Disaster relief work of 1953. He served in the 3rd Battalion, The

23040868 Guardsman Norman Durham

Police Cadet Norman Durham first left in the police wagon - East Coast 1953

Coldstream Guards throughout his two years of National Service and was stationed at Wellington Barracks, London, Purbright and Pickering. Norman performed spells of guard duty at Buckingham Palace, St. James' Palace, the Tower of London and the Royal Mint. He was also present on two Trooping the Colour Parades and was promoted to the rank of Lance Corporal.

Norman spent thirty years in the local police force as a Police Constable and Detective Constable. He worked on scenes of crime and, in that capacity, he was required to visit his old Deputy Headmaster Mr O J Kind, who unfortunately, had been burgled. 'Scrounger Kind'

who never forgot a pupil's face, greeted him with: "Hello Young Durham!"

Sir William Brockington, who had been Director of Education for no less than forty-four years, finally retired on 30 September 1947. He had held office longer than any other Director in England and had made an enormous impact upon Leicestershire, being responsible for the reorganisation of elementary education in the county between the two World Wars. He was deservedly Knighted in 1946 for his services to education both nationally as well as in Leicestershire. Aged 76 years when he retired, but still extremely active and alert, he was remembered with affection by all who served with him.

'Brock' as be became generally known, had left his mark not least on the South Wigston Schools whose existence and ethos were attributable to his vision and foresight after the conclusion of the Great War.

Sir William Brockington was succeeded as Director of Education by Stewart Carlton Mason who had been educated at Uppingham School and Worcester College, Oxford, before commencing a teaching career. He later joined the Board of Education Inspectorate and, in 1944, became involved in the Authority's development plan for implementing the requirements of the Education Act 1944. He was appointed to take up his duties on 1 October 1947.

During the Academic Year 1947-48 the school leaving age was raised to 15 years in accordance with the provisions of 'Rab' Butler's Education Act 1944.

The standard of rugby football played at the Boys' School was renowned locally and became acknowledged further afield when, on 13 March 1948, Leslie Armston (4A) of Croft, the school's rugby captain, was selected to play for the England Schoolboys' Team in the International Schools Rugby match with Wales at Cardiff Arms Park. He was accompanied to the game by Mr E.H. Johnny Churches, P.T. and Games Master, who was obviously very proud of the recognition given to one of his young protégés.

The result of the match was Wales 11 England 18 and Armston featured prominently throughout the game. The *Leicester Mercury* (15 March 1948) described his performance in the following terms: "Apart from fitting adequately into the high powered scheming of the English forwards, he scored a brilliant try. Seizing upon a loose ball, he swerved around two opponents and dummied his way through to score".

Leslie Armston
(Leicester Mercury)

This was the first time that the English International School Boys XV had defeated the Welsh Schoolboys at Cardiff. In receiving his international cap, Leslie Armston carried on the great tradition of pupils from South Wigston in representing their country and he became number nine on the illustrious list of boys to play for England.

The girls too maintained their prowess on the sports field. They excelled and maintained high standards of achievement at athletics in the Mid-Leicestershire, the County Sports and the All-England sports in addition to continued success at rounders and netball.

Harvesting work continued throughout 1947. Parties of boys and girls volunteered for potato picking work on local farms. In July 1947, a group of forty boys accompanied by members of staff, attended a two week Harvest Camp at Beaulieu, Hampshire. The account of the camp was vividly described by B. Clayton (4A) in *South Wigston High School: The First Fifty Years*.

They were accommodated in tents and slept on palliases filled with straw. "Reveille" was sounded by bugle at 6.30am, blankets had to be folded and the contents of the tents put out for inspection. The camp offered a mixture of hard work, discipline plus time for fun and exploration. Trips were organised to the Isle of Wight, Beaulieu Abbey and excursions to the New Forest. This proved to be a great adventure for many boys whose horizons had been limited to the confines of Leicestershire throughout the six long years of the Second World War.

On 7 January 1948, Mr James Joyce commenced duties at the Boys' School as Metalwork teacher. This was the first time the teaching of the subject had been possible since the department had been closed down at the outbreak of war some eight years earlier.

In early 1948, the Headmaster wrote an article explaining the new School motto, "**TO KNOW AND TO GIVE**" which had been introduced just before Christmas. The motto, which had been put forward by Mr Leslie Wild, Art and Crafts Master was, Mr Harrison explained, to give aims for everything the school did. The two aims, **TO KNOW** by which he meant the gathering of knowledge and understanding together with **TO GIVE** the significance of which was the giving of friendship, help, skills and advice to others. The interconnected aims were seen as enabling pupils to give of themselves for the use of other people. These noble aims were destined to inspire generations of children at the South Wigston Schools.

Chapter Three
Second Generation
(1948 - 1958)

Monday 8 September 1948 heralded the new autumn term at South Wigston Secondary Modern School and one can well imagine the thoughts of children returning after the long awaited summer holidays were over. A mix of emotions no doubt abounded with some newcomers feeling more than a little trepidation on entering the building. Would they ever find their way to the many classrooms snaking off the long corridors on two floors? Would they ever see their friends who had been streamed into different grades? Were the tales of existing pupils returning to be believed? Leaving the cosy environment of the Junior School in Timber Street and Bassett Street to begin their 'adult' education was challenging but those inner thoughts were seldom noticed as the streets of South Wigston came alive with excited voices making their way to the gates. Others were transported from many outlying villages by bus and it is only when history is revealed that we become aware of the friendships being formed between the sexes on those journeys. It is ironic to remember the strict rules of 'never the twain shall meet' without stifling a wry smile. In both the Girls' and the Boys' Schools a close guard was maintained on activities by masters and mistresses yet some innovative charges still managed to develop innocent friendships and evade detection. Some later married their childhood sweetheart as we shall see and one little girl wending her way on this eighth day in September 1948 was one of them.

It was intended that the message was indelibly printed in the brain. Boys were an alien species not even to be viewed from a classroom window overlooking the sports field. On the boys part it would appear that 'boys will ever be boys' as the stories related in the previous chapter tell us. Daring incidents kept the masters extremely busy and caused some quite serious consequences. This could explain why some girls were reluctant to take showers and were given a slap to coax them in. They were told in no uncertain terms 'not to be so silly'. One girl remembers being asked if she was a freak and the battle to avoid the ordeal raged with all manner of excuses being put forward. Some remember running alongside the showers at speed

being as dry when they came out as when they went in. For girls who had brothers and boys who had sisters one assumes that easy relationships existed in the home but for those who did not, what sort of image of the opposite sex did they carry with them? One supposes that it would be viewed as quite natural but in the post war period when many children grew up without their fathers or older male relatives 'the alien species' idea may have nurtured all manner of inhibitions. This strict edict did not only apply to the children as one female member of staff recalls secretly passing cups of tea through the classroom window to a male contemporary outside. It is quite fascinating to learn that fear of the Head's wrath extended beyond the children. Most of all they had respect for each other's positions and apart from the few wild spirits the children respected their elders too.

How significant the children of 1948 - 1958 were to the history of this book. Only twenty four years earlier one can look back at the fresh faces of that newly clad uniformed group of girls looking out from the photograph. Whatever their achievements, their academic success, some of those innocents had produced the second generation marching forward to school on this day and brothers and sisters would later follow. How much different from their mothers would these childrens' school lives be? How would they turn out? Let us see how the next decade treated them.

We know that very soon after their inauguration into the school system, interaction with teachers would dictate their future learning ability. Class sizes were so much larger than the present day and absenteeism vigorously investigated. Children were told that a 'Board Man', officially known as the Attendance Officer, would be checking habitual non attenders. The passing of the 1880 Elementary Education Act committed the local authority to the enforcement of compulsory education. These officers were employed to gather information regarding absenteeism or truancy and were an important link between school and home in monitoring patterns of attendance. In school the registers were called each morning and passed to the Deputy Head at the end of each day for inspection.

The house system continued as described in the previous chapter and Captains and Vice Captains were chosen. House marks for good work and order marks for misbehaviour determined the house winners. Discipline was well maintained and supported by the rules of the house system.

For the boys entering school their houses named in the previous chapter were equally important. Boys excelled themselves at South Wigston School and some became very famous in the world of rugby playing for England. They also played cricket, and were excellent athletes continuing their sport long after leaving school. Remembered too was the caretaker Mr Sutton who had valiantly cleared up the mess left by countless rugby players.

Both boys and girls proved that they were fierce competitors as they faced other schools in the county and won their trophies repeatedly. It is notable to record that three pupils actually became teachers in the Boys' School after completing their education. These were Mr Jack Cooper, Mr Joyce and Mr Lunn.

Mention here must be made of the retirement in September 1948 of Captain Ernest George Fowler who was the architect responsible for the design of South Wigston Secondary Modern Schools and many other schools in the county. He served as the architect to the County Council's Education Committee for forty years.

Music was enjoyed in both schools as soon after the autumn term of 1948 had begun the girls found themselves auditioning for the Junior and Senior Choirs. So many past pupils have remembered the music mistress, Miss Molly Vann and singing with gusto 'Nymphs and Shepherds' and 'Jerusalem'. Great emphasis was placed by Miss Vann on 'nor shall my **sword sleep** in my hand'. Remembered too is 'The Trout' by Schubert and Schumann's 'Merry Peasant'.

Boys had recorders and violins in their school and an account in *'The Wasp'* magazine states that some very weird noises were heard coming from under the doors. Mr Ken Harris the Music Master is well remembered by boys as an inspiring influence. Introducing classical music in class gave a life long appreciation of music to boys with no musical talent at all. John Reeve, known to his friends as 'Rev', remembers an enjoyable visit to London during his four years in school visiting the Boosey and Hawkes Instrument manufacturers. A very informative article by K Swanwick of Form 3A appears in the December 1951 issue of *'The Wasp'*. He brings alive the manufacture of woodwind and brass instruments.

Many people over the years will be familiar with the name of Eric Pinkett who is renowned for his influence in founding the Leicestershire Schools Symphony Orchestra. Mr Pinkett was appointed in November 1947 as the County's Adviser for Music in Leicestershire and South Wigston Secondary Modern School was one of seven schools chosen for visits. Mr Pinkett's role as the first adviser and enthusiasm for music was intended to inspire teachers and pupils to achieve excellence as musicians. South Wigston was the home of the Premier Drum Company producing percussion instruments and in the mid 1960s began producing glockenspiels, xylophones and tambourines for school orchestras. Charles Moore's Music Shop and the band were notable additions in the community also. It is recorded that parties of boys visited both of these establishments and that a Music Society was created. Mr Harris on one occasion had secured the services of Mr Tharp who with Mr Roper and Mr Cousins delivered a very interesting lecture and recital with flute, oboe and piano. Logged also is a visit with Mr Harris to the Barracks to hear the Band of the Royal Leicestershire Regiment. It is amusing to read today from Mr Eric Pinkett's book, *'A Time to Remember'* his memory of Mr Harris as on one occasion he is said to have asked Mr Pinkett, 'if he knew that his orchestra was playing out of tune'? Today everyone is aware of the success of the Leicestershire Schools Symphony Orchestra and the wonderful times that schoolchildren have enjoyed together. By testament of many boys we know too what a wonderful asset Mr Harris was to South Wigston Boys' School.

Nineteen forty eight was a memorable year in many ways. A Girls Training Company (GTC) was formed at school and the girls met on Monday evenings. Cadets trained in rolls, parades and drills and enjoyed a very varied programme. First Aid, Home Nursing and National Dancing, Home Management and Civic Affairs were just a few of the courses. Visits to youth hostels and camps were made and some girls trained to be non commissioned officers. (NCO's.)

National events of 1948 would have been of importance to the boys and girls in their history and

GIRLS TRAINING CORPS (GTC) L to R Eileen Withers, Maureen Baldry, Mavis Clark, Miss Tebbutt, Shirley Cole, Gloria Clark, Pat Martin, Miss Doherty, Sheila Smith, Dorothy Barfoot, Margaret Hensman, Jean Thompson, Jean Carter

physical education classes. Topical discussions on the British Empire would almost certainly have included the assassination in January of Mahatma Ghandi. For sporting enthusiasts in the schools news of the Olympic Games in London would surely be an inspiring event to follow. How the wheels of time have turned as the children today will be keen to train for the 2012 Olympic Games once again in the capital and in Leicester itself; the current debate rages on whether or not a statue of the Indian spiritual leader, Mahatma Ghandi should be erected in the city.

Closer to home a sad event touched the hearts of everyone in South Wigston School as they learned in April of the death of a past pupil, Andrew Lawson Robinson. Reported in the boy's own magazine 'The Wasp', at twenty one years of age; Andrew was serving with the Parachute Regiment. Before joining the Army Andrew was described as 'a quiet unassuming character with artistic gifts. A pleasure to teach'. It stated that some of Andrew's work could still be seen in the Art Room and recalled his article entitled, 'My First Parachute Jump'.

The death in November 1948 occurred of Mr William Meredith Mew who had given forty eight years service to South Wigston Boys' School. He is described as 'a friend to all'. Recalling his brilliant blackboard work, incredible skill at mathematics, fund of general knowledge, one could always ask 'WM' for advice. Staffroom members recalled his dry humour which dispelled any cloud on the horizon.

In the Girls' School the drive to raise funds was especially focussed as events were organised regularly. Their aim was to raise enough money to buy a film projector. By the Christmas Fair the grand total for 'The Great Projector Drive' stood at £275.00. To the delight of everyone it was possible to obtain a Bell Howell 601 Sound and a G B film strip projector. The girls were very proficient at fund raising and had the support of teachers, parents and trades people in the community. All manner of events took place. A Bring and Buy sale raised £5.00 for the Doctor Barnado's Home whilst jumble sales, whist drives, plays and concerts were arranged. Country stalls displaying plastic jewellery, vegetables and flowers all took their place with jam making, pickles and chutney amongst the flowers and fruit. Items from the art and craft department were plentiful and varied with very colourful designs and one can imagine how industrious the girls and mistresses were in achieving success.

November 1948 saw the soon to become school leavers escorted on an educational visit to Dunmore and Sons Biscuit Factory and Orson Wright's Boot and Shoe Factory situated in Canal Street, South Wigston. The street was a thriving thoroughfare of industry offering employment to many.

Both the Junior and Senior Choirs were in excellent voice as they participated in the Christmas Carol Services. Performances of 'Footsteps in the Blackout' was staged by fourth form pupils, 'The Stolen Prince' by Form 1B, A Nativity Play by Form 111C and 'Michael' by Form 111B. Drama was very much enjoyed by the pupils and the audiences.

At the Christmas Fair which was officially opened by Mr A W Holmes, Chairman to the Governors, four hundred parents and friends were having tea served by third year girls in their pink and white housecraft uniforms made by their own fair hands. All delicacies having been made in the housecraft lessons too included sandwiches, scones, cakes and trifles.

At the final Assembly in the Boys' School tributes were paid to the Assistant Caretaker, Mr Sutton on his retirement. He had been with the school since 1939. Mrs Betty Hodges, School Secretary, left for new employment in Leicester. The year closed with the Past Pupils annual reunion and dance.

Not until January 1949 did the schools resume business with all the new resolutions of staff and pupils alike either failing or achieving their goals. School is seen as a stable environment for most children but at the same time it is a moving community as they inevitably come of age and seek employment. Many teachers have been recorded as moving on to other schools but most have left their mark and been remembered. On the first day of the term Miss Margaret Clarke began her duties as the new Boys' School Secretary and on the last day of January the boys attended a special Assembly when Mr Johnny Churches left the school. Congratulations were extended on his recent marriage. Mr Churches moved on to Westcotes School in Leicester.

On the last days of school it was common practice to collect teachers and friends autographs vowing never to forget each other and wishing everyone well. Most people can remember their schooldays and name teachers. Geoffrey Garlick, a pupil in the Boys' School named almost all of them during his time there.

It is quite poignant to recall some of the memories expressed throughout this decade.

At the end of April 1949 Mr Harris and Mr Joyce accompanied a party of boys on a cycling holiday to the Cotswolds and Mendips staying in youth hostels. In June the County Education Department paid half towards laying of new concrete paths for a garden to be constructed on waste land and ploughed field in order to grow flowers, fruit and vegetables. This became an enjoyable part of school life. New classrooms near the Clinic had already become a feature to accommodate the growing numbers of children attending the schools. Over time the use of the Primitive Methodist Chapel rooms on Countesthorpe Road were also used for this purpose.

Sport has always been a source of pride in both the Girls' and the Boys' School and continues today in the tradition.

Christine Riley competing in the final of the Girls' School hurdles

Christine Sharpe, nee Riley 1946 - 1950 is recorded as the winner of the one hundred yards sprint and high jump also representing the county at the All England School Sports at Port Sunlight in Cheshire. Christine also played in the rounders and netball teams.

Shirley Tebbs nee Wilson, Head Girl in 1949 remembers her academic course for the East Midlands Educational Union Examination and the following year the Northern Universities Certificate in which she obtained Distinctions. Shirley admits to being quite shy in those days and recalls with dread her duty as Head Girl taking the Friday morning services at school. The Library was her classroom but she enjoyed art and needlecraft with Miss Constance Wright who wanted her to continue her studies at Loughborough College.

Enjoying swimming and music Shirley played the piano for 'Grey' house and was once complimented by Mr Eric Pinkett when she played for the school choir. Teachers in Shirley's memory are Miss Norah White in her green P E tunic, Miss Pogson and Miss Gardner, domestic science and a teacher named Clarice who had a wonderful contralto voice.

Remembering Mr Westhead's visit to the school from the County Education Department a job was selected for Shirley. Starting two days later, Shirley had no holiday after leaving school. It was Mr Westhead's role to find suitable school leavers employment.

March 1950 'Legs Eleven'. L to R Doreen Watson, Shirley Wilson, Sheila Clarke, Mary Wray, Ann Waldron, Betty Singleton, Irene Trolley. Barbara Handford

Having learned to play the saxophone and clarinet later Shirley was offered a place in Ivy Benson's Band but turned it down as she had recently married.

The boys' talent at rugby is well documented and cricket teams were also formed. Swimming, boxing, even basketball was introduced and many outstanding sportsmen have emerged from South Wigston Secondary Modern School. Senior boys helped Mr Chapman to prepare and seed the ground in order to lay a new concrete cricket square and Mary Herbert nee Wray in the Girls' School remembers the tennis courts being constructed. Mr Chapman has been described over the years as an excellent groundsman and one who through his care of the new field deserved every bit of praise for his dedication.

Fourth year boys still found time to write to boys in South Africa, America and France. The intention was to promote good relations between nations. Both boys and girls had pen friends corresponding over many years. The boys school orchestra appear to have progressed well having enlarged its numbers with Mr Pinkett's violin class. Boys playing flutes, clarinets and cornets were teaching younger boys to play in readiness to take over from them as 'school leaving terms' dawned. During March and April girls accompanied by Miss Vann enjoyed a Schools' Orchestral Concert at de Montfort Hall and over a hundred girls and many staff saw the film 'Hamlet' at the Granby Street Cinema in Leicester.

Shirley Wilson left, Betty Singleton right

Leaving school in 1949 Margaret Nobbs known in class as Nobby, became a Girl Guide Leader. After a short period at Blacks Shoe Factory on Saffron Road, Margaret was employed at British Telecom for thirty four years. Her interest in all ranks of the military stemmed from the age of four years when her grandfather, Captain Nobbs allowed her to play with his medals. Margaret's collection of cap badges, uniforms and military hats acquired over her life time eventually was one of the biggest in the country. Margaret gave many entertaining talks on the subject.

Margaret Nobbs with her military memorabilia

From *The Magazine of the South Wigston Secondary Modern School for Girls* 1949:

The Vision

Walking through the pastures green,
We had a vision of a stream.
With rippling waters, clear and blue
And mossy banks all wet with dew.

Looking down the stream we spied,
Two pure white swans puffed out with pride
Which gently glided from our view
Down distant streams to pastures new

But when the sun began to rise
The vision faded from our eyes,
And all we saw were pastures green,
Gone was that little rippling stream.

Maureen Moore, Margaret Gooder,
Jennifer Payne. Form 111A

In January to April 1950 Deputy Head, Mr Walter Higgins who was appointed to South Wigston School in 1938; took up a temporary Headship of the Whetstone Church of England Primary School pending a permanent appointment. In 1951 he took his place as Head Teacher at Latimer Street County Junior School, Anstey. After a very successful career in Education, in which he became Head of four schools, he was consulted by architects on a revolutionary open plan school in Oadby and later was honoured by the Queen with an OBE.

Leaving school in 1950 Clifford Shephard was one of the school's rugby stars. As a wing forward it was reported that if he won a place in the England Schools Rugby Team they would complete a hat-trick of International caps since 1948. Clifford was competing for the Midlands against the North in the Newcastle Trials. For the record three South Wigston schoolboys, Les Armston, Pat Hunt and David Hillsdon played for England.

Pat Hunt

Clifford's memory of his schooldays is clear. His love of sport overshadowed other subjects. Remembering Mr Skinner, Clifford says that he was a wonderful person giving lots of encouragement. Mr Churches also was fanatical about the game and the two teachers together were magnificent.

On leaving school Clifford's first job was with 'British United' moving on to 'English Electric'.

National Service took him into the Royal Air Force. Working for Everards Brewery and Harvey's Wine Merchants Clifford spent twenty years with Mitchell and Butler's Bass Company in Birmingham.

Clifford's wonderful association with the Leicester Tigers continued. He has represented rugby at all levels. Having represented the Leicestershire Alliance Colts and then the County 1st team Cliff made his debut for the Leicester Tigers against Coventry in 1955. Such was his success that he was offered professional terms with Barrow Rugby League Club.

Cliff represented the Tigers 1st team on one hundred and forty six occasions and scored thirty six tries. On occasions he played with the redoubtable John Elders. He has continued his involvement with the club by coaching the young Swifts side and also as Team Secretary for the Tigers' Extras over the last sixteen years. For the last twelve years he has acted as the 1st Team Secretary and Kit Man. Travelling with the team to the Millennium Stadium in Cardiff to the Tigers versus Brieve and the Munster matches he has seen four Heineken Cup Final matches and

Clifford Shephard scoring a try for Leicester Tigers against the Harlequins

travelled to the Stade de France stadium, Paris with the team. His long association with the Tigers has spanned fifty years and Clifford has enjoyed every single minute of them.

A very memorable development in education legislation took place in 1951 with the introduction of the General Certificate of Education (GCE) O and A Level Examinations. These examinations were intended mainly for grammar schools so at South

Wigston Secondary Modern School fifth form pupils could count themselves fortunate in having the opportunity to take them. These exams replaced the School Certificate and the Higher School Certificate.

In 1951 Mr N Penney accepted a Commission in the Royal Air Force and in that year one boy leaving school remembers Mr Penny, the maths teacher as an ex Lancaster pilot. Peter Hollis had made his own special mark on the school himself running at Port Sunlight twice and achieving fourth place in the finals but then became the new England record breaker in the 440 yards championships at Southampton.

Peter Hollis 440 yards. England Junior Champion

CHAMPION Peter Hollis, of South Wigston Secondary Modern School, has something to look pleased about. He ran 440 yards in 54 seconds in the Schools' A.A.A. championships at Southampton to set up a new all-England junior record. (See page 9).

Highlight of three excellent performances was that of Hollis in the junior boys' 440 yards. In his heat he equalled the England record of 54.8 seconds and went on to set up a new record in the semi-final of 54.4.

CAME FROM BEHIND

Not content with that the South Wigston champion came from behind in storming fashion to win the final and become the England champion in the excellent time of

Three excellent performances made news headlines. In the Junior Boys 440 yards he first equalled the England record of 54.8 seconds then went on to set up a new record in the semi final of

Peter Hollis with fellow representatives from
Leicestershire Schools who competed in the
All England Championships

Peter Hollis with his championship cup

Peter Hollis running for South Wigston
Boys' School

54.4 seconds. Not content with that he came
storming from behind to win in the final at the
schools AAA championships at Southampton to set
up a new All England record of 54 seconds.

Peter remembers many school friends and
teachers. He names Mr Brearley for geography and
relates the teacher explaining on a cycling tour on
the Isle of Wight with Mr Harris and their party the
reasons for the scars on his face. Mr Brearley had
been a navigator and had survived two air crashes.
On one occasion in a Lancaster the plane had a
serious fuel supply problem in two engines and
could not maintain height. Only five out of the seven
crew survived. On the second occasion in the
Hebrides the plane ran out of fuel. Mr Brearley
sustained burns to his face.

Mr Leedham is recalled as the pioneer of some
kind of 'Learning Machine', Mr Davis as a very kind
hearted man and Mr Joyce who introduced square
dancing into the school. This activity was popular
and enjoyed after school.

On leaving school Peter sustained a serious
motor cycle accident on Saffron Road when he was
involved with a brush with a car. Whilst Peter was
thrown to the ground his motor cycle travelled
ninety yards alone up the road and demolished one
of the schoolmaster's, Mr Orson Kind's, gate post.
Peter remained in hospital with his injuries for
eleven weeks.

Peter tried his hand at various jobs eventually achieving a place on a mature student's course in Engineering at Huddersfield Polytechnic. Qualifying he taught in schools in Leicester until finally teaching general subjects to pupils with learning difficulties and behavioural and emotionally disturbed problems at Marshfields School in Peterborough.

Peter's wife Dorothy nee Walden from Braunstone attended South Wigston Secondary Modern Girls' School leaving in 1953. Dorothy recalls Miss Gaskell who became Mrs Miller and Mrs Hames who she believes left the school for Morcambe. Dorothy spent two years as a nursery assistant. She spent a year in technical school before entering Cheshire County Training College in Crewe. Dorothy finally taught at Hazel Street School before moving to St. Mary's Infant School in Leicester.

L to R Monica Tibbles, Mary Gamage, A N Other, Gillian Getliffe, Dorothy Walden

One pupil who entered Miss Mawby's Form 1B at the Girls' school 1947-1951 travelled by bus from Braunstone. With two sisters and two brothers at home Sylvia Jervis nee Pacey can remember no problems at all with her contemporaries seeking out the company of boys. No bullying or misbehaviour is remembered and Sylvia credits this to the strict discipline meted out by Miss Walker who regularly watched the girls leaving school for home at the end of each day and woe betide anyone not wearing their beret.

One embarrassing incident sticks in Sylvia's mind when she arrived late for morning Assembly wearing a bright yellow jumper. Spotted and rebuked by Miss Walker four hundred pairs of eyes were turned upon her.

Recalling Miss Constance Wright Sylvia has never forgotten the skills she was taught of 'threading a sewing machine'. Days too spent helping at the Nursery in the 'Clinic' are remembered.

Sylvia after learning shorthand and typing with Miss Davies left the school in 1951 continuing for a further year at Miss Goddards Commercial Training School situated on New Walk in Leicester. Her first job was at Thomas Cook's Travel Agents in the Shipping and Forwarding Department which dealt with the return of dead bodies from abroad. Burial in England, Sylvia described as a very lucrative part of business. Thomas Cook's services in the early days dealt more with business trips than tourism.

Leaving school also in 1951 was Margaret Thompson nee Hipwell. A past pupil of Ravenhurst Junior School, Margaret spent two years in Miss Mawby's form and two years with Miss Evans. She was a keen rounders player and also sang in Miss Vann's choir. In her last year Margaret studied commercial subjects with Miss Davies but she is especially remembered by other pupils for her wonderful trumpet playing on the school stage. Margaret's first job was with Jones and Shipman who sent her for half day training sessions at Miss Goddard's Commercial School. However, Margaret's ambition to continue her music saw her accepted into the Gracie Cole Band in London. Margaret's professional name became Margaret Martin. The band travelled the country entertaining

Margaret Hipwell extreme right playing with the Gracie Cole band

South Wigston Girls' rounders enthusiasts 1950. Margaret Hipwell back row, 4th left

the United States Air Force at various American Air Bases. Margaret eventually moved on to play with the Dinah Dee Band.

Miss Hutchinson, later Mrs Swierczek, recalls, 1948 - 1954 'Happy Memories, a wonderful experience and a beginning that eventually spanned thirty seven years of teaching domestic science'. Her first contact with South Wigston Secondary Modern School for Girls' was as a student teacher on final teaching practice spending November 1948 under the expert tuition of the Head of the Domestic Science Department Miss Winifred Gardner. In the autumn of 1949 she joined the staff. She recalls that Leicestershire schools taught domestic science to a precise syllabus, the Leicestershire Plan; a well designed and thoroughly planned course of lessons was controlled by the Head County Organiser, Miss Sack and her colourful and encouraging assistant, Miss Broughton. The syllabus started with personal hygiene, simple anatomy and laundry. The teacher acted as the role model with the class of girls with their feet in bowls of water and Dettol. The school nurse proceeded to carry out a nit, flea and bug inspection later producing a list of names. Miss Hutchinson describes the domestic science room as a single storey extension with large windows adjoining the main school block overlooking the playground on one side and the school garden on the other. The cookery room contained very large wooden tables, large stone sinks with wooden draining boards, two large commercial gas stoves,

one electric cooker and a real joy, the coal fired range prepared by the caretaker each morning. Cookery was taught around the meal culminating in sitting down to eat a properly set lunch. In the 1950s the subject was offered for 'O' level in the General Certificate of Education.

Mrs Swierczek also remembers playground duties, lunchtime duties involved saying Grace, overseeing orderly dismissal from the dining room. The success of the lunch was judged by the amount of waste food left in the 'pig bin'. It was the duty of the cookery section to supply the staff with mid-morning break and on one occasion a disgruntled student laced the tea pot with salts of lemon. These salts were used to remove iron stains from linen and as a result a few staff had an uncomfortable day. The dreaded school inspections were feared but recorded by Mrs Swierczek as an occasion when they excelled with an A grade. She looks back with 'pride and joy, that I cut my teaching teeth in such a well run school with Miss Walker the Headmistress at the helm'. The school also ran evening classes for adults where Mrs Swierczek taught domestic science whilst her husband learned French with the boys Headmaster, Mr H K Harrison.

The South Wigston Evening Institute was founded by Mr Leslie Wild in 1953 and was very popular. An annual exhibition of work was held in March 1955 with a social and dance on the same evening. The prospectus for the summer session 1955 offered a choice of subjects on two evenings each week. On Wednesdays, Shorthand (Speed) with Mr L W Sharp, Shorthand (Elementary) with Miss J M Bodycote, Typewriting, Folk Dancing with Mr J B Joyce, Athletics with Mr J Elders, DLC (Diploma Loughborough College) Photography for Beginners with Mr W Davis and Dressmaking with Miss H M Richardson. On Thursday evenings German was taught by Mrs A Kind. Other courses were offered in different years as Miss Constance Wright taught Decorative Stitchery. Her pupils created work to be encased in trays and fire screens amongst other articles. Mrs Olive Chapman made her own wrought iron garden gates at the school. The Evening Institute ended in 1958 being transferred to Guthlaxton and was very much missed at South Wigston.

Henrietta Shultka nee Joyce remembers enjoying her cookery lessons with Miss Hutchinson. Hettie as she was known was a prefect. Girls appointed as prefects were easily identifiable by wearing a yellow sash. Regarded as responsible pupils in this position Hettie was on occasion chosen by Miss Walker, Headmistress, to take messages outside of the school. Hettie was summoned one day to take a letter to the Commanding Officer at Glen Parva Barracks on Saffron Road. She was allowed to take a friend with her and on arrival at the barrack gate the pair were quite overawed to be challenged by the sentry on guard duty pointing a rifle, demanding, 'Who Goes There'?

The years nineteen forty nine and onwards into the fifties are very memorable in both the Boys' and the Girls' Schools. One pupil following in the footsteps of her Aunt and Mother was Carol Shuter nee Garnett. Carol's Aunt Winifred Billing taught English for five years but left the school as Carol

Sentry on duty at Glen Parva Barracks, Saffron Road, South Wigston

entered in 1949. Miss Billing had moved to South Wigston during the war years to be nearer to her sister Ethel Garnett nee Billing who taught biology. Having attained her degree at Bangor University, Miss Ethel Billing secured a post in South Wigston but was forced to relinquish her teaching on her marriage to Ernest Garnett, the local Tobacconist and Newsagent. Mrs Garnett did supply teaching during the war years whilst the men were away. Both sisters originated from Wales. Carol's entry into the A stream at South Wigston saw her learning French. In her last year Carol studied shorthand and typing in the Commercial Class offered.

From *The Magazine of the South Wigston Secondary Modern School for Girls. 1951*

The Cuckoo

The cuckoo is a lazy bird
She sings a song that's quite absurd,
And when she's sung it through and through,
She starts again and echos you

She lays her eggs in other birds' nests,
And then she has a little rest,
She sits alone in another bird's home
Until again she starts to roam.

Delia Wright. Form 11A

David Dryden attended South Wigston Secondary Modern Boys' School 1950 - 1953. His family was evacuated to Leicestershire during the war from the East End of London. David travelled to school from his home on Hillsborough Road, Glen Hills and says his family was quite poor. They had very little money. He remembers he had to wear his father's shoes stuffed with cardboard to protect his feet against the wet

Taken by Miss Sowden c1950 Henrietta Joyce extreme right, on the back row

that soaked in from the holes in the soles; the shame and discomfort that this caused him is still vividly recalled. David's sub-standard footwear encouraged other boys to ridicule him, making his three miles journeys to school even more wretched. More happily he remembers the popular childrens games of the time naming snobs, conkers and collecting cigarette cards.

David admits that he was lazy at school and says he learned little while he was there. It did nothing to motivate him. He describes himself not as a late developer but a very late developer. Mr Joyce the metalwork teacher however, encouraged him and he successfully made a metal coat hanger in class. This positive experience may have had some influence on David's later choice of an engineering design career.

Many of the school teachers of the day and the subjects they taught are remembered. Though his methods would not be approved nowadays, David can thank the school for making him a life long non smoker. He was one of the many boys who used to have 'a crafty drag' in the playground toilets. Mr Harrison (the Head Master) caught these smokers one day and gave them all a good thrashing. David was caned on his arms, legs and hands staying silent throughout his ordeal. He has never smoked again from that day forward not even while he was in the Army despite pressure from his mates. It was an effective deterrent.

David's life and prospects changed for the better when he joined the Royal Corps of Signals at seventeen and a half. David was trained as a Radio Technician. He served for nine years reaching the rank of Sergeant serving in Germany, Hong Kong and Singapore and then seeing active service in Borneo and Sarawak.

On leaving the Army David persued a career in Electronics and Radar with Marconi Radar. Subsequently he was appointed Chief Technician with the Department of Engineering, University of Leicester. He held the post for twenty seven years. Highlights of his time there included helping to rebuild the Palestinians economy by teaching satellite reception to students in Gaza and the West Bank. Of the many designs David has created his most well known is

David Dryden in Gaza 1995

probably the Fruit Fly Amplifier. David's Fruit Fly Amplifier is used in universities around the world to explore learning, genetics, etcetera, all the UK's universities use this particular design if they need such equipment.

In February 1952 a report by Her Majesty's Inspectors of Schools for the Girls' School, states that the work of the Headmistress (Miss Walker) is marked by her successful determination to fulfil the varied needs of the school and by her fine contribution towards making it a gracious, vital community.

Reminiscences of Mr Jack Cooper, Physical

South Wigston Secondary Modern Girls' School Staff 1950s. Identified: Miss Morris, Miss White, Mrs Holm, Miss Walker, Miss Wright, Miss Vann, Mrs Catterson, Mr Morse, Mrs Winder, Mr Baker, Mrs Baker, Miss Fawcitt

Education Teacher span 1949 - 1959. Recalling two Headmasters during his time there Mr Cooper names Mr H K Harrison and Mr Mark Rutherford as being gentlemen of the highest order but with very different styles. Discipline was strict, working hard and playing hard. However this did not stop some of the boys dismantling Mr Rutherford's bicycle and throwing it in pieces on to the school allotments. It is remembered that Mr Rutherford, a man who abhorred violence, did on that one occasion thrash the culprits.

Mr Cooper writes of 'a remarkable fine staff'. Mr Orson Kind, the Deputy Head, and three others who went on to be Headmasters were Mr Walter Higgins, Mr Ken Harris and Mr Mark Hollis. Mr John Leedham and Mr Gerry Brearley became Lecturers at Loughborough College. Mr Les Wild became Mr Rutherford's Deputy and other high quality teachers were Mr Hugh Every, Mr Horace Place, Mr Trevor Lord, Mr Bill Davies, Mr Jack Beddoes, Mr Lunn and Mr Tweed. Mr Cooper remembers Miss Warren and Mrs Hull as working in the 'kennels' a term for the Horsa Huts close to the school clinic. All of these teachers contributed to a happy staff room where shove halfpenny was in evidence at break and dinner intervals.

The HORSA Programme, (Hutting Operations for the Raising of School Leaving Age) was introduced after the war as a result of the raising of the school leaving age to fifteen and the rise in numbers of school teachers emerging from training colleges. New school building programmes nationwide led to the erection of around seven thousand Horsa Huts.

South Wigston being a hot bed of rugby footballers is recalled when Mr John Elders, Mr Howard Wallace and Mr Alan Blackhurst joined the staff. Remembering capped boys for England Mr Cooper speaks of Les Rainbow and a boy named Hook, Pat Hunt and David Hillsdon. A boy who Mr Cooper felt should also have been selected was Mick Hanney.

On the last day of the summer term 1952, Deputy Head to Mr H K Harrison, Mr O J Kind retired from South Wigston. Teaching at South Wigston since 1920 Mr Kind's service to the school spanned over thirty years. A tribute in the boys magazine, 'The Wasp', states how very sorry they all were to see him leave. In all activities of the school Mr Kind had

Mr O J Kind

given his full support and encouragement to others.

A native of Countesthorpe, Miss Ellen Morris, history and drama teacher in the Girls' School; has been given so many accolades by the girls. 'Amazing, progressive, so helpful, fantastic' are just a few of the phrases freely given to describe her. Miss Avis Fawcitt joined the staff in 1952 and is remembered too as a wonderful music teacher even composing some of the scores herself. With Miss Molly Vann's excellent training of the choirs, it is clear that South Wigston Secondary Modern School was so lucky to have the three very dedicated ladies. The achievements in choral verse speaking, drama and musical talent are illustrated in many of the photographs and the self confidence that pupils acquired well equipped them for life far beyond their schooldays.

Reading the testament of Brenda Phillips school days illustrates perfectly the sense of belonging that the verse speaking, music and drama groups surely felt. Brenda emphasises 'I loved it, I really loved it from day one'. She was chosen by Miss Morris to participate in the Choral Speech Group and stage productions. Brenda admits that personally she didn't think about much else. Miss Fawcitt was her form teacher and Brenda reveals that they were a very close knit class loyal to Miss Fawcitt and each other. Miss Fawcitt knew how to get the best out of each one of us says Brenda remembering nostalgically all the children gathering round the piano to practice for a concert or a music festival. On hot summer days they would sit outside the prefabricated huts where their classroom was situated to finish their work. Brenda writes that the choir was entered for many music festivals and South Wigston was almost hated by the other competitors as they knew before they started that

South Wigston would walk away with the winners cup every time. This was due to endless practice to perfect their art. Many lovely photographs illustrate the work of Miss Fawcitt who produced the music whilst Miss Morris was the stage manager. Brenda remembers the dedication they all felt towards their work and on one occasion acting as trees in brown and green costume, they waved their arms in the wind endlessly and never faltered. *'The Four Pictures of Christ'* a cantata written by Avis Fawcitt and Ellen Morris was performed in Saint Thomas Church and remembered clearly is the image of Sue Townsend, dragging the Cross up the aisle as she played Jesus. A massive production with all the followers at her side reciting perfectly the words they had learned so well, The cantata, an experiment of choral orchestral music, drama, mime and choral speech depicts four phases in the life of Christ. The Nativity, the Ministry, Crucifixion and the Resurrection.

TWO TEACHERS WROTE MUSICAL PLAY

THE FIRST of three performances of "Music Come: Strangely," a musical play written and composed by two o the staff, was presented at South Wigston Girls' Secondar; Modern School last night by a cast of 50 pupils.

Miss E. Morris, English and history teacher, wrote the script, and Miss A. Fawcitt, junior music mistress, set it to music.

The play, in three acts, tells of a boy violinist who hears strange imaginary music, and is driven away by the villagers.

His experiences in the world of music develop the theme of the play, which is that music needs to be interpreted in the light of human feelings and emotions or it is a cold, colourless thing.

MISS A. FAWCITT

MISS E. MORRIS

Miss Avis Fawcitt with some of her aspiring musicians C1950s

This was repeated in many churches at the time.

There is no shortage of pupils to relate their glowing memories of their music lessons, journeys abroad to drink in the culture and entertain. Rosemary Pratt and Sheila Bailey Watts nee Jones are just two other very enthusiastic past pupils who will never forget the happy days spent in this wonderful world of music. Rosemary writes that Miss Vann a resident of Blaby and Miss Fawcitt not only taught within the school but devoted many hours of their own free time teaching them to sing in the Junior and Senior Choirs and play instruments in the Orchestra. With Miss Morris they were a truly dedicated trio who brought excellence to the school.

Rosemary Pratt 1953 - 1958 was in both the Choral Speaking and Drama Groups. Three plays she performed in were, 'Music Comes Strangely', 'Doctor Faustus' and 'Peter Pan'. She remembers well the wonderful flower fairy costumes made by Miss Constance Wright for the productions and the girls who wore them. Gillian Everitt as Bluebell, Pat Beadle, Wild rose, redheaded Margaret David was Marigold and Shelia Bailey Watts nee Jones, Snowdrop.

Rosemary's holiday with the group to Switzerland also is remembered fondly and the first day she entered South Wigston Secondary Modern School too.

A chilly Autumn morning she was one of several girls boarding the Harris Company Bus from Braunstone. The girls were all dressed in brand new uniforms from Grahame Gardner the school outfitters in Leicester. Rosemary remembers that it cost parents a fortune as there were no 'off the peg'

Miss Fawcitt's school orchestra c1950s

Avis Fawcitt conducting 1950s Marion Whait, Jane Bellamy, Nan Kennard, Arnold Goodyer, and A N Others

shops they could use selling garments to school regulations. Lined up in the playground on that first morning the girls in 1A were collected by Miss Constance Wright who was to be their form mistress. They very soon discovered that Miss Wright was also the Deputy Head. Their first task was to write out their timetables which included learning French and Mrs Holm's greeting over five years, 'Bonjour, mes enfants. Assayey-vous' is still ingrained in the memory. The first article the girls created using a sewing machine in their form mistress's needlework class was a PE bag but hockey, netball and tennis with Miss Pat Giles were not Rosemary's favourite sports as she cannot recall any of the rules of the games being passed on. On one Parents Evening Rosemary's mother was told that she lacked interest. Her Mother's response was not to worry as long as she can run to catch a bus for work.

Form 1A was taught English Language and Literature by Miss Morris and later Mrs Holm where they studied much poetry and classical works. Rosemary relates the 'curious' way of teaching arithmetic by Miss Carroll who she believed was really very kind. If a girl looked worried sweets were readily handed out. The following term Miss Carroll was succeeded by the Scottish, no nonsense, Mrs Rosemary Catterson. Rosemary admits that after the ease of the lessons with Miss Carroll, under the tuition of Mrs Catterson she very soon discovered that she was indeed 'the world's worst pupil at maths' after all. No more diving under the table for sweets now as geometry, fractions, decimal points, logarithms and equations were pounded into their heads. This resulted in the maths sessions for Rosemary becoming very fraught. Other memories include Mr Ron Baker teaching science, chemistry, biology and gardening. Some classes recall standing three deep around the tall bureau in the science laboratory when a cockroach was handed round by Mr Baker for inspection, Bunsen burners which must be very carefully handled as they flared into life and very simple Litmus paper tests for acid and alkaline. Also remembered by girls is the instruction Mr Baker gave not to eat the apples from the trees as they had been sprayed and could be poisonous. Mr Baker was well aware that the apples had already been 'scrumped'. Pupils loved to be outside especially on summer days and the gardening classes

were interesting. Children whose parents and grandparents owning or renting plots for allotments were quite knowledgeable and who knows whether a budding Gertrude Jekyll or Lancelot Brown was in the making?

Three Art teachers were Miss Blenkhorn, Miss Larby and Mrs Hall. History was taught by Miss Morris and Miss Biard. Rosemary found domestic science uninspiring with Miss Gardner as they were grouped into parties of six to scrub the floor. Cabbage and jacket potato was their first cookery dish but by the fourth year they had progressed to stews and cakes. The pièce de résistance was the Christmas Cake which took three weeks to create. The cake, the home made almond paste which turned out to be quite expensive to buy the almonds and on the third week the icing to finish it off. By the end of the three weeks Rosemary recalls that the girls were truly sick of it.

Rosemary's abiding memory of Miss Walker, Headmistress, is related with some amusement. On one occasion the choir were required to sing for one of the school Governors, Alderman Curtis Weston who resided in South Wigston. On the school stage the choir came to a line in their song, 'Drop thy pipes, thy merry pipes' when a group of builders outside the school let fall a load of scaffolding. The back row of the choir started laughing and the next day Miss Walker had them all on the stage to sing it again. They came to 'Drop thy pipes' and again could not control their laughter. This resulted with the ruler across their arms.

On leaving school boys were encouraged to join the 'Old Boys Association' and to this day a number of them still meet but the season of 1948/49 proved to be a record. They were faced with placing the 'Old Boys' in 'the top flight' of Midland rugby clubs. The success of the team was put down to 'the virile qualities of fifteen players'. Alan Davies is recorded as their first centurion closing the season with 118 points. The Junior Alliance were proud to boast the talents of four members who were selected to play for Leicestershire versus the East Midlands at Bedford. These were Terry Whittaker, Leslie Armston, Roy Scarlett and Mick Harris. Congratulations were heaped upon Patrick Hunt as he was selected to play for England. In 1951 in the under fifteen group, David Hillsdon was selected to play in the full back position for England versus

Miss Fawcitt's orchestra in the Gymnasium c1950s

Wales in two schoolboy international matches. The first in March of that year was at Gloucester at the Kingsholm ground where the score was lost 3 - 6 and the second in April at Cardiff Arms Park where they drew 11-11. David writes that he feels very fortunate to have been educated at South Wigston where good manners and discipline were important attributes. Having worked all of his life in the building trade David spent thirty three years as a Managing Director of a building firm but still enjoyed playing all sports in his leisure time. He has made many

David Hillsdon pictured at the school in his England rugby kit 1951

friends during his varied sporting days.

In 1953 the young John Elders joined the staff of the Boys' School where he taught mathematics and physical education. He remembers well the enthusiasm of the boys and staff alike. He was also persuaded by the past students to run an athletics club. At the same time Mr Elders was playing for the Tigers whom he went on to captain, and Leicestershire. After leaving South Wigston in 1955 he taught at Alderman Newton's Grammar School in Leicester prior to accepting a post at the Royal Grammar School in Newcastle-Upon-Tyne in 1957 where he stayed for the next twenty five years. His invitation to coach the England team in 1972 was national news and he remained the England coach for the next three years.

At this time David Cawthorn was fourteen years old and recalls that his Mechanical Drawing Teacher, Mr Trevor Lord, suggested that he might like to join his hockey group. David says that this decision changed the direction of his life for ever. The South Wigston mixed team was esteemed amongst the best in the county. Recalled are some of the 'lovely characters'. Laurie Holland, a speedway rider with the Hunters, Percy Bernard, and Fred Seymour. Playing also for the school cricket team David

Mr Rutherford back left, John Elders back right, with the 1953 school rugby team

South Wigston '7' A Side Team competed in the schools' '7's finals at The Leicester Tigers Ground 1953

names Robin Whait, Tony Rogers, Clawson and Wale from Blaby and Hill from Birstall. The problem was, 'no girls'. As Head Boy David had certain privileges along with the prefects on dinner duty. The connecting corridor alongside the kitchens leading into the girls' dining room was too tempting

an opportunity to miss. Whilst kitchen staff were preoccupied with clearing away and washing up the 'brave hearts' were able to steal at least two or three minutes scurrying through the narrow passageway to make liaisons with the girls who were waiting. David left South Wigston for Kibworth Grammar School and Westminster Teacher Training College qualifying for his post as a Physical Education Teacher. He became the England National Indoor Hockey Team Manager and Coach for fifteen years and an Official for many international tournaments and national events.

Not to be outdone girls excelled at athletics, hockey, netball, rounders, tennis and gymnastics participating in many county sports days. Anne Hammonds nee Cansick particularly recalls the vaulting horse when more rotund girls unable to leap over acted as 'catchers' on the other side. Physical Education mistress, Mrs June Bull nee Sowden's memories are recorded here. She writes that on joining the staff of the Girls' school in 1949 how lucky she was to have Miss Norah White as Head of Department. Described as an excellent teacher Miss White passed on many of her teaching skills and enthusiasm and Miss Sowden said that she could write a three year memory in praise of Miss White. Girls practiced hard to gain places in teams and Miss Sowden particularly remembers staying three nights a week in the summer term to train for the area sports

The school rugby team of 1955. John Elders standing left, Mark Rutherford centre

England Indoor Hockey Team v West Germany, Bristol February 1977. David Cawthorn, Coach and Team Manager standing left. Result: England 6 West Germany 10

The Girls' Netball Team 1949-1950. L to R back row, Iris Hastings, Janet Granville, Dorothy Weston, Maureen Baldry, Christine Riley. Front Row, A N Other, Margaret Elsey

and the thrill of achievement when one of the girls came first in the under 15 National Long Jump competition. Sport played a major role in school life but the academic and commercial skills were vigorously taught also. Girls learned shorthand and typing and secured many responsible posts in various offices in Leicester. The East Midlands Education Union Schools' Certificate was the culmination of the fifth formers and dreaded by some pupils.

Joan Robinson and John Reeve recall the years 1949-1953 where they daringly met on the school playing fields. John recalls his lessons with Mr Trevor Lord, Mr Leedham and Mr Jack Cooper. Memory of 'Smiler Higgins' who whacked the boys and the advantage the boys took of Mr Davis's poor eyesight as they brought stink bombs and lizards into the classroom is still clear. John a good rugby player achieved a place at the Coventry Trials at Counden in a bid for selection to the England side. Joan, a keen sporting enthusiast remembers her visit to Loughborough where she participated in the Hurdles Trials.

After leaving school John joined the Royal Air Force, later working at the Co Operative Society. Joan was first employed as the Junior School Secretary afterwards working thirty four years at the

The wedding of John Reeve and Joan Robinson at Saint Thomas' Church, South Wigston 27 July 1957

Royal Infirmary. Joan and John celebrated their Golden Wedding anniversary in 2007.

The death of King George V1 on 6 February 1952 brought sadness to the country. The announcement made in the schools has been remembered as a very sombre occasion. In the streets outside people appeared to be quietly attending their business of the day. Very soon afterwards the proclamation of the new Queen Elizabeth 11 turned the nation's thoughts to the future Coronation of 1953. This was an occasion when the county schools excelled themselves with musical talent.

In May 1952 one hundred and twenty girls visited Windsor Castle. Two weeks later South Wigston Girls' School won the shield at the Area Sports at Hinckley for the third year running. Ending the term, on 2 July, thirty boys camped out in Charnwood Forest.

The new term September 1952, the Arts Department in the Boys' School were pleased to see the installation of a kiln into the bicycle sheds.

On 19 December in the Boys' School a special Assembly was arranged in order to say goodbye to their Headmaster. Mr H K Harrison left to take up his new appointment as Head of Roundhills Secondary Modern School, Thurmaston, Leicestershire.

In January 1953 Mr Mark Rutherford was welcomed into the Boys' School as their new Headmaster. Mr Rutherford BA was previously Headmaster at Boroughbridge County Secondary Modern School in Yorkshire. He was very supportive of Stewart Mason, Director of Education for Leicestershire and the future plans for the county schools. The new Headmaster became known by many as 'The Gentle Quaker'.

Valerie de Soto nee Ward 1949 - 1953 recalls her very good English, history and geography teachers,

Miss Ellen Morris, Mrs Evans and Miss Vann who tested her singing ability with the difficult 'trills' of 'Rolling Down To Rio'. Enjoying rehearsals at de Montfort Hall, Valerie was selected as one of eight girls to sing in the massed choirs in the great 'Elizabeth to Elizabeth' pageant. The octet also sang together on stage. The pageant, 1558 to 1953 was a Coronation Festival and a tribute to Her Majesty Queen Elizabeth 11. Six hundred children in costume from the County Schools, a choir of five hundred together with the Orchestra and the Military Band of the County School of Music was directed by Mr Eric Pinkett on the 20th and 21st May 1953. In addition to contributing to the choir, a number of boys from South Wigston Boys' School participated in the 'Boer War' scene at the pageant. Other scenes portrayed various historic events in Leicestershire.

Elizabeth to Elizabeth Programme Cover

Elizabeth the First 1558-1603 Elizabeth the Second 1952-

On 22 May the school closed for the Whitsuntide holiday but 'The New Testament' commemorating the Coronation was presented to every school child by the Gideon Society. Valerie still has her copy.

The Coronation of Queen Elizabeth took place on 2 June when insessant rain did not dampen the country's spirits. The following day one hundred and fifty South Wigston pupils and ninety pupils from Kibworth Grammar School attended the Coronation tea and each received a gift of a Coronation Beaker.

Sporting activities which had been arranged for the evening were cancelled due to the weather conditions. Later in June the Chairman and Vice Chairman of the Glen Parva Parish Council attended the school to present the pupils of their parish with 'The New Testament' or a spoon. Finally, all of the schoolchildren watched the film 'The Early Life of Queen Elizabeth' and other films of the Royal Family.

In July Valerie also took part in the childrens opera by C. Armstrong Gibbs, 'The Great Bell of Burley' which she enjoyed very much. Three consecutive evening performances were given to packed audiences in the School Hall and one matinee performance to members of the South Wigston and Oadby Evergreen Club and Enderby Modern School pupils.

Anne Hammonds nee Cansick remembers taking part in this production also when she was taken to Nottingham Theatre to be fitted out with her costume.

Recalling Miss Field for gardening Valerie was taught about the type of soil. By placing a square of soil on paper and drawing round it, the amount of shrinkage could be measured as the soil dried out. The garden was divided by paths and the areas of soil between the paths was designated for different growing, vegetables and flowers. The centre of the garden was planted with beautiful roses and the girls were told the different varieties and names one of which was Sam McGredy. At the time horticulture was an important addition on the curriculum the teacher holding a degree in the subject. Natural

The Great Bell of Burley. Valerie Ward pictured extreme right, back row

history was taught also alongside science and biology by other teachers.

Miss Wright awarded a bottle of Lavender toilet water to anyone showing knitting skills which Valerie won for producing a blue cardigan.

Most of all Valerie expresses her gratitude to Miss Davies, the Shorthand and Typewriting Teacher who gave her students excellent skills for their future secretarial careers. Practice exercises on Underwood and Imperial Typewriters to music tested their dexterity enabling them to pass many examinations.

On leaving school in 1953 Valerie secured a post in shorthand and typing at the Local Education Authority in Grey Friars, Leicester. where the pioneering Mr Stewart Mason was already in place. He was destined to become famous for the re-organisation of primary and secondary education in Leicestershire. 'His Leicestershire Plan' or the 'Leicestershire Experiment' started in 1957 was the beginning of Comprehensive Education and the abolition of selection at the Eleven Plus Examination. This would have a profound effect upon South Wigston's and the County's children. In 1960 Valerie became the Secretary to the Professor of Obstetrics and Gynaecology at the University Hospital, Seattle, USA. On her return to England she worked for the Officer in Charge, Royal Army

Back row, L to R Josie Goddard, Beryl Newell, Glenda Watkiss, Valerie Ward, Jean Shore Front Row, L to R Maureen Williams, Miriam Middleton, Janet Mortimer, Janet Wright, A N Other from Blaby

Ordnance Corps (RAOC), Manning and Record Office, Ministry of Defence. Later Valerie was employed as Secretary and Office Manager for the Office for Standards in Education (OFSTED) based on Tigers Road. South Wigston. Valerie finally ended her career with Social Services.

Joan Welsh nee Hipwell left Ravenhurst Junior School in 1950 and travelled from her home on Narborough Road South by bus to South Wigston Girls' School where she stayed until 1954. Miss Constance Wright is well remembered for her needlework classes which Joan enjoyed. She found the classes relaxing and liked Miss Wright but everyone knew they could not 'mess about' being

Leicestershire Schools Symphony Orchestra which performed at The Hague

made to listen and learn. Joan loved gardening, cookery and music and remembers Miss Walker's keen sense of cleanliness insisting that the girls pick up discarded litter.

Joan was selected to play the violin whilst a pupil at Ravenhurst Junior School by Eric Pinkett. Eventually she played for the Leicestershire Schools Symphony Orchestra. Mr Pinkett supplied the violin and Joan's mother paid two shillings and sixpence a week until £2.10 shillings was reached. Taught by Mr Pinkett Joan's first piece was 'Twinkle Twinkle Little Star'.

As a pupil at South Wigston Secondary Modern School, Joan rehearsed with her violin at Quorn and Birstall Schools on Saturday mornings. She describes Mr Pinkett as 'always smiling, a lovely man'. The children visited various schools to play and were accompanied by different school teachers from the schools selected.

Eventually Joan travelled to The Hague in Holland and Essen in Germany with the orchestra and remembers being billeted with a German family. Allocated on arrival she did not know who she would be going home with. Living near the River Rhine one family Joan recalls could speak no English. A particular memory is of the maid who cleaned her shoes for her. An exchange visit to England saw two boys at Joan's home but she only recalls one of their names which was Klaus.

Peter Davie also left South Wigston Secondary Modern Boys' School in 1954. He was one of many children attending from Ravenhurst Junior School in Braunstone. He particularly remembers a fellow Ravenhurst pupil, Irene Granger who attended South

Joan Hipwell

Wigston Girls' School as she won the England Schools Long Jump event of 1952-1953. He recalls the Headmaster Mr Mark Rutherford refereeing rugby matches, the formation of the Old Boys Athletic Club and the Young Farmers Club together with cross country running. As a member of the Young Farmers Club organised by Mr Hollis, the gardening master, Peter recalls much discussion, films and visits to various farms being made. Cycling trips to Wales and Lands End led by Mr Ken Harris are very much remembered too.

Studying for two years for his General Certificate of Education Peter sat the examinations in his last year. His Advanced Level Exams were taken at Leicester Technical College consequently moving on to Loughborough College for a Teacher Training

Course. His first appointment was at Lutterworth Secondary Modern School given to him by the former South Wigston Music Master, Mr Ken Harris. Later moving to Wycliffe School, Peter finally became Principal of the residential college for Adults with physical disabilities, Prospect Hall, Birmingham.

David Burley 1951 - 1955 confirms that school discipline was very strict. He recalls Clayton's Bus Company bringing him to school from Countesthorpe. The company of Astill and Jordan from Ratby was also used. Some children living in Countesthorpe have said that it depended upon the location of their home whether or not they qualified for the school bus service. The unlucky ones were required to make their own way. Boys were not allowed to enter school until lines were formed in the yard and to stop dead in one's tracks at the whistle blow. Good conduct was overseen by prefects on door and stair duty but on one occasion David was seen to ruffle up the hair of the Deputy Head Boy, Dickens. This was observed by Mr Leedham on playground duty and for this David received 'three of the best' with a shortened cricket bat. The punishment was meant to teach him respect. A slap across the face was not unknown to be metered out by Mr Place in class if it was felt necessary. Most classes David recalls irritated Mr Place by 'bumping' which brought forth the command, 'Stand up the boy sitting next to the boy who is bumping'.

Once inside school boys marched in an orderly quiet fashion from room to room for lessons and queued outside. David enjoyed cross country running and remembers that boys had their gardening plots to attend to with Mr Hollis. Also the task of stone picking was undertaken at the top field in preparation for rugby.

Many past pupils remember Miss Constance Wright as someone who kept strict order. Pupils excelling in needlework sailed safely through their lessons and enjoyed them. Today they thank Miss Wright for the excellent skills that she taught them in dress making and decorative stitchery. Others feared the hand that would on occasion snatch and toss their work aside in disgust or the quick retort, 'donkey' and slap that jerked them to attention as they were instructed to unpick their mistakes. Jean Betts nee Beardall recalls making a blouse and receiving a thump in the back for her work. Jean's sister Iris also attended the school but was in Mrs Vrolijk's class for needlework. Susan Burnham nee Townsend a pupil, remembers Miss Wright humiliating her in front of the whole class for work which was considered not to the required standard. Susan admits that needlework was not her favourite subject but it is ironic that on leaving school Susan's first job was with the School Outfitters, Grahame Gardner. She hastens to add though, 'definately not as a tailoress'.

The needlework classroom situated on the upper floor had a large circular window facing the main road. Brenda Phillips recalls that during her time the girls would open the window with the long window pole before Miss Wright entered the room in order to witness the expected response. 'Girls, close the North Window. We do not have the North window open'. This practice amused the girls throughout the term without apparently Miss Wright being aware. At the end of the afternoon lessons pupils living at Blaby were allowed to line up at the door a few minutes in advance in readiness to catch the early bus. A plot was hatched. Each week two extra South Wigston girls joined the queue to escape resulting in the queue growing ever longer as the term advanced. Brenda reveals that she was not one of the culprits who repeatedly punched Miss Wright's hat in as it hung on the cupboard door as they hurriedly left. These children indeed were daring individuals. It is known today that the teachers themselves were in awe of Miss Wright's authority as they often struggled to calculate their registers on time to arrive on Miss Wright's desk by the end of the day's lessons.

In February 1953 children were raising money for the relief of the East Coast Flood Fund when it was estimated that three hundred people had lost their lives.

'The Wasp' reports of a Youth Music Festival for the South East Area in March 1953. The success of four boys winning first place was recorded. K Swanwick, trombone, A Langford, violin, M Bown, violin, and J Wilcox, vocal. The Brass Quartet was also awarded first place. The successful soloists went forward to the County Festival in which K Swanick won a bronze medallion. He was subsequently chosen to accompany the County School of Music to Germany eventually becoming a student at the Royal Academy of Music.

A most terrible crime was committed on 22 May 1953. A twelve year old pupil of South Wigston Secondary Modern School, Janet Mary Warner, was murdered at Blaby. The incident shocked everyone in school and in Leicestershire. Janet was identified by her school tie and it is with great sadness that it is remembered here. Joseph Christopher Reynolds was hanged on 17 November at Leicester Prison and was buried within the prison walls. He was the last man to receive the death penalty in Leicestershire.

December 1953 saw both South Wigston Girls' and South Wigston Boys' from their respective Fifth Forms at the BBC's broadcast of 'Childrens Hour' in Birmingham.

Mrs Marion Baker nee Hughes 1953 - 1992 joined the staff of South Wigston Secondary Modern School in September 1953 after completing a post graduate year at Cardiff University. Mrs Baker was one of four to join the staff at that time the others being Esther Biard, Judith Larby and Mr Ronald Baker. Miss Hughes intention to return to Wales to teach was changed as in 1955 she married Mr Ronald Baker. He was a native of York but they made their home in Leicestershire where they raised their two sons. Mrs Baker's memory of Miss Walker the Headmistress, Miss Constance Wright, Deputy Head, Mrs Holm, Miss Vann and Miss White is clear. She remembers Mrs Roberts and Miss Fawcitt teaching in 'the prefabricated huts' by the clinic. Mrs Baker says that she will always remember her first form, a lovely group of girls in their second year. Many of the girls with others have kept in contact with her over many years especially at Christmas which she loves. Mrs Baker recalls the pantomime written by the Physical Education Teacher Mrs Cockroft's, mother. They sang the popular songs of the day and Mr Friis the maths teacher at the time was a most unusual fairy godmother with a luxuriant beard and a pink tutu. One Christmas the whole school walked to the local cinema to see 'The Wizard of Oz'. During the last week of Christmas carols were always sung in the dining room as a thank you to the kitchen staff. Mrs Baker recalls Miss Vann's very good choir and the whole school having to stay behind after the last lesson of the day if a hymn was poorly sung at morning Assembly which took place in the gymnasium. On one occasion Miss Vann asked Mrs Baker to teach the girls a song in the Welsh language. Although Mrs Baker admits that it is a very hard language to learn the girls mastered it and sang beautifully the song to the tune of the Christmas Carol, 'Deck the Halls with boughs of holly, tra, la la la, la; la la: la la'....

Coaches outside near the school clinic had to wait to take children home so everyone put heart and soul into the singing in order to get away quickly. Mrs Baker recalls the rota system where staff escorted pupils to the coaches from the school yard, alongside the field to the parking area bordering the Countesthorpe Road end of the school premises. This duty was enjoyed in the summer months but dreaded in winter especially if a coach had not arrived. This was then Miss Walker's duty to investigate the missing coach as many bus companies over the years have driven children from varying villages.

Enjoyed were the end of term hockey and netball games played by staff versus pupils and Mrs Baker writes that it was a caring school with good standards and good discipline.

Mrs Baker worked through many systems, streaming, setting and mixed ability and has very happy memories of her time there.

More appreciation for the enrichment of her life comes from Carole Williams nee Simpson. Carole a pupil between 1953 - 1958 was a member of the choir taught by Miss Molly Vann and the orchestra with Miss Fawcitt. Competing in the Leicester County and City Music Festivals they travelled to Nuneaton and Lincoln. They were very successful on many occasions. Practicing on Thursdays and Fridays (lunch time and evenings) they flourished. They were joined by the boys at times and the drama group with Miss Ellen Morris. Carole's memory of the cantata, 'Four Pictures of Christ' was performed at Braunstone Church in July 1958.

Carole feels very privileged that in the 1950s when few people owned cars, on Thursday evenings after practice, they were all transported home to Blaby, Glen Hills and Braunstone in Miss Fawcitt's car. Carole recalls great fun due to a dodgy petrol guage. It was not unknown to have to get out and push to the nearest garage. Eventually the 'kind and caring Miss Fawcitt' bought a brand new van. It was never as exciting but always greatly appreciated. Carole will always remember Miss Fawcitt, Miss Vann and Miss Morris and says if it were not for their teaching, 'my life would not be so enriched'.

Sheila Bailey Watts nee Jones 1953 - 1958 describes herself as a shy girl and one who failed the Eleven Plus examination at Blaby Junior School. Introduced in 1944 in the Butler Education Act this examination tested children's ability in arithmetic, writing and logical problem solving. On passing the examination it determined whether or not a child would earn a place in a grammar school but in failing the option was for a secondary or technical education known as the Tripartite System. Over time this examination became resented by large numbers of people who saw the examination as an unfair process. For Sheila Jones and David Buswell the news of failure was a shock to all who knew them both at Blaby as they were considered as 'two of the brightest in the village' At that time Sheila herself felt a failure too but as it turned out the opposite is quite apparent.

Sheila remembers South Wigston Girls' School as 'second to none, a fantastic school, strict but fair with an equal amount of things to share in'. Sheila's form mistress for three years was Miss Wright. Despite Sheila hating needlework she has good memories of Miss Wright and says that thanks are due to her that she can now make her own clothes. On reaching class 5A with Mrs Holm the girls designed their own summer uniforms. The pale blue dresses were worn with their yellow prefects sashes. Sheila was one of the girls who were given first year pupils from Fry House to mentor. Other teachers remembered are Mr Ron Baker for general biology and Mr Wignall for maths who apparently was very accurate at hurling the blackboard rubber at miscreants. Sheila participated in many dramatic productions put on by Miss Morris and Miss Fawcitt. The list includes 'Dr Faustus', 'Everyman', 'The Bell Ringers', 'Goblin Market', 'Harlequinade' conducted by Eric Pinkett and quite a serious interpretation of the 'The Bach Family'. She remembers well her visit to Norway with the County School of Music when Mrs Pinkett acted as chaperone to the children. In Norway Sheila took part in the 'Ballet Mime' which was also enacted in the County of Leicestershire at various venues. Whilst Mr Pinkett was the County Adviser for Music, Mr Alfred Bradley was the County Adviser for Drama and was involved in many of the County School of Music productions.

Mrs Dorothy Holm 3rd Left, back row Sheila Jones 3rd Left, front row

Sheila's family had moved to Bristol leaving her in lodgings until after she had completed her GCE O Level examinations. She remembers the kindness of Miss Walker, the headmistress at this time who took an interest in her welfare. Sheila was very sad to leave South Wigston school and moved on to take her A Level examinations in Colston's Girls' School, Bristol. The school was traditional and strict having connection with the Merchant Venturers of Bristol who first endowed a school for the children of mariners. Sheila missed the open fields of South Wigston. The new school was cramped in comparison and parents were required to sign a document which disallowed children to visit Bristol in the evenings. Sheila has no regrets that by failing the Eleven Plus Examination she was sent to South Wigston Secondary Modern School in place of the grammar school at Kibworth. She obtained teaching qualifications at Nottingham and for a time taught in Anstey, Leicestershire. She has many happy

Sheila Jones centre back with friends

On the sports field

memories of her school friends and a collection of photographs to treasure.

David Buswell spent his last year at Blaby Junior School in 1952 with the knowledge that he would sit the Eleven Plus Examination in May 1953. David writes that he had no real qualms about taking the examination as he had always enjoyed school and had found no particular problems in lessons. David felt no disappointment in failing the Eleven Plus as he recalls that although everyone else had expected him to pass he had given it little thought.

His entry into South Wigston Secondary Modern School for Boys' in September 1953 was preceeded by David's mother taking him to Jaques Outfitters in South Wigston for his obligatory school uniform. As recommended she had purchased one hundred and forty four name tags to sew on to every item of the new clothing. A third year boy in Blaby warned David that he would suffer an initiation ceremony on his first day at the school when he would be ducked under the tap outside the woodwork shop and not to struggle or it would be the worse for him. Sure enough on his first day of school the warning given came to fruition but to David it was 'a weak affair'.

Travelling on the normal service bus from Blaby he was dropped off in front of his new school and he assesses that there must have been approximately one hundred and thirty new entrants, the first year boys being instantly recognisable wearing their short trousers. David was allocated into the A form and Wycliffe House. His house master and English tutor was Mr R. Sibley BA and David remembers him as 'a brilliant and enthusiastic teacher for whom he did his best work'. On the third day the boys were introduced to the gymnasium where Mr Jack Cooper and Mr John Elders explained to them the great Rugby tradition of the school. Mr Elders asked for a show of hands on who would like to play for England? David remembers only one response but a little more enthusiasm when asked who would like to play in the school team. David thinking the

question on who would play for England inappropriate learned later that the school had produced three schoolboy internationals in 1948, 1949 and 1951.

Having been selected to attend Trials in his Junior School for the Mid Leicestershire Schools Football Team and played on several occasions, David's choice now was between rugby or hockey. He chose rugby and who better to teach it than John Elders? After much practice throughout the winter David played scrum half wearing his No. 9 shirt, black with one gold band across the chest, and enjoyed it. David was awarded his large size school badge with 'Rugby' embroidered upon it and wonders to this day how Mr Elders managed to create such a good team out of the raw recruits he was dealt.

David participated in cricket and athletics and learned to swim at the Oadby baths wearing pyjama bottoms. His maroon coloured woollen swimming trunks held water weighing half his body weight.

David did well in all academic subjects except arithmetic and French with Mr Beddoes. He loved music but for some unknown reason did not hit it off with Mr Harris. Mr Harris recognised David's singing ability and wanted him to join the choir. Not fitting in with the macho rugby playing image, David declined. Mr Harris's low marking of David's work did not improve matters and ultimately David decided that Mr Harris and George Frederick Handel could both drown in the 'Water Music'.

David remembers that school discipline was legendary believing that apart from natural good manners and respect for ones elders, 'fear and threat' may have contributed to good behaviour. Never did you dare to tell your parents of any admonishment. David's description of the conventional caners, edge of the ruler wielders and Mr 'Spitfire' Lord with his cat-o-nine tails made from basket weaving cane evokes quite an image with the blackboard chalk and rubber throwers. David remembers only one personal incident in the gym when Mr Elders failing to find the culprit of one misdemeanor gave the whole form one sharp stroke of the leather ended climbing rope across their backsides. Wearing only thin PE shorts this certainly left its mark.

David decided to leave school without taking his O Level GCE examinations. He was interviewed at school by a visiting Youth Employment Officer and later at their location on Pocklington's Walk. In due course a letter was handed to David by the Headmaster from the Headquarters of the East Midlands Gas Board in Leicester for interview. Later David was offered a post as Junior Clerk in the Commercial Manager's office.

On the last day of term ten of the boys were invited to the Headmaster, Mr Mark Rutherford's room where they stood in a semicircle round his desk. After confirming that they all had jobs to go to, Mr Rutherford said a few words, wished them success in their chosen careers and shook hands. Half an hour later David's schooldays were over.

Lance and Ellen Davis at 'The Man's Shop'. Blaby Road, South Wigston. Lance and Ellen also worked on school uniforms at Jaques the Tailors, South Wigston

John Penlington's School days 1952 - 1956 are recorded thus.

John also failed the Eleven Plus Examination at South Wigston Junior School and on his first day at South Wigston Secondary Modern Boys' School; he was initiated by a ducking under the tap. John writes that this must have been expected as in Assembly in the Headmaster's welcoming address he offered towels to those who needed to dry off. Dressed in his new uniform, a black jacket with a badge, (three stars of wisdom and a book of knowledge) on the breast pocket and grey short trousers, he sat dripping and listening to the instructions given out. As well as the allocation to classes John was also allocated to 'Burnaby' house. Competitive achievements were fought for and John remembers the glass cabinet in the corridor being full of gleaming silver trophies. When John left the school four years later their cabinet was empty. John played rugby at school later playing for Syston, South Wigston and the Police.

Recalling the 'girls' John admits that the only time they ever saw them was on sports days when they came out in white blouses tucked into navy blue knickers or on hot summer days at lunch times when they were allowed out on to the field. For talking in class John was sent to Mr Rutherford, the Headmaster's office where he received 'six of the best' with the cane. Some time later he was sent again for the same reason. His friend accompanied him to plead his case. John was given only three of the best. His friend received three also for his cheek. On one occasion their tutor left the class for a while. The boys took the opportunity to place a book above the door, leaving it slightly ajar so that it would fall on their teacher's head on his return. Seeing through the windows to the corridor, Mr Lord, a strict disciplinarian walked by. John reveals that this was the last person you would want to enter the room. Puzzled by their good behaviour and silence Mr Lord did enter and the ambush worked a treat with the book falling squarely on his head. After a half hour's interrogation, no one owned up. They were all given detention but unfortunately the book had a pupil's name in it. The culprit was led away by the ear and returned rubbing his backside.

John remembers one Physical Training Teacher used a plimsoll instead of the cane. The plimsoll was stolen and thrown into the canal on the next bus trip out. John was taught woodwork, metalwork, and gardening and remembers well Mr Horace Place as a congenial, elderly rounded tutor who could always during lessons, be persuaded to deviate and talk about the love of his life, growing tomatoes.

John's last teacher was Mr Scotson whom he believed to be Canadian. They were quickly reprimanded if they used any American slang as they believed that Mr Scotson was not favourably disposed to Americans.

John participated in his final year in the Gilbert

Mr Horace Place. South Wigston Secondary Modern Boys' School from 1945. Founder, Whetstone Juvenile Choir, Choirmaster, Whetstone Male Voice Choir, Barwell Choral Society and Barwell Male Voice Choir Conductor, Barwell Wesleyan Church Choir. Since 1945 Choirmaster and Deacon at Whetstone Congregational Church

and Sullivan production of 'The Pirates of Penzance'. Strangely he portrayed a policeman. John left at the age of fifteen years with no qualifications but had a good grounding in the three R's, history, geography and tomatoes. John went on to become a Senior Police Officer. Now retired from the service he has written one book, *'The Best Time Is Now'* *(The Ups and Downs of a Police Career)* and has been successful in having a number of articles published in magazines.

John Penlington 1954

It is recorded that in February 1954 six double decker buses took all staff and pupils to the Savoy Cinema in Leicester to see the film, 'Conquest of Everest'. In April Mrs Vrolijk and Mr Ron Baker escorted thirty four girls to Holland for one week's holiday.

In the Boys' School the McRobie Trophy was awarded to the First Year Rugby Team for their unbeaten record that season and in September in the

Girls' School there were now eighteen pupils in the Fifth Form.

September 1954 saw the new arrival of Miss Joan Elliott later to become Mrs Pechey. Mrs Pechey's memory of Miss Walker is of a very fair and caring Head Teacher who was very supportive of newly qualified staff always keeping a very tight ship. Mrs Pechey, Domestic Science Teacher, remembers well the room with wood everywhere. Table surfaces, chopping boards and the dreaded draining boards which all had to be scrubbed at the end of each lesson. The best part of the room was the teacher's high desk with step up seat from which she could survey the whole class. Towels and dish cloths had to be boiled at the end of the day. Mrs Pechey played hockey for the 'old girls' and went with a party to Insbruck in 1956 and to Spain in 1958. Staying in a school in Austria the pleasure of warm duvets was a new experience. At South Wigston School the boiler room was the link between the two mirror imaged schools. No mixing of the girls and boys was allowed. In the five years that Mrs Pechey taught at South Wigston Girls' School she can only remember entering the Boys' School on one occasion to see Mr Harris. Remembered is Mr Baker and Mr Morse in the Girls' School. Mrs Pechey left South Wigston School in 1958 to take up an appointment at the newly built Hamilton High School where she had 'a big say in the equipment in the cookery and needlework rooms, Bliss'.

Rosie Taylor nee English 1954 -1958 looks back on 'many happy memories' of her schooldays. First impressions of the very large school she had entered in comparison to the Bassett Street Junior School are clear. The first three years were spent with Miss Norah White as their form mistress, the final year with Miss Molly Vann. Rosie says it was a real novelty to constantly change classrooms for the different lessons. There were forty girls in the class and Rosie made friends with many of the girls from different areas in the county who were bussed in.

Rosie enjoyed dancing once a week at lunch time in the Boys' Hall and remembers playing netball in a thick snowstorm. The girls could hardly see the ball and were freezing in their navy PE knickers and Tee Shirts. Breaking a few Bunsen burners is remembered in the science lessons. Rosie's favourite subject was arithmetic and every Friday afternoon in her last year she was allowed to calculate the

The Senior Girls' Choir. Miss Molly Vann front row, extreme right

registers whilst the rest of the class studied Religious Instruction. Rosie was excused this lesson as she was a Catholic.

One of Rosie's best memories was visiting Switzerland with the school. Her leaving day was very sad as the girls all collected autographs.

From January to Easter 1955 children and teachers alike were suffering from Influenza. School life continued with many successes in music and sport. Visits to the cinema and de Montfort Hall were enjoyed. The Past Pupils Association was flourishing winning the County Dramatic Trophy. In September they performed 'Berkeley Square' to an audience of two hundred.

In July 1955 Mr Harris, Deputy Head in the Boys' School left to take up his appointment as Headmaster at Lutterworth Secondary Modern School. He was succeeded as Deputy Headmaster by Mr Leslie Wild.

On 1 October 1955 The National Union of Teachers, (NUT) held a Refresher Course at South Wigston Girls' School. The course was opened by Mr Stewart Mason, Director of Education and Sir Robert Martin, Chairman of the Education Committee. Mr Chuter Ede was the Principal Speaker. Three hundred people were in attendance. James Chuter Ede was elected to Parliament on three separate occasions and served in the wartime coalition Government holding junior ministerial office as Parliamentary Secretary to the Board of Education. Having studied at Christ's College,

Cambridge and working for a time as a teacher, Chuter Ede became active in the National Union of Teachers. He was closely involved in the drafting of the Butler Education Act and was created a life peer becoming known as Baron Chuter Ede of Epsom.

Baron James Chuter Ede of Epsom

In December 1955 boys learned of a road accident involving two of their masters. Mr Davies and Mr Beddoes were travelling home on Saffron Road when their car was in collision with a military vehicle outside Glen Parva Barracks. Both masters were seriously ill in the Leicester Royal Infirmary. The sad news of Mr Beddoes death occurred a week later without him ever regaining consciousness.

Mr John Morse, a very tall Welshman spent four very happy years at the school from 1955 to 1959 and taught Religious Instruction and geography.

Wearing his mortarboard he is well remembered in the Girls' School as he swept along the corridors in his flowing black gown. Brenda Phillips recalls the class standing by their desks in silence as he entered the classroom. Looking back on the nineteen fifties it seems quite unreal in today's integrated society to remember the Catholic children who always 'sat outside' in the cloakroom usually during morning assemblies. Their faith did not allow them to participate in the prayers and hymn singing which brought the rest of the school together each day.

Christine Colebourn nee Silk 1954 - 1958 came to school by bus from Kirby Muxloe but with a group of school friends often walked home after school. Their route took them from Saffron Lane via Wigston Lane, Dog Lane, Coalpit Lane Narborough to Ratby. Christine remembers Mr Morse along with other teachers already named. Miss Thompson taught her for needlework, Miss Priestley for PE and Miss Gardner for domestic science where they attempted to make Swiss rolls with no flour. Christine played rounders, hockey and netball and participated in choral verse speaking and Bible reading. At the Edward Wood Hall in Leicester Christine was presented with a certificate for her recitation 'To A Water Fowl'. She also enjoyed her school trip to Flushing, Holland with the school orchestra. At school someone took in a little bottle of Evening in Paris and the girls were all made to wash it off in the showers.

Mr Morse recalls Miss Walker as a very strict but fair disciplinarian for whom he had 'a great deal of affection and respect'. At that time Mr Morse was one of only three men in the Girls' School, one of which was the caretaker. Mr Morse believed that the way to kindling the interest of young people was through out of school activities. His memory of the bicycle ride and consequent hike through Bradgate Park is still clear also the badminton and tennis clubs played on the tarmac school playground. Reprimanded were the girls who 'spyed' through the locked keyholes into the boys changing rooms. The last ten minutes of the geography lessons at the end of the day were usually lost as girls attention wandered to the long crocodile of boys wending their way to the bus park beyond the Horsa Huts. The classroom located on the first floor gave an excellent view as the boys were allowed to leave that much earlier than the girls.

In the long holidays Mr Morse remembers his camping visits to Hathersage in Derbyshire where a marquee and living tents would first be erected. Cooking over wood fires still makes his eyes weep at the thought. The highlight of the holiday was the sheep trials.

Other years were spent at Innsbruck in the Austrian Tyrol. The party was quite large and split into three parts like 'Ceasar's Gaul'. Mr Morse took his party walking in the mountains singing pop songs of the day. 'I love to go a wandering, 'fal dee ree, fal dee ra'. On their return they learned of a national incident. Another of their group had not 'kept off the grass' in a public place. The instruction had been in German which resulted in the party being locked in the cells for three hours. Mr Morse recalls another occasion when the girls attempted to learn his college songs in the fluent Welsh language. 'Sir Jasper and the foggy foggy dew'. Mr Morse's last year saw him organising a trip to Pineda on the Costa Brava. A long train journey setting out at four in the morning on one day and arriving in the evening of the next. There were many memorable events including the 'Corrida of the Bulls'. On the first evening after dinner which was always accompanied by wine, 'my trusty Sancho Panza' the indomitable Mrs Scruton, would ensure that 'all were present and correct'. Checking all rooms, one door remained firmly locked and no amount of banging could raise the occupants. The hotel keeper borrowed a ladder, picked his way over the balustrade only to discover the four girls sleeping soundly after over indulging themselves in the 'vin de table'.

The second week celebrated the fiesta of the local saint with dancing in the town's large central plaza for three nights. The dances were all variations of the traditional Catalan dance called the Sardana. Very soon the girls became very adept at the complicated steps under the expert tuition of the seventeen year old youths. When the new school term began Mr Morse's spare time was taken up by translating the many romantic letters received by the girls from the Spanish young boys.

1956 was a memorable year when in April Mr Curtis Weston presented GCE Certificates to several girls. In May girls gave a fashion show wearing gowns they had made themselves from Simplicity patterns and many talks were given to school leavers.

Visit to Josiah Wedgewood Potteries, Stoke on Trent c1956. Mrs Hall Left, Mr John Morse Right

One very memorable occasion is recorded in *The South Wigston Secondary Modern School For Girls Magazine*. A music festival was planned to take place at the de Montfort Hall on 18 and 19 May to celebrate the eightieth birthday of Sir Robert Martin in recognition for all of his work as the Chairman of the County Council Education Committee. Most of the schools in the county were represented as over a thousand children took part. Several girls sang in the massed choir and Jennifer Clarke, Form 111 writes that songs were learned from Miss Molly Vann. At the end of the Festival 'A Fine Old English Gentleman' was sung. The event concluded with a speech delivered by Sir Robert.

In September at the beginning of the new term Miss Norah White was absent from school having been hit by a loose pig trailer. This resulted in three weeks away from school. In October a pupil in the Housecraft Room suffered an accident when she lit the oven. The gas blew back into her face singeing her eye lashes and hair. She also sustained slight facial burns and burns to her arm.

1957 heralded a new dawn for the South Wigston Girls' and Boys' School. Less than twenty years since the school's grand opening, their name was to change. Mrs Baker recalls that under the 'Mason Plan' South Wigston Secondary Modern School was renamed to South Wigston High School. The Director of Education for Leicestershire was known to be very forward thinking and promoted Comprehensive Education. A consequence of this change meant that children were transferred from South Wigston at the age of thirteen to Guthlaxton and Countesthorpe Schools. It did however mean the loss of the General Certificate of Education Examinations at South Wigston.

Mr Mark Rutherford explains in 'The Wasp' that the Eleven Plus Examination has been abolished. This meant that children would go straight to the High School from the Junior School rather than to a Grammar school at the age of eleven. There would be no passes and no failures. Children who may have been destined for the Grammar school would now attend South Wigston but the loss of a Fifth Form at South Wigston was also a consequence. Children wishing to take examinations and stay on at school would transfer three years later to Guthlaxton. The full implications of the new arrangements were not expected to be fully operational until 1959.

The 1950s are recognised as the era when Stewart Mason backed by very innovative staff and the local authority made his mark. The time was ripe for

Brenda Phillips still playing the drums with The Orpheans

Miss Avis Fawcitt and The Right Worshipful The Lord Mayor of Leicester, Councillor Mary Draycott February 2006

change. At Leicester University the education system was under scrutiny. Professor Robin Pedley's book *Comprehensive Education A New Approach* (1956) was quoted freely in the House of Commons debate leading to a conference with him and the Education Minister to discuss his proposals.

As a direct result of the re-organisation by Leicester Education of County Schools into the High School/Upper School System, the Leicester Orphean Youth Orchestra was formed from the South Wigston Past Pupils Music Group and Miss Fawcitt. As the children moved to Guthlaxton School at thirteen they themselves wanted to continue with Miss Fawcitt and the music they so much loved. The group joined together with Miss Ellen Morris's Past Pupils Drama group entering small events and competing in the County and Midlands Festivals. It is significant today to note that as new systems are again on the horizon at South Wigston High School, the Orpheans are still entertaining and raising money for charity. In 2008 over fifty years will be celebrated with Miss Avis Fawcitt still voluntarily teaching music to enthusiastic children.

School trips continued to be enjoyed in 1957. February saw sixty girls at Wembley to see the International Hockey Match. During the month of August one party of girls visited Austria whilst the following week another party visited Switzerland. The boys trip to Switzerland that year was hampered by the French railways being affected by strike action.

Other occasions out of school for the boys were visits to the Auster Works at Rearsby, the John Bull factory and a day in London.

The Past Pupils Association continued to flourish as in May of 1957 they won the Hilton Trophy for the third year running for drama for their production of 'Quality Street'.

At the Area Sports at South Wigston the trophy was again won by South Wigston only having lost it one year out of eight.

Pupils from South Wigston Boys' School will remember their days of National Service and in particular 485654 Regimental Sergeant Major Harold Brown, stationed at Glen Parva Barracks. He was known as 'Topper Brown'. RSM Brown enlisted in the regular Army on 11 January 1932. He served with the 1st Battalion the Royal Leicestershire Regiment and took part in the Korean War.

The last boys to be called up for duty were on 31 December 1960.

Topper Brown's daughter Ann attended the Girls' School at South Wigston until her Father's posting took the family to Barbados.

The first of March 1958 saw the South East Leicestershire Youth Music Festival take place. Adjudications were held at the Boys' and Girls' High Schools, South Wigston and the Winning Competitors Festival Concert at the Abington High School in the evening. The Chairman was Mr Richard L Bishop, South East Area Youth Advisory Committee and the Announcer was Mr Roger R Richmond. The eight Adjudicators came from various towns in the Midlands and organisations

MERITORIOUS SERVICE MEDAL FOR R.S.M.

Regimental Sergeant Major Harold (Topper) Brown

AFTER witnessing the passing-out parade in which 95 N.C.Os and recruits took part at Glen Parva Barracks today, Lord Cromwell, Lord Lieutenant of Leicestershire, declared: "The marching and arms drill I have seen today might well compare with that of the Guards Regiments."

The recruits have just completed ten weeks basic training at the Royal Leicestershire Regiment depot. Some are expected to join the 1st Battalion of the Regiment in Khartoum, and others will be transferred to the Royal Lincolnshire Regiment.

A feature of the parade was the presentation of the Meritorious Service Medal to Regimental Sergeant Major H. Brown.

Already the holder of the Good Conduct Medal, Sergeant Major Brown has 23½ years' service behind him. His only break from the Regiment was in 1941, when he left to become the first R.S.M. of the 1st Parachute Regiment, with which he served for two years.

He has served all over the world with the Tigers, but has been stationed at the depot for the last two years. And although he can now leave the Army, Sergeant Major Brown, who is 4? will probably remain in the Service until he is 55.

Lord Cromwell presenting the Meritorious Service Medal to R.S.M. Brown, at today's Glen Parva passing-out parade.

---

participating numbered twenty two.

Categories listed were Instrumental, Piano, Vocal Classes, Verse Speaking, Bible Reading and Folk Dancing. The Festival Office was situated in the Girls' School, South Wigston also a hot lunch time meal in the Girls' dining hall. Light refreshments and anyone bringing their own sandwiches were directed to the Boys' dining hall.

On 9 May 1958 Queen Elizabeth 11 and the Duke of Edinburgh visited Leicester. This was celebrated by the children all rushing to the city to catch a glimpse of the Royal Couple.

On Saturday 19 July 1958 the 'Leicester Advertiser' reported on the 'Performance of South Wigston Teachers' Sacred Cantata'. The performance, 'Four Pictures of Christ', was written and produced by Miss E Morris and Miss A Fawcitt. The cantata was presented by one hundred past and present pupils of the school in conjunction with the newly formed Orphean Youth Orchestra at St. Peters Church, Braunstone.

Also presented in July at school was 'Nymphs and Shepherds' and two French plays.

As the decade 1948/1958 closes in July 1958, it is apparent that many visits to factories, museums. cinemas and theatres was broadening the outlook of school children from South Wigston giving them insight into life outside of their protected environment. A party of boys was taken to visit the Houses of Parliament and they were met by Sir John Farr, the Conservative Member of Parliament for the Harborough Division.

Freedom experienced on cycling and camping trips in the English countryside and more adventurous journeys to foreign lands far exceeded the experience of the last generation's children who had suffered the awful effects of war. Travels abroad for the majority of parents had mainly been with the fighting forces. Boys called up for their two years National Service after leaving the South Wigston School, if not directly involved in the Korean War in 1950 or the Suez Crisis in 1956; would have only a taste of military life.

The wonderful accounts in both the Boys' magazine 'Wasp' and the 'Magazine of the South Wigston Secondary Modern School For Girls' give the most informative and delightful accounts of school life. Far too many to record here. Articles and poems display the excellent standard of English illustrating enthusiasm and love of their art.

The haunting sound of childrens voices singing together in morning Assemblies or in concert still have the power to bring a tear to the eye. Hymn number 24, 'Praise my soul the King of Heaven', in the little red book, 'Prayers and Hymns for Use in Schools', was sung with regularity as it was said to be Miss Walker's favourite.

It is said that 'school days are the happiest days of your life'. Days to be cherished and remembered with pride always.

Chapter Four
Was Adrian Here?
(1958 - 1968)

'Was Adrian here'? A question we may never find the answer to but one in which we challenge you all to consider. During this decade we now know that one of the most famous pupils of our time passed through our school. Sue Townsend nee Johnstone is revered nationwide for the creation of 'Adrian Mole' and has been described as one of Britain's best selling authors.

We ask again, 'Was Adrian Here'? Every school child has probably passed him in one school corridor or another. Who was he? Where was he? Unlike Peter Pan, Adrian has moved onwards and upwards but somewhere in South Wigston High School the spirit of Adrian still lurks. He is there with Pandora Braithwaite. Which reader will recognise him? Could it be in the discovery of Pandora, we will unmask Adrian?

On 10 September 1958 a staff meeting was held in South Wigston High School prior to the official opening of the new school term on the 11th which began the academic year. As decreed by the rules of the Leicestershire Plan, it was reported that sixty one boys and twenty four girls did not return to South Wigston Schools on this day having transferred to Guthlaxton Upper School. One hundred and seven girls had been absorbed into industry whilst a small number had moved on to Teacher Training Colleges.

As well as the new pupils entering South Wigston on that day there was also a new master making his debut at the Boys' School. Mr Charles Edward Geach Thomas was appointed as a Teacher of Art and his connection with the school spanned thirty five years. He became known fondly as 'Ted' Thomas and recalls that at South Wigston, music and art were extremely good.

Mr Thomas was born in Falmouth and completed his education at the West of England College of Art, Bristol. On arrival at South Wigston he found the art rooms were situated in the old nursery block next to the Girls' tennis courts. Although at the time the Boys' and Girls' Schools were separate, Mr Thomas saw the girls and the girls staff every day due to the location of his class rooms. Mr Jones ran classes One and Two and Mr Reid, Three and Four. The PE lessons would be quite visible. For most other staff male and female paths rarely crossed.

Recalling the school duty of escorting their respective bus queues to the buses parked by the school clinic at the end of each day, Mr Thomas actually met his future wife who had come to the school to teach PE. Miss Margaret Cox, was also escorting her charges to their bus. Miss Walker's strict rule of 'no fraternisation' of the sexes somehow was lost in the bus queue. Miss Cox left the school after just over a year when she was appointed to a post at Beaumont Leys School but Mr Thomas and Miss Cox married in 1962.

Part of Mr Thomas's duty was to teach PE and he undertook some refereeing at the Saturday rugby matches. Becoming involved in many extra curricula outdoor activities he was soon going out on Mr Tom Pell's (Head of PE) camping and canoeing excursions.

Mr Thomas describes his first experience of a trip which took place in the summer of 1959. He and Mr Pell and two senior boys set off as an advanced party to set up camp for forty to fifty boys who were to spend a fortnight on the activity holiday on a farm on the banks of the River Wye a few miles upstream from Ross on Wye. They bought some provisions and did some preparation when they learned that the pantechnicon bringing the tents and equipment had broken down and would not be arriving until the next day. The boys and accompanying staff were already on their way by train so improvisations had to be made. A metal grid was found by Mr Jenkins, the farmer. Placing this over some stones provided their stove. The farmer also produced a cast iron jam kettle so the evening meal of a good warming stew was prepared.

The sleeping quarters was an open sided barn with plenty of straw bales but part of that was fenced off to accommodate a few young bullocks. Mr Thomas vividly remembers waking up to bovine snuffling rather close to his ear and seeing the tousled head of a young boy appearing from a straw lined feeding trough. 'Was Adrian Here'?

The next day all of the kit arrived and they spent a very successful fortnight in temperatures up to 93 degrees Fahrenheight. (33 Celsius)

Mr Thomas describes the strong tradition of

operetta in the Boys' School including performances of Gilbert and Sullivan favourites. Mr Paddock, Head of Music, composed his own at times and one remembered piece was based on Charles Lamb's story of the origins of roast pork. Mr Thomas was responsible for designing and making the scenery part of which was to make a straw hut. This had to be transformed into a quick scene change into a blackened shell. All went well during the performances at school but on an occasion at Guthlaxton one of the scenery changers got his jersey hooked up on the shell and was left stranded upon the stage. At the time the boys were expected to sing and all of the male and female parts were taken by the boys.

In October 1958 an accident occurred when Mr Leslie Wild, Deputy Headmaster in the Boys' School and Head of the Evening Institute, was moving a piano with the help of some boys. The piano fell over backwards injuring Mr Wild and Calvin Townsend. It was discovered at the Royal Infirmary that Mr Wild had broken his toe in two places and that Calvin Townsend had broken bones in his foot. The piano which had been hired by the Evening Institute Operatic Society was found to be not as well constructed as the school piano and in turn could easily be caught off balance. It would appear that Calvin Townsend was quite unlucky as four months later he was in the wars again when he switched on the classroom lights. His finger was burnt by 'a flash of light from the panel'. Needless to say this matter was immediately dealt with by calling the County Council's designated electrician.

The winter months of 1958 record much absenteeism due to illness. Miss Walker attended a Head Teachers' Conference at Brockington School. Over the years Miss Walker carried out numerous visits to various schools, colleges and official meetings.

A staff meeting was arranged in mid-October in the Girls' School to discuss Christmas Examinations and End of Term Activities.

In November a meeting of High Schools' Head Teachers for Hinckley and Wigston was hosted in the Girls' School at four in the afternoon.

Early in December school examinations began but later that month pupils enjoyed their house netball matches, a prefects party and a visit to the cinema to see Danny Kaye in the film, 'Court Jester'. On the last day of term a carol concert was held in the morning and the school concert in the afternoon.

January 1959 saw Miss Walker accompanied by Mr Friis go to view the new arithmetic teaching methods in action at Glen Hills Primary School whilst at the end of January Dr. Braine, Deputy Director of Education for the London County Council together with Mr Pulbrook, visited South Wigston High School to observe something of 'The Leicestershire Experiment'.

The first term of 1959 continued to see the girls participating in the choirs and choral verse speaking classes and entering into the South East Area Music Festival held in the school. The Past Pupils Drama Group continued to flourish

At Easter 1959 a party of twenty eight boys visited Switzerland accompanied by Mr Leslie Wild and Mr Cooper. Soon after arrival they enjoyed the cable railway ride into the snow capped mountains close to their hotel. At the top they spent time watching the skiers and snowballing in the sunshine. Mr Cooper and a few of the boys descended the mountain on foot from the half way station. The following day they journeyed by train up the Jungfrau. Graham Wood and David Hardingham of Form 2A write in 'The Wasp' of the magnificent views, the Sphinx Observatory and the Ice Palace. The last day was spent at Montreux.

School life continued until the summer term with all of the normal activities.

In July Bronte and Fry Houses in the Girls' School celebrated their achievements in winning the most points at the Kenwood Swimming Baths. Drama and music students continued to bring many accolades to the school.

In the Autumn Term of September 1959 a new arrival on the staff in the Girls' School was Mr Aubrey Burl. Mr Burl writes that Miss Walker, the excellent Headmistress gave him responsibility for history throughout the school with the responsibility also for teaching Latin to the Alpha stream only. The class consisted of twenty eight to thirty very bright girls.

Alicia Parker nee Slater recalls many of the teachers mentioned between 1958 - 1961 particularly Mrs Holm who taught her Latin. Alicia studied this subject for three years in the Alpha stream.

Mr Burl describes the school as a well disciplined quiet school, socially mixed, but orderly; a rewarding place in which to teach. It comfortably passed a General Schools Inspection.

The Headmistress encouraged well-planned out of school activities. Mr Burl recalls that one Easter Miss Walker led a party to Rome for the occasion of the Pope's address. It was In fact Easter 1960 when joining Miss Walker and Mr Burl, Miss Wakefield, Miss Randall and Miss Garner together with twenty seven girls visited Italy. They travelled to Naples, Capri, Sorrento and Amalfi. To stand in the thronged Vatican Square to hear Pope John XXIII during their five days in Rome must surely have been an historic occasion. Ostia, the harbour city of Ancient Rome, and Tivoli an ancient town were also visited.

Under the Mason Plan there was a week's break during Whitsuntide and twice school groups visited the Dordogne for morning visits to churches, castles and fortified mediaeval towns. Afternoons were often spent bathing in the Dordogne whose river passed under the balconies of their small country hotel. The girls were encouraged to speak French and were sent out to the local shops to buy the picnic lunches.

During term time Mr Burl remembers the brass rubbing excursions to Leicestershire churches. Wanlip and Bottesford were two. He recalls that transparencies are in existence of the girls on their knees heel-balling the images.

On 4 July 1959 the school enjoyed their twenty first birthday reunion. One thousand tickets were sold. Set tea in the Girls' dining hall and a buffet in the Boys' dining hall was arranged. An afternoon performance of folk dancing by all classes was given and the Senior Choir and School Orchestra gave renditions. Form 11G performed 'The Sleeping Princess' and Form 1G, 'The Princess and the Woodcutter'. A dress show in the evening together with a performance by the Past Pupils ended the celebration. A profit of seventy five pounds was raised.

In July Mr Morse conducted three parties of girls on an educational visit to London.

On 24 July the school closed for the summer holidays but sadly seven members of staff were not returning. Miss E Morris and Miss A Fawcitt both left to take up posts at Hamilton School. As recorded, 'Miss Morris, history, English and drama,

outstandingly taught'.

Miss A Fawcitt. 'music, orchestra and English. Miss Fawcitt built up the orchestra from scratch'.

Other teachers to leave were, Miss J Elliott, Mr J Morse, Miss O M Bailey, Mrs Cockroft and Mrs Wright.

Joan Hogarth nee Robertshaw 1958 - 1962 recalls her memories of school life. Joan was awarded many offices at school. She was Vice Head Girl to the Head Girl, Jackie Marriott. A prefect in Fry House, House Captain and Games Captain, Joan was obviously a very popular pupil. On Monday mornings it was the duty of the House Captains to read out the names in Assembly of any girls who had gained order marks for misbehaviour during the previous week. This method of shaming an individual and incurring the anger of very competitive house members helped to ensure good discipline. There were also many privileges for attaining the role of prefect. They were allowed to enter school via the front main door as the teachers did and to use the centre stairs. In winter prefects could remain inside school and Joan admits that it was very good to be warming oneself by the radiators whilst unavoidably 'smirking' out through the window to the shivering onlookers on the outside. A badge of office would be worn on the uniform for each title so Joan had four badges. She recalls wearing white panama hats in the summer and navy blue velour hats in the winter months. Navy blazers were worn with pale blue ribbon round the edge and the school badge on the pocket. Pale blue dresses with white trim were worn. Satchels were part of the school kit but work was always left in the form room desk as pupils moved from room to room to their other lessons. Only home work was carried home at the end of the day. Today Joan observes the heavy kit bags carried by the school children to and fro everywhere.

With some amusement Joan recalls the occasion in which a number of Fourth Year girls were reprimanded by Miss Walker. The girls had attended school in fashionable net petticoats which added volume to the skirts of upper garments. The girls were instructed to stand in a line on the stage in front of the whole Assembly whereupon Miss Walker pulled down every girl's petticoat. The offending items were confiscated until school was over for the day.

Joan joined Miss Morris's drama group and has many memories of her friends in the class one of which was the famous 'Adrian Mole' creator, Sue Townsend nee Johnstone. Joan has some vivid memories of pranks they played and still keeps in touch with many of the girls.

in Joan's last year she studied commercial subjects learning to touch type. There were no computers in school at that time and learning to set tabulations and the use of Tippex is well remembered. Pitman's Elementary examined the skill of the shorthand pupils.

Joan left the school at Easter 1962 after taking the College of Preceptors Examination. Historically the College of Preceptors dates back to 1846 when it was founded by a group of Brighton schoolmasters as the Society of Teachers. They were concerned regarding standards within their own profession. The College of Preceptors was incorporated by Royal Charter in 1849. The College originally awarded qualifications to secondary school teachers and pupils.

producing surgical spirit and cotton wool. Miss Walker's inspection passed without incident as the girls offered forth their beautiful natural nails.

Shirley participated in the drama group. 'The Princess and the Woodcutter' which was produced to celebrate the school's twenty first birthday and 'Oliver's Island' were two productions put on by Mrs Dorothy Winder. Shirley took part in both.

Today Shirley is a Methodist Local Preacher and one day a week is involved in the Chaplaincy at Leicester Royal Infirmary. This supports patients with religious, spiritual and pastoral care.

The Princess and the Woodcutter
Margaret Rose, woodcutter, Shirley
Gardiner, princess

Joan Robertshaw, Sue Johnstone and Class 4A 1958-
1962 celebrating their 25th anniversary reunion

Shirley Kendall nee Gardiner recalls that she was also in the same class as Sue Townsend. Shirley's fear of Miss Walker's announcement one morning to inspect girls' finger nails caused great consternation for herself and two friends. The previous evening they had very carefully painted their nails with nail polish even though they knew that it was strictly forbidden to wear it at school. Mr Baker, the science master saved the day by

Oliver's Island. Left Margaret Rose as
Oliver, Shirley Gardiner as Jill

Linda Bartholomew nee Allen 1959 - 1964 recalls her first day at South Wigston High School for Girls'. After the security of Bassett Street Junior School she writes that 'the big school was quite a daunting prospect but exciting too'. She describes in detail the uniform and as many girls have said, hated wearing the horrendous beret emblazoned with the school badge. Prefects stood on guard at the school gates each morning ready to report anyone who did not have the dreaded things firmly on their heads. Linda and her friends used to slap the berets flattened like pancakes as far back on their heads as possible holding them in place with hairgrips on either side. Living dangerously they would only put them in place on their approach to Saint Thomas Church hoping that the prefects were not looking in their direction. Linda and her friend Shirley also recall the fashion of the frilly underskirts which had to be removed as their uniform could not billow out beyond two inches.

Linda's first form teacher in 1A was Mr Horst Briel, Head of Geography. Linda describes Mr Briel as seeming huge with floppy dark hair and intensive blue eyes whom girls 'drooled' over. One of Linda's favourite subjects was English with Mrs Winder who graciously informed them that her name was pronounced as in 'Windermere'. Miss Vann was another favourite vigorously rolling French vowels at them. History was greatly enjoyed with Mr Burl who she says besides throwing board rubbers and chalk at them, brought civil wars to life by allowing them to re-enact them in the classroom. Rulers became swords and window poles transformed into pike staffs. He certainly had the knack of making history interesting. Linda recalls that a number of years ago whilst watching a television programme about Stonehenge, there was Mr Burl as the presenter. The acclaimed Dr. Aubrey Burl, famous archaeologist and renowned author specialising in megalithic monuments and rituals, large as life on the screen.

Linda recalls many of the teachers, and taking home her carefully prepared cookery dishes in straw Gondola baskets. After sitting the College of Preceptors Examinations Mr Jobling, her art teacher, taught them how to dance the Madison and the Twist one afternoon in the hall. This was a day or so before the girls left school and to quote Linda, 'Cool teacher or what'? This she says was a delightful

L to R Mr Horst Briel, Dr Aubrey Burl, Mr David Nutt

change from prancing round doing the 'Bolero' for Miss Cox.

In her final year Linda's dream came true as she entered the commerce classroom taught by Mrs Sullivan. The girls fought to get the best typewriters but Linda ended up with a battered Remington. For hours they struggled to type to music to gain rhythm dreaming of becoming a millionaire's PA. Mrs Sullivan informed them that a good secretary could take down a dictated nursery rhyme in shorthand and then type it back without realising what she had produced.

At the end of the last term in the summer of 1964 Linda and her friends were 'Beatles' crazy, Form 4A put on a Doctor Kildare sketch in the End of Year Concert. Doctor Kildare was 'The' programme to watch on television and was famous for its 'freeze framing' when the credits rolled and advert breaks. The girls tried to include this in their sketch. The storyline was built around an operation and Gill Whaite who played Dr. Kildare even managed to find a side fastening white jacket like the TV. original. Heart, lungs and kidneys were borrowed from the school laboratories as props. Carol Buddin and Linda played young lovers in their advertisement which was about how 'BURLBRAND Cigarettes' help keep you calm during those special dates. (history). Linda recalls it seeming funny at the time and Mr Burl graciously roared with laughter.

Linda's proudest moment at South Wigston High School for Girls' goes back to her first year in form

1A where she managed to attain 97% in her French exam. The exuberant French mistress, Miss Vann, was so impressed with her achievement that she presented her with the French version of Beatrix Potter's *Peter Rabbit - Pierre Lapin*. Proudly Linda took her prize home to show her parents, little brother and four year old sister, Beverley. Linda recalls that this was a token to treasure for the rest of her life, to show her grandchildren. Her sister Beverley found the book and illustrated pictures with her own crayons with disastrous results. How ironic it is that she has grown up to be the present Headteacher's secretary. Finally, Linda says, 'Be on your guard, Mr Gary Toward'.

John Breen left Ravenhurst Road Junior School on Turnbull Drive, Braustone and was transported to South Wigston High School by Woods Coaches, 1959 - 1962. John lived in fear of missing the school bus as the route to South Wigston would have taken him into Leicester to catch a second bus, (L8) and out again to South Wigston.

John's memory of the bus route to school is clear especially when alighting at Countesthorpe Road. The path to school vividly reminds him of his ordeal at the 'Clinic' which he had to pass. On one occasion John was suffering in tremendous pain from Verrucas. He remembers the long queue of boys suffering with the same agonising problem all waiting their turn for treatment by the doctor at the Clinic. Obviously the Verrucas were cauterised as John recalls the 'burning sensation' and there was no privacy as the act was carried out in front of everyone. The showers were blamed for the outbreak at the time. The only 'prize' for Verruca sufferers was that they were allowed to 'hobble' a little slower on the cross country runs.

John recalls a mixture of friends coming from outlying villages as well as South Wigston. He names, Roy Sherwin, Stephen Gill, Anthony Gray, Philip Bairstow, Paul Huddlestone, Stuart Coles, John Stevenson and two other boys whose surnames were Mildred and Parry. The boys were always addressed by their surnames by the masters.

The masters John remembers are Mr Wild wearing his long cloak and Mr Rutherford, the Headmaster, Mr Glenton for art, Mr Pell. and a very strict science master. Recalled is the Hungarian goulash and blancmange at school meal times when they sat eight to a table. The scramble for a place if a boy was late was fearful as food was expected to have run out. Boys ran a tuck shop at break.

A particular memory is the 'shoe inspections' for cleanliness. The vaulting horse and the climbing frames in the gymnasium and the core subjects and swimming is recalled but John's best subjects were history and French. He still has a fish slice which he made in the metalwork class and a bookcase which still in good use, has stood the test of time. This was made in the woodwork class.

Visiting the Ritz Cinema, the Third Years saw the film. 'Around the World in Eighty Days'. John enjoyed his time at South Wigston remembering 'Wigston South' Railway Station, the signal box and train spotting as a hobby. On leaving school he joined the Enquiry Office at the Midland Red Omnibus Company at Coventry transferring to Leicester some months later. He has completed forty three and a half years with the company which has changed hands more than once.

In September 1959 the school celebrated its twenty first birthday. The occasion was marked by the composition of a school hymn which had been written by Norman Davis based on the school motto, 'To Know and to Give'. The music was composed by Ralph Paddock in May of that year.

To Know and to Give

'Lord with thy presence fill our school, inspire our work
Watch over our play, shape every thought, mould every word
Guide every minute every day
Teach us the joy of knowing Lord, And to thy use
Our Knowledge bend, Guide those who teach us so to lead,
That learning with wisdom blend
Teach us the joy of giving Lord.
Let kindliness from learning spring
That we may grow more like Thy son, Who for our sake gave everything.'

Taken from the 1959 September *'Wasp'* is the following article which was said to be of interest to most boys at South Wigston, It was written by a boy who left South Wigston in 1957.

Impressions of Guthlaxton School

When a group of boys from South Wigston

Secondary Modern School entered Guthlaxton for the first time on 9 September 1957 it was the beginning of the new venture for them. These were the boys who had decided that a GCE Certificate was more important to them than starting work immediately with no qualifications.

As many of you know our school is one of two in the County that has adopted the Leicestershire Experiment. Its success will not really be known until the forthcoming GCE examinations are over, but taking the school as a whole it has so far run excellently, much of the praise goes to the Headmaster and staff for their efforts to put Guthlaxton on the map. In the Fourth and Fifth Years where the experiment comes into operation, the boys and girls have settled down very well after conquering of co-education, which to many of them was a new thing.

When arriving in your fourth year you are placed in a class where the subjects suit you best, which, on the whole is better than judging you by your all round ability. The names of the forms speak for themselves. 4 English, 4 Maths, 4 Crafts, 4 Practical and 4 General. The 4 being the year you are in and the word following it denotes what type of subjects are entailed.

The school itself is one of the most impressive buildings imaginable, as many visitors both from England and overseas have said. The nucleus of the school, is, as it should be, the most impressive, in the form of a large and modern Assembly Hall adapted acoustically so that speeches, of which there are many, can be heard quite distinctly. There is also a balcony at the rear in which further children can be seated.

The foyer, or dining hall, is also modern with contempory wallpaper and glass swing doors, which are visible from the road. The library is a treasured possession of the school for it not only has several valuable pieces of furniture but a rapidly growing collection of books as well.

The two Gymnasia are very well equipped, one has a built in high jump pit in the floor besides elementary equipment such as beams and ropes. The showers are so inviting, with hot and cold water, that few boys ever miss them, as I recall they did at Wigston.

The classrooms themselves consist of six labs an art room, woodwork and metalwork room, two lecture rooms, one of which contains a 27 inch television and various other classrooms that only entail text and exercise books. All of these rooms are fitted with thermostatic heating equipment, green blackboards, which are less tiring for the eyes, and tiled floors.

Next come the school grounds, which could be compared with any parkland for they are not only extensive but have many fine trees scattered about them. There are two soccer pitches, one rugger pitch, two hockey pitches, tennis courts, a cricket pitch, several rounders pitches, and a four forty yards running track. The school has plenty of sports equipment with which to put these facilities to use.

When I tell you that the opening of the school was as splendid as the building itself you will understand what I mean. This was an important occasion for it not only gave us wide publicity but marked an important milestone in the short, but full, history of the school. There were several eminent people on this occasion, most prominent of whom was Sir John Cockroft, OM, KBE. who performed the opening ceremony. In his stimulating speech Sir John said that the country had a great demand for scientists in many different spheres and that it was a school such as ours that could provide such men.

Boys from South Wigston have played no little part in this experiment and their achievements in school activities are quite admirable. First and foremost come their achievements as scholars, an activity in which we fared very well. On entering the school five South Wigston boys were immediately placed in with the grammar school stream and soon worked their way to the top half of the class. These boys, along with several others are now attempting six or more subjects in the GCE this June.

In the school itself four of our boys, Bray, Green, Hill and McNally were made prefects at the commencement of their second year at the school.

In the sporting sphere we upheld our strong tradition and at first the school rugger team consisted entirely of South Wigston boys. Tarry played for the County. Ainsworth gained his county colours and several boys represented the school in the county sports held at Manor Road. Several boys gained a place in the school football team as well although they had not played the game for several years.

All concerned with the school agree that much of

its success has been due to the enthusiasm, progressiveness and understanding of our Headmaster, Mr M J Oliver, MA. who has made it his duty to know every child personally in the school. This policy has induced amongst the pupils a bond of friendship which is needed before any school can progress beyond the stages of establishment.

If any of you are thinking of entering into this scheme I thoroughly recommend it to you but as a last piece of advice may I say that you must come with an industrious outlook, which will, in turn present you with the many things the school can offer.

Michael McNally

On 2 October 1959 Miss Walker and Mr Friis attended the Mount Grace School at Hinckley to hear the Dr. Dienes address on mathematics. At the end of November Mr Biggs and Mr Williams from the Education Research Foundation attended South Wigston to observe the new maths methods in action.

Examinations and Christmas celebrations, visits to Coventry to see 'Great Expectations' ended the school year in the Girls' School.

During the holidays in the Girls' School renovations were being made to the second science room. Pupils returned to new furniture and fittings which had been added.

January 1960 started badly as many of the teachers were absent suffering various illnesses. Supply teachers were brought in to assist.

In February Miss Walker attended a meeting at Hastings High School where 'The Crowther Report' was under discussion. The report focussed on 'Fifteen to Eighteen' year olds recognising that sixth forms were designed to prepare young people for university. It also recognised that state school pupils were being given an education of a more general nature enabling girls to enter nursing and teaching, professions, and boys leaning towards banking, insurance and law. In 1959 examinations for A levels were not required for some professions, training beginning at eighteen years of age.

During the year Mr Howard hailing from Tasmania joined the school for a term on his way back home to Canada taking a very full part in school affairs. He arranged visits and prepared a memorable verse speaking performance for the forthcoming music festival. After leaving the school it appears he was teaching English to the Eskimos.

Sport was always very much a part of school life for the girls as well as the boys. In March 1960 Mrs Scruton with four other teachers took charge of one hundred and seventy girls on their visit to Wembley to watch the International hockey match. In the evening they enjoyed 'Alladin' at the Coliseum.

In every edition of the school magazines reports are religiously recording the scores and achievements of competitors in rugby, cricket, swimming, athletics, hockey, cross country running and basketball. Throughout the years the various houses are vieing for the trophies to fill their cabinets. Clubs spring into action to serve most interests with chess, fishing and aeroplane modelling becoming very popular. Athough sporting trophies are coveted the Work Cup seems genuinely important too.

In August Mr Tweed, the woodwork master left the school after teaching there since the opening in 1938. Pupils were sorry to say goodbye.

During the summer holidays alterations to some classrooms was carried out. The domestic science room was reorganised and a third science room created. An additional needlework room was added and work was carried out on a new small classroom to the new Primary building being constructed. Major electrical work was being completed for the organisation of lighting equipment.

Mrs Christine Kenney recalls the early years at South Wigston Secondary Modern Girls' School 1960 - 1964. When she began in 1960 there were nine new staff members. Mrs Kenney trained as a Top Junior, Lower Secondary Teacher at Homerton College, Cambridge and previously taught at Westcotes School in the city of Leicester. Her impression at that time was that the South Wigston children took much for granted being very materialistic even though they were poor. Mrs Kenney remembers the children being bussed in from Braunstone until the Winstanley School was built.

Each Monday morning Mrs Kenney recalls that the teachers were required to hand in a blue record book of their detailed teaching plans for the week which was signed by Miss Walker. This practice was discontinued by Mr Rutherford when the schools became amalgamated. The children who were leaving school at fifteen years stayed at South Wigston. Others moved on to Guthlaxton earlier.

Recalling 1962 -1963 Mrs Kenny spent a very cold night at the school under canvas. This was arranged under the leadership of Mr David Nutt, in readiness for a camping holiday.

After Miss Walker's retirement Mrs Kenney writes that the school gradually became mixed. With others, Mrs Kenney on occasions taught in the Boys' School. She taught PE and English to the girls and Religious Education to the boys. When the school finally integrated she was one of the first teachers to have a mixed class of pupils.

During Mrs Kenney's thirty years at the school, she also taught children with special needs. She describes this work as very rewarding. Mrs Kenney explains that over the years attitude and provision have changed. Children with learning difficulties were usually placed in the bottom set. At this time Dyslexia was not recognised. Mrs Kenney attended one of the first lectures on the subject at Nottingham University but it was still many years before it was accepted. Today children are tested and have individual programmes and support according to their difficulties. She writes that in the 1980s children with extreme difficulties were withdrawn in small groups of six for maths and English but 'twilight' children did not have this support. Children with very severe learning difficulties were sent to a special school many of which have been closed and the children are now with support in the main stream school. There are still at least two schools for children with behavioural problems. In Mrs Kenney's thirty years at South Wigston she cannot recall many children with physical disabilities. One boy had a hearing problem. He brought a microphone to the lessons which the teacher had on her desk. One girl with crutches attended and at that time there were no lifts or ramps in the school.

Mrs Kenney taught children in groups of six mainly English and maths. On one occasion at a Parents' Evening a parent came to her to say, 'he now reads the paper'. Mrs Kenney revealed then that 'you know that you are on the right track'.

Teaching until 1993 Mrs Kenney also served under four Head Teachers. Miss Walker, Mr Rutherford, Mr Norris and Mr Bothamley.

The start of the September 1960 academic year saw the new appointment of Mr David Nutt. Mr Nutt had trained as a chemist and worked for six years at an Atomic Energy Plant north of Preston in Lancashire.

As a chemistry teacher Mr Nutt taught fourth year pupils in readiness for their College of Preceptors Examinations. This appointment in turn gave Mr Ron Baker the opportunity to teach physics whilst Stella Andrews taught biology. There was no chemistry syllabus at this time and as a result of this the three teachers pioneered a trial school for the Nuffield Sciences. The trial spanned two to three years before the County adopted it.

Mrs Baker recalls that Mr Baker with the others produced a Teachers' Handbook to introduce Nuffield Science Courses to the High Schools. He also organised trips to Weiskirchen in the Saarland region of Germany with Mr Brannan, Mrs Larkin, Mrs Thompson and Miss Williamson.

Mr Nutt was seconded in 1967 for duties as the School and Community Counsellor. Mr Andrew Fairbairn, deputy to Mr Stewart Mason, Director of Education, was progressing a new innovative plan to establish counsellors in all Leicestershire Upper Schools and High Schools. Schools were allowed extra time for this venture and Mr Nutt was the first person to be involved at South Wigston. Spending a year at Reading University, Mr Nutt was sent on the new course jointly run by English and American advisers. On his return to South Wigston, the Headmaster, Mr Mark Rutherford was very supportive of the project.

Mr Nutt's role as School Counsellor led him into various kinds of problems in the community. Meeting parents in order to help the children and families took many hours in and out of school hours at weekends in South Wigston, Blaby and Eyres Monsell. Health issues were invariably part of the problems and Mr Nutt worked in conjunction with Doctor Kind situated on site at the School Clinic. Medical and welfare problems were shared also with Social Services and psychiatrists in order to gain professional help.

Mr Nutt recalls time at South Wigston School when together with Mr John Orton, Head of Design, set up the outdoor activities. He recalls Miss Walker the Headmistress sitting in the playground selling tuck to the pupils to raise money for new equipment. Miss Walker allowed Mr Nutt to take over this duty

Mr David Nutt with his class teaching how cosmetics are made

which he organised by allowing the children to sell from inside the chemistry laboratory. They sold the tuck through two of the windows to the children outside. This venture was a properly organised affair with orders being brought in from the Cadbury and KP suppliers.

Recalling Miss Constance Wright as a force to be reckoned with, Mr Nutt gives an account of an occasion close to his first Christmas at the school. Himself with other male staff, John Orton, Stuart Friis, Aubrey Burl, Horst Briel and Ron Baker; were talking inside the toilets with celebratory drinks when Miss Wright banged furiously upon the door, named each one of them in turn shouting, 'I know you are in there' and demanded that they come out immediately and produce their registers for her inspection.

Streaming was part of the school system in that a series of options were available to the pupils. French was the main denominator with Mrs Holm on the girls side and Mr Ron Griffiths on the boys. These two were eventually amalgamated. Choices were chemistry, the sciences or history and geography.

In 1961 Mr Andrew Napier Fairbairn became

deputy to Mr Stewart Mason, Director of Education. Mr Fairbairn was born in Watford in Hertfordshire. He became a chorister at Winchester Cathedral and attended the Pilgrim School. He went on to Ardingly College in West Sussex and won a choral scholarship to Trinity College, Cambridge. Mr Fairbairn had a life long appreciation of music, particularly singing.

Mr Fairbairn served in the Second World War and his distinguished war record earned him the Military Cross when in Normandy, outnumbered by the enemy; he led a platoon and captured a vital bridge also taking many prisoners. Eventually he did become a prisoner of war himself.

Mr Stewart Friis became part of the Professor Dienes work on Logics in Mathematics using wooden blocks as a visual representative of a counting system. The blocks in multiples of ten were aids in teaching the decimalisation of the currency.

In December 1961 Mr Stewart Mason, Director of Education visited the school informing that Mr Friis was to be given a part time County appointment. He was seconded in the following January 1962 to take up County Maths research work eventually becoming one of the first Maths Advisers in the

Mr David Nutt with South Wigston Girls' School camping group

country. He also became a founder member of the National Association of Maths Advisers and wrote several books on modern algebra.

Dr Dienes Mathematics was to be retained on the curriculum.

Mr Nutt accompanied pupils to the Cairngorms for camping holidays and every year they raised money to buy their kit. Girls carried heavy rucksacks and pitched the tents. Mr Nutt also visited Derbyshire and other venues with camping groups.

Mr Nutt was responsible for setting up the very unique South Wigston Youth Club which was applauded by Bernard Harvey, Further Education Officer for the Wigston Area. Members met in the evenings from four O'clock until ten O'clock and a local band practiced on stage. Disco dancing was popular and Christopher Lingard, Christine Curry the Laboratory Assistant and Janet Freestone nee Davies helped enormously. Eventually Mr Christopher Lingard took over responsibility for the club.

Cyril Statham, Assistant Caretaker, Mrs White, Assistant School Secretary, Hilda Davies, Cook, Mrs Jeffreys, Assistant Cook, were all very well remembered members of the school too by Mr Nutt.

The number of outside activities reported in *'The Wasp'* was formidable and the scope ambitious. The Headmaster Mr Rutherford and Mr Thomas took a party of boys to Switzerland. A party of eighteen boys toured the continent in dormobiles driven by Mr N Cooper and Mr Davis. Six countries were covered in seventeen days. Forty boys visited the Lake District with Mr N Cooper, Mr Rainbow, Mr Thomas and Mr Wilmer for a climbing expedition. A party of thirty boys later went to Ross on Wye for

camping and canoeing. Several members of staff were present on this trip. The staff and the Outdoor Activities Committee expressed their gratitude to the many fund raisers which made it possible to purchase the school dormobile. It is notable too that canoes were being constructed in the Canoe Club. Memories of canoe practice at the open air Kenwood Swimming Baths are recalled by Mr Thomas as a rare treat. Most of the older boys spent long days swimming in the pool at Knighton. They were taken in a fleet of double decker buses. On the last occasion they took some canoes for extra fun and practiced 'eskimo rolls' clambering back into a capsized canoe.

Mr Thomas writes of the Young Farmers' Club which was in existence on his arrival in post. He recalls that it somehow came to him to run it for a while. He thinks that someone discovered that he was a farmer's son. Some boys from the village schools lived on farms lending some authenticity to the title but there were several lads from South Wigston and Glen Parva as well.

There were some successes in Public Speaking Competitions with other schools and they also ran some other activities from the art room. They did some work on the allotment or garden on a section of the school field near the bike sheds. The garden was maintained largely by boys from what was then known as the Remedial classes. These children needed extra help with their academic work led by Mr Jones and Mr Reed. A live hedge divided the garden from the field and vegetables and flowers were grown.

One Saturday morning a pet show and competition was staged in the school playground. Mr Thomas recalls a lad arriving with a Rhode Island red hen at the end of a length of binder twine. He can also remember someone's rabbit escaping having to be rescued before it fell prey to one of the pet dogs on show and under various degrees of control.

Was Adrian here?

In those days the cane was still used as a form of punishment along with the less severe detention. Mr Thomas admits that this was a problem for pupils living in outlying villages. Mr Wild, the Deputy Head was the one who administered the cane rather than Mr Rutherford, the Headmaster. Some may remember the slipper being used as a more immediate response to a misdemeanour. With the amalgamation of the two schools in 1964 such corporal punishment was looked upon as unacceptable in mixed classes. Mr Thomas believes this was even before it was officially banned. With amalgamation the style of things changed somewhat. The old fashioned slipper and cane went out. More use was made of debit and credit marks like the already established 'blacks' and 'ambers' in the boys' school based on the school colours. Even on Mr Thomas's arrival at the school he remembers a well established house system which made for some fiercely contested matches especially at rugby and of course at the annual sports day. House points were also given for academic work. At the amalgamation of the schools the names were changed to local parks and estates, Bradgate, Belvoir and Wistow. Recalling the 1970s Mr Thomas writes that a more comprehensive pastoral system was introduced and so many activities and assemblies were based on year groups that the house system lost much of its status. Year Heads for example were given extra pay but there was nothing for a Head of House. Therefore the House System seemed superfluous and Mr Thomas thought it a waste of time and resources to run both. Competitive sport and other activities were then organised between classes in each year group.

Mr Thomas recalls that Mr Pell built up canoeing as a popular activity even making the canoes. They were made on moulds with fibre glass and resin and the nursery block art rooms became the construction centre when the schools amalgamated in the sixties. Canoeing practice took place on the canal at the end of the school playing fields. A gate was built into the fence to make access easier. Mr Thomas recalls the time when two of them from the boys staff went canoeing at lunch time with two members of the girls staff. This was in the early days when the canoes were two- seater canvas ones. This was also an early instance of the younger generation of staff breaking the unspoken 'no fraternisation rule'.

Although pupils left South Wigston School for Guthlaxton it is significant to note that contact was still maintained as many of these students successes in the General Certificate of Education was reported in the school magazine. Some sense of loss appears to have been felt as the children moved on to the Upper School at a crucial stage in their development. Echo's of sadness resound through the pages. Seeing a pupil blossom is rewarding for the teacher but at the same time the further development is missed.

A major music event took place in Saint Thomas Church when the Annual School Carol Service was held. It was described as a very impressive ceremony with an even larger orchestra than usual. At the evening performance the Wigston Choral Society joined with the boys in their carols also contributing The Hallelujah Chorus and John Elliott sang solo in a new carol composed by the school music master, Mr Paddock.

At the area Music Festival the choir was judged equal second whilst the brass ensemble came first qualifying them to compete in the County finals.

The following term the school entered the Loughborough Music Festival securing a second place with the band and a first with the ensemble. The Frankland Shield was retained for the second year.

The orchestra became a pit orchestra playing nautical selections during the school play, Treasure Island. John Elliott was recorded as having a good year. He was placed first in festivals in Leicester, Loughborough, Kettering and Northampton. He was at the time currently rehearsing for the County School of Music production of Menotti's opera, 'Amahl and the Night Visitors' and did secure the lead role.

The school notes of Autumn 1961 - 62 look back with sadness in the Boys' School as two deaths of their members of staff are reported. In January Mr Tom Jones died suddenly. A person who could not be ignored many powerful memories are felt by many. Remembered is his delightful tenor voice in Assembly, his passionate argument in the Staff Room and his disarming laugh. It is very clear that Mr Jones was going to be missed so much.

A few weeks after the start of term Miss S R Kinaston, teaching science to the boys in her first post, died after a road accident. Miss Kinaston had impressed the boys with her likeable and lively personality. Five other male teachers left the Boys' school for pastures new including Mr Every who apart from his war service, had been in post since the opening.

Many more outside visits are listed for the year with the inclusion of holidays in Guernsey, the Science Museum in London and visits to theatres to see Shakespearean plays were also enjoyed. It is remarkable to note how many clubs existed for the boys too. These included chess, train spotting, photography, geography and woodwork.

At this time fourth year boys were also preparing for the Duke of Edinburgh Awards which involved map reading, climbing and First Aid. The projected holidays for the future year included sailing on the Norfolk Broads, walking in Scotland and more canoeing camps.

March 1961 saw Miss Walker attending a science conference and in the summer with Mr Burl, Miss Corrigan and twenty seven girls she headed a visit to Innsbruck and Salsburg. Taking in the Stubai Valley, a folklore evening at Innsbruck, a visit to the salt mines and a marionette theatre; all kept the children entertained.

By October there was some unrest with some teachers in both the Boys' and the Girls' Schools regarding salaries.

A Careers Convention was held on one evening in November when representatives from the Army, Navy and the Royal Air Force were in attendance together with other industrial and agricultural managers. One hundred and sixty parents from South Wigston Boys' and Girls' Schools, Abington and Bushloe High Schools came to listen to the many speakers.

The speakers came from Brooksby Hall to promote horticulture and agriculture. Major P J Jackson, Army and WRAC, Mr J P Watkins, Recruiting Officer Royal Navy, Marines and WRENS. Squadron Leader D M K Atterley, RAF and WRAF, Mr P Browett, automobile and agricultural engineering, Mr A E Hall, building trades and apprenticeships, Mr A Clark, boot and shoe, Dr, Foden. clerical work, Loughborough College, Mr R Gill, Managing Director, Midland Dynamo, Mr John Smith, Wathes. Radio and television, Mr P Baines, Further Education Leicestershire County Council, Miss E Brayshaw, Leicester Branch of the Hairdressers Federation, Mr D Woods, Managing

Director of Two Steeples, Mr Copson, Jones and Shipman. Miss A Sheen, Matron of Markfield Hospital, Mr A Cave. Leicester Master Printers, shop work represented by the Chamber of Trade.

The Convention was run in three sections in order that parents could visit three speakers. Guests were entertained in the staff room and light refreshments served to parents in the dining hall. The list and choice of employment was quite vast.

In December 1961 a meeting in the library with representatives of the Transport Department and County Education Committee to discuss transport problems of Blaby and Glen Hills pupils took place.

At a Governors meeting on 7 February 1962 notification of Miss C M Wright's resignation was received to take effect at the end of the summer term.

A memorandum was received on the forthcoming plans for the 'Mason Plan' to take effect. Mr Stewart Mason, Director of Education visited the staff of both the Boys' and the Girls' Schools to inform them of the proposed amalgamation of the Boys' and Girls' schools into one single co-educational school which would take place in 1963 or 1964, on Miss Walker's retirement.

Miss Walker attended the annual picture sale in early March held at the Winstanley School in Braunstone. With her allocated art allowance she was able to purchase a picture entitled, 'The Nuns at Chartres' and 'Monica', a sculptured head by Willi Soukop. Willi Soukop regularly exhibited at the Royal Academy. Other meetings listed in March for Miss Walker include, 'Head Teachers at Brooksby Hall Farm and Institute', 'Teachers for retarded pupils at Gartree High School', an 'Accident Sub Committee' at The County Rooms and regular 'Q.E.S.S'. meetings.

In March an address was given by Major Randall, Queen Alexandra Royal Army Nursing Corps to third and fourth year pupils. In the same month Mr Curtis Weston, the Reverend Neil Robinson and Mrs Stapleton, School Governors, attended a special service in the Girls' School. They were invited to present the certificates to successful pupils attaining their College of Preceptors and Pitman's Shorthand and Typing Examination passes.

In May at Hamilton School Miss Walker and Miss White attended a conference on sex education and at the end of May Miss Runswick gave her third address to fourth year leavers on the subject and boy friends. At the School Clinic pupils received tuberculosis vaccinations.

In June, Mr Baker, Mr Nutt, Mr Orton and Mrs Andrews took thirty girls camping to Hathersage near Sheffield whilst Mr Burl, Miss Corrigan and Miss Harris took fifteen girls to the South of France.

Mr Horst Briel was appointed Junior Education Lecturer at the National Housecraft College, Leeds in July which meant that he would leave South Wigston at the end of the Christmas term.

18 July 1962 was a memorable occasion for Miss Constance Wright when a presentation was made to mark her retirement. Miss Walker and all members of staff, Mr Broadhead, Miss Broughton and Miss Sack, from the County Education Department, most of the Governors, Mr Rutherford and a large number of past pupils attended. Refreshments were served by the kitchen staff and made in the domestic science room. Miss Walker paid tribute to Miss Wright's devoted service for fifty years as a county teacher, thirty years as First Assistant or Deputy Head and presented her with a gold watch and bracelet. Mr R C Weston, during his speech commented to the amusement of the audience, 'that Miss Wright had been a lady who had been 'right' all her life'. Mr Weston along with Mrs Pedley, Chairman and Vice Chairman of the Governors after paying tribute to Miss Wright presented her with a transister radio and Ann Bee, a past Head Girl. presented on behalf of the Past Pupils Association, a pig skin handbag. A week later at a musical evening by the girls, a travelling clock and bouquets were given.

Miss Wright had given fifty years service to the children for a National Savings Fund for which she had enjoyed a visit to a Buckingham Palace Garden Party. Savings of very small amounts were taken and on Miss Wright's retirement, Mr David Nutt took over the reins.

A party of twelve girls attended the Rutland Youth Camping Site at Yarwell. They enjoyed canoeing and swimming.

A Rambling Club was formed in the summer of 1962 by a number of girls. Many enjoyable weekends were spent at this activity accompanied by Mr Nutt, Mr Orton, Mrs Andrews and Christine Kenney nee Jeays.

Mr Nutt carried out an interesting and comprehensive survey of the general life interests of the pupils.

The new term, September 1962 saw Miss Norah White's appointment as Deputy Head take effect.

One late night in early November Miss Walker, Mr Rutherford, members of the Governing body, the Welfare Committee and the local constabulary met outside the school to consider the road traffic dangers to the children on Blaby Lane. Continuing their discussion in the Head's room culminated in a further meeting a few days later to consider the moving of the bus stop and the possibility of a lay-by opposite to the Constone Works.

The Christmas break was celebrated one afternoon with community singing and impromptu sketches by the staff and pupils.

Once again January started with illness in 1963. Due to this and one of the staff having a serious operation, Miss Walker took the maths classes.

In the middle of the month a very happy reunion of the Past Pupils Association occurred when many past and present members of staff attended also.

Miss Walker's visit to the Grand Jury Room in Leicester for a meeting on accident and prevention was followed two days later by the transport problems outside the school coming a little closer to a solution. Mr Swann, County Education Department, Mr Curtis Weston, representatives from Blaby Parish Council and Blaby and Glen Hills parents, Midland Red Transport Department, Miss Walker, Mr Rutherford and Mr Harris all came together. Eventually the lay-by was created outside the school.

April saw Mr Burl and a party of girls at the ancient church of St. Mary de Castro in Leicester as part of their history lesson. Church architecture was introduced for study also.

Staff saw a film on the Duke of Edinburgh Awards Scheme and later that month Miss Faggo attended the school for two days to instruct the staff on the scheme.

Films were also shown on the Design for Living Scheme and Form 1V was taken by Mrs Winder for a tour of The Post Office and the Telephone Exchange.

Lunch time dances were arranged by the girls in order to raise funds for the Freedom From Hunger Campaign. Various events and concerts were organised too.

At a presentation in the library in July on the occasion of Mrs Holm's retirement; a member of the staff since the opening of the school and a teacher in the Central and South Wigston School for over thirty years, was presented with a slide projector and case by the staff, Past Pupils presented a watch, and pupils gave a bracelet and coffee percolator. The Governors presented a book token. It was stated that the school had lost a valuable and devoted teacher.

The new term in September 1963 was of historic importance. The first year students were amalgamated for the first time. New entrants which consisted of fifty seven girls and sixty boys were allocated into mixed classes and the old adage, 'never the twain shall meet' ended.

At the end of the month Doctor Skemp visited the school. He conducted a maths lesson with the first year pupils.

Mr Christopher Lingard's memories of South Wigston School span eleven years, 1963-1974. Born and educated in Bedford he transferred to the City of Leicester Training College. Applying to the County Education Authority at that time for a teaching post he was appointed as a Science Master at South Wigston High School.

Mr Lingard first taught science to the mainstream pupils later transferring to teach the less able children in the remedial section. He remembers that there was no national syllabus then. The curriculum was organised by the schools and students would be working towards achieving success in the various Examining Boards.

Over the years the phraseology for the remedial section has changed. Some children need more help than others for a variety of reasons and in many cases some problems are not well understood. Mr Lingard's experience of a child with autism was one such case but the pupil gained much help from Mr Lingard. When the need arose to seek outside advice on an occasion, he was told after a visit to the school, 'not to worry. as you have it taped here'.

Mr Lingard concentrated on the basic training of the 'Three R's' and remembers a child with a serious hearing problem. Sitting in the front of the class it was still very difficult for the child to hear but he was able to lip read a little. Mr Lingard said that the other children would help by tapping him on the shoulder and pointing him to face the teacher again.

A system of banding, streaming and setting was used in the mid 1960s to teach children of mixed abilities. Putting pupils into broad ability bands represented a balance of ability level. Splitting pupils into hierarchical groups was defined as streaming. These children would stay in the same group for all of their lessons but setting meant that putting children of similar ability together for certain lessons; resulted in individuals placed in the top set for one subject and a lower set for another subject.

A number of Chinese children in the Wigston area were allocated to Mr Lingard, Mr Pell and Mr Read in order to help them learn English. One of the ways in which this was achieved was by taking the children out sometimes by car. By pointing out various objects the children began to understand. Mr Lingard admits that the other children in school were the main educators. Very soon the Chinese children picked up the language that way.

As a result of the success with the Chinese children, South Wigston School remarkably acquired a worthy reputation and Mr Lingard recalls that children began to arrive for language help from Abington and Bushoe Schools.

Recalling the organised summer trips for the children to Guernsey with Mr Tom Pell, Mr Lingard participated in at least nine of them out of the eleven years he was at the school. One occasion is recounted vividly as they were awakened in the early hours from their tents by a violent thunder storm. In the middle of the field the insulators on the overhead electric power lines were hissing and crackling angrily. Help was quickly sought by Mr Lingard and Mr Pell and a repair team arrived.

In September two students, Miss Smith and Miss Farrell commenced duty to observe and teach backward readers for a time. They also gave help with English lessons.

Miss White and Miss Vann attended a conference at Loughborough on 'Programmed Learning'.

At the beginning of October at a Governors meeting the resignations of Miss Walker and Mrs Winder were received. They were to take effect on 31 December 1963. Miss Walker expressed her thanks to an able and loyal staff. The dawn of the Co-educational system at South Wigston under the Headship of Mr Mark Rutherford was in sight.

On 11 November, Remembrance Day, Mr Halifax, Her Majesty's Inspector, visited the school to observe Mr Punshon teach Form 1A maths and Mrs Winder with Form 4C. He spent the afternoon in the Boys' School

At the end of the autumn term goodbyes' were said to Miss Walker. After twenty years service her retirement marked the end of an era in the history of the school. No more would the girls and boys be separated. It was hard for pupils and staff to believe that Miss Walker was leaving as one put into words the thoughts of so many that 'Miss Walker is South Wigston'. The ideals and standards she set for so many was recalled and the happy times spent together. On the evening of 12 December, School Governors, Members of the County Education Committee, Heads of contributory schools, past and present members of the teaching staff and domestic staff and past pupils gathered in the school hall to pay their tributes. The gift of candelabra was presented from the Governors, a fire screen from past pupils, glass tumblers from the domestic staff and a clock from past and present members of the teaching staff. The present pupils made their presentation of a tray, a toast rack and a cruet on the last morning of the term.

1964 was a turning point in the history of South Wigston School but also changes were taking place in the structure of education. The Department of Education and Science was created in 1964 merging the offices of the Minister of Education and Minister of Science. These titles were to change again later.

It was felt that the new High School needed a new magazine so the *Viking*' was born and Mr Thomas designed the cover. To mark the first issue the Headmaster, Mr Rutherford submitted an article which follows.

'1st January 1964 is an important date in the history of South Wigston High School for it was then that the former Boys' and Girls' were amalgamated into one co-educational school. The County Education Committee took the decision to make the schools one legally but quite obviously much more is required (and will shortly be done, I hope) in adaptations or additions to the buildings before the feeling of being two separate schools disappears. But buildings alone do not make a school; a good school has its own special spirit and I therefore welcome this first number of a new School magazine as a publication that expresses excellently the new spirit there is among us. It is a truly united effort - the first effort since January that did not have its origin in either the former girls' or boys' school. Long may it flourish!'

M Rutherford.

Next to 'marry' were the 'Houses'. At an inaugural meeting in February, the former 'Grey' and 'Wycliffe' houses joined forces to become 'Bradgate' house. 'Bosworth' was formed by coupling 'Fry' and 'Burnaby', 'Nightingale' and 'Beaumont' became 'Belvoir' and 'Bronte' with 'Montfort' became 'Wistow'. At last, after twenty six years, 'the twain SHALL meet'.

When the two schools were amalgamated Mr Thomas recalls that the boys and girls numbered a thousand pupils. Mr Thomas moved with his colleague Mr Glenton to the art rooms in the East (girls school) wing. They taught mixed classes from the start except the boys and girls crafts were taught separately until 1970 when they became a Design Department. Mr Thomas became the Head of Department. Prior to that in 1966 Mr Thomas had become Head of the Art Department.

One obvious result of the two schools joining forces was the addition of a new school hall and music block with the updating of boys and girls changing rooms. This also provided the school with an enclosed quadrangle. Much later on Mr Thomas assisted Mr Bothamley in planning the landscaping of the area. Prior to this there had been a very modern metal sculpture reminiscent of a whirlwind there which disappeared suddenly one summer holiday.

The Whitsuntide holiday which fell in mid May was very memorable for a group of pupils and in particular Julie Staples as they travelled to the Cairngorms in Scotland with Mr Nutt, Mr Burl and Miss Lex. For the first week on arrival at Glenmore they lived in four caravans and a number of tents. There were about ten girls to each caravan sharing the domestic duties of cooking and cleaning. The main party split into two groups, A and B and on the Monday morning group A set off for the Lairig Ghru, interpreted as 'The Gloomy Pass'. Hiking by road through Rothemurchus Forest they left the road and followed the mountain down to the Gloomy Pass which lived up to its name in the wind and rain. The party sheltered in the Sinclair Hut built in memory of a man who died there. Miss Lex cooked a meal before they headed back to the road spending the night in Army ski huts. Sitting around a huge log fire Mr Burl told ghost stories!

The next morning Group B set off to make camp by a huge patch of snow in Coire Ant, Sneachda. The next morning the mountains were shrouded in mist so after the teachers had taken breakfast in bed to the girls they had to break camp.

Group A visited a neolithic burial ground, Clava Stone Circle. From there they walked to Culloden Moor, the famous battle ground of the Jacobite rebellion before visiting Inverness.

At the end of the first week the party with all of their equipment moved into the Norwegian Huts opposite the camp site. The views of the snow capped mountains, the blue lochs and the pine trees could be seen from the bedroom windows. The party swam in the loch, danced to their own records and visited Mr Lindsay's gift shop.

The successful hockey team of 1966. Back Row. L to R. Susan Wilson, Wendy Kinnear, Tina Dalby, Moira Massey, Wendy Wood, Jennifer Davis. Front Row. L to R. Susan Pritchard, Jill Ecob, Vivienne Crutchley, Susan Walker (Captain), Christine Smith

Mr David Nutt with four of the girls outside the Norwegian Huts in the Cairngorms

The following day the senior party made camp at the Coire-an-Lachan where they pitched tents for the night and sang specially composed songs round the camp fire. In the morning they set out to conquer the second highest mountain, Ben Macdhui where they saw three reindeer herd and ptarmigan. They met the junior party the next day at camp. The holiday ended

with a party where the shop owner, Mr Lindsay did a Highland Fling. The following day they left for home taking memories of a wonderful holiday with them.

In 1965 The Certificate of Secondary Education (CSE) was introduced for Secondary Modern pupils. This was to cater for those students not sitting GCE O Level

In April 1966 competing against twenty eight schools in the City and County, South Wigston High School were the proud winners of the schools under thirteen hockey tournament. The team captained by Susan Walker, who played left back, met Guthlaxton School in the final. It was a close game with South Wigston winning on two penalty corners, no goals were scored. Although South Wigston Girls had come close to winning in the past, it was the first time they had taken the honours in recent years.

The death of Miss Walker on 18 July 1966 came as very sad news. Only three years since her retirement and the years which should have been enjoyable relaxing years were denied. Miss Walker had remembered the school to the end as she had left instructions in her will bequeathing a legacy of £100. The money was intended for the purchase of a picture, sculpture, decorative window or a piece of furniture preferably for the new chapel or hall: or some equally desirable purpose that the Governors shall see fit.

Taken from the *'Golden Jubilee'*, *'The First Fifty Years'* a record for 1966 informs,

The Truth About Teachers

"The majority of you who read this article, will have only seen your teachers in the classroom, unless you were asleep, in which case you will not have seen them. Well, we have seen them in that forbidden place, The Staff Room. For every day we prepare their tea for them. It appears that tea is the vital fuel needed to drive teachers; if their supply runs short they become even more crotchety than usual and to quote one of them, 'like dehydrated peas'. The male staff, however grown up they appear in classroom, are all young at heart. Listen Boys! Remember those water pistols that disappeared into teachers' pockets and desks, They didn't take them to save the other unfortunate pupils from a drenching, but to play with them during their dinner break. We have all been threatened by a large gentleman teacher, with a red water pistol in one hand and a green one in the other. Another thing, did you think that those teachers sat there all dinner hour dutifully marking that work which we all struggled to finish the night before? Not much they don't, instead they sit about either gossiping, sleeping or playing cards. Mentioning cards, we would like to say we have never heard such a row as the card players make. We are unanimously agreed that however the staff appear on the surface, they are really quite human underneath and we should know, shouldn't we?

The Long Suffering Tea Girls.

Was Adrian Here?

By 1967 the first year juniors were decimalising the currency. This activity would well equip the pupils for Decimalisation Day which was on 15 February 1971.

In May, Mr Paddock set the poem, Casey Jones to music for the orchestra, speech, choir and percussion. He entered the work into the Composers Competition at the Leicestershire Music Festival. Sir Michael Tippett, composer, was the adjudicator and awarded it second prize.

January 1968 started well for the pupils with a number of visits to enjoy. The first one escorted by Mrs Kendall and Mr Davis was to the Phoenix Theatre to see 'The Three Musketeers'. 'Treasure Island followed at the Belgrade Theatre with Mrs Kendall. Mr Pell and Mr Alster took a party to view the Wigston Fire Station whilst Mrs Garrett and Mr Smith escorted pupils to the Royal Albert Hall in London for a gymnastics display.

February saw children with Miss Davis and Mr Rose on a visit to the de Montfort Hall to hear the Birmingham Symphony Orchestra and many more outings of interest continued to be enjoyed until the summer when it was arranged that a party of eleven boys and eight girls would go youth hostelling in Scotland. They would be taken by Mr Nutt, Mr Kelly, Mr Lingard and Miss Pole to see Loch Lomond. During the trip they would visit the Clyde, Inverness, Edinburgh and the Cairngorm area. Whilst there they would view a hydro electric power station.

In browsing through the *'Viking'* it seems fitting to include two very moving items from the children of 1968. In all of the girls and boys magazines over the years there have been so many that inspire but here are just two.

The Horse That Was Never Mine

There he was, standing on a small hill like a majestic King with his head held up high. His black coat gleamed and shone like a newly polished shoe as the sun glared down on his smooth shining back. The picture was like a silhouette with his black form against the grey sky. That was the horse that was never mine. The stallion turned and looked over his domain, then he suddenly galloped down the slope as graceful as a ballerina but as strong as a lion. That was the horse that was never mine.

His eyes were glaring like wild fiery furnaces as he turned and saw me. He trotted up to me and calmed down like a gentle lamb. He pushed his muzzle into my hand and I felt the warm air blowing from his nostrils. We stayed in this position for a while until I realised this paradise had to end. I stroked this creature of the fields and felt tears run down my cheeks as I watched him standing there, the horse that was never mine.

Elizabeth Brewer.

Hamble River

The river flowing gently
Glides smoothly on its way
To join the busy Solent
Where ocean liners lay

In the warmth of summer
I can play in my canoe
And if I paddle softly
I can watch the moor hens too

The lip lip of the water
As it touches the shore
Says to me softly
Have you been here before?'

On the Hamble River
Once upon a time
Were built the great oak ships
That sailed in Nelson's line
                              Philip Hunt

In April 1968 Mr Burl and Mrs Kendall accompanied a group of first years and fourth years on a day visit to the prehistoric site of Avebury in Wiltshire.

In May 1968 to June of that year the student riots in Paris sparked similar reaction in England with sit-ins at colleges. It began in France between students and university administrators and the police who inflamed the situation further leading to street battles. There followed a general strike by students and strikes throughout France by ten million workers having an enormous social impact on the country. High school student unions spoke in support of the riots and rallied at the Arc de Triomphe in great numbers.

Mr Thomas recalls that some of the local South Wigston High School pupils felt the need to join in. One break time on a fine summers day some of the older pupils decided that they would not come back into school and staged a sit down strike. There was consternation amongst the staff when the children would not respond even to the orders from the Head and Deputy. However, form tutors went out and persuaded initially their more amenable pupils that they had had their fun and needed now to return to work. Gradually their resolve weakened and the protest melted away leaving the prime movers 'high

and dry'. They were given some punishment but as it was their last term they were not too upset. There was a more troublesome disturbance at Guthlaxton at about the same time. Mr Thomas recalls 'the bush telegraph working before the days of the mobile phone'.

Trouble hit the headlines in May as the *Leicester Mercury* reported *'DISCIPLINE DEMAND BY WIGSTON PARENTS'. It stated that,'an emergency meeting of governors of South Wigston High School is to be held to discuss the row which has flared up between the Headmaster, Mr Mark Rutherford, and a large number of parents of children at the school. A member of the board, the Rev. N Robinson told the Leicester Mercury today that the meeting was to have been held this afternoon but it had been found necessary to cancel it because a sufficient number could not attend. It would now be held at a date in the future when the majority of governors could be present. Relations between the Head and some of the parents began to deteriorate round about Christmas when children came home with stories of alleged incidents at the school. According to one parent girls' blazers, skirts and blouses had been ripped and girls had been seen running along corridors in their underslips. As a result of the childrens tales a petition was signed by over one hundred adults demanding more discipline. Wishing to remain anonymous for fear of victimisation the parents did not go ahead with the meeting but sought assistance from the Blaby Ratepayers Association. The Chairman of the Governors, Mr Curtis Weston was unobtainable by telephone. Mr Rutherford said that he was unable to comment until he had heard from the parents'.*

Recently reported in the *Leicestershire Chronicle* it stated that. *'The scenes could have been peeled straight out of the chaotic corridors of Saint Trinian's. All that was missing was a mutiny from the ramparts and a vexed Alistair Sim clutching his hands. In the summer of 68 South Wigston High School was a lawless, feral seat of education, and the pupils' parents enflamed by increasingly torrid tales of woe. Forty years since Lorraine Forman nee Norman was at the school but as far as she was concerned there were no tears in her uniform. Less still can she remember young girls gamboling down corridors in their underwear. She doesn't remember discipline being lax at all. The Headmaster Mr*

South Wigston Staff 1960s

Rutherford was a gent and his deputy Mr Wild was a much stricter taskmaster. Lorraine recalls a narrow escape after playing a game of cards but being of quick wits she made her safe exit via an open window. Lorraine was fourteen and ready to leave for Guthlaxton. She was not allowed to wear trousers even though they were freezing in the winter. Some of the girls took up their hemlines to shorten their skirts and the teachers were always referred to by their surnames unlike her brother's school at Countesthorpe College.'

Mr Thomas commenting on the situation today recalls the headlines as a storm in a teacup. He believes that a few high spirited school leavers decided to celebrate their departure with some sort of high jinx.

It would appear that the much talked about 'free expression' of the nineteen sixties was very soon 'knocked on the head' at South Wigston High School.

Forty years ago in the summer of 1968 John Rawlinson wrote in the *'Viking'* a short article entitled, *'Looking Back'.* It is interesting historically but also to note the enormous pressure of decision making at that age regarding whether or not to transfer to Guthlaxton. It was often very hard for some children not to follow in the footsteps of their friends. The article follows.

Looking Back

My four years at this school have been very happy ones. The most enjoyable years were my second and third years, and the most successful career-wise is my present fourth year.

When I first came to this school I didn't like it at all. It was a very tough school, especially the fourth years. The teachers were tough, they had to be. I didn't get a very good start in my first year because I was ill and I had to have the first six weeks off from school and from that bad start I never really caught up with the time I had off.

In my second year I had a very good time. I hardly missed a day at school and I had a very good form teacher named Mr Gardiner. He was a great fellow! I think the second was our hardest work wise; nearly every night we would have at least two homeworks and on Friday nights we would have about five subjects. In my four years here, I can honestly say I have never forgotten to do my homework although my brother used to do my French.

My third year was a very pleasant year. We worked very hard all the year round and this was the year I gained recognition for my soccer. I was selected to play for the area team. This was the year also I had to make up my mind whether I was going to transfer to Guthlaxton or stay here. It was a big step to take. Should I go with nearly all of my best friends or stay here and try to make something of a career in soccer. Luckily for me, I made the right decision. I was again picked for Mid-Leicestershire and what a great time we had! We made it to the Sixth round of the English Schools Trophy. I travelled to Bedford and Swansea twice and we beat Swansea Boys at Vetch Field. We went to Southampton and lost that time 3-1 at the Dell but it was still a great thrill and experience to play. I also made friends - plenty of friends I shall never forget. I was then picked to play for the County and I won a cap for playing for them. Also I have had a very successful year with Wigston Fields, where we were runners up in the league and I was in two cup finals.

I must say how much the PE staff at this school has helped me, especially Mr Smith, Mr Lingard and Mr Stabler. I'd like to thank these people very very much.

Where are you now, John Rawlinson?

L Parry another pupil reflects on his departure from South Wigston to Guthlaxton in:

Meditations by the Canal

'As you sit by the waters edge in the calmness of midday your memory seems to surge back in time. You suddenly become unaware of the surrounding noises as you gaze into the water. and then as you gaze, you are reminded of the things you will miss when you leave this school to go on to Guthlaxton. You imagine that your friendships at this school will be lost when you leave, those friendships which you have had for three years will be split up'.

L Parry

Looking back over this chapter one may have glimpsed the spirit of 'Adrian Mole'? He has surely captured the soul of every boy and mesmerised readers far beyond this nation. He is not as elusive as we think! He is timeless. He is everywhere.
He is hiding in the hearts of men.

To the boy himself, 'We love you Adrian Mole'.
To Pandora, 'Be kind'.

Colleen Jefford extreme left second row. Miss Walker, Headmistress, middle row centre

Janet Bigger 1952-1956
Janet's four children
attended the school 1970s
and later two of her
grandchildren

1940s

1941 class photograph

Joan Robinson and friends.
Rounders team 1950s

A day out. Mr Penny left back, David Gill 6th back,
Norman Durham 7th back, Mr Cooper right back

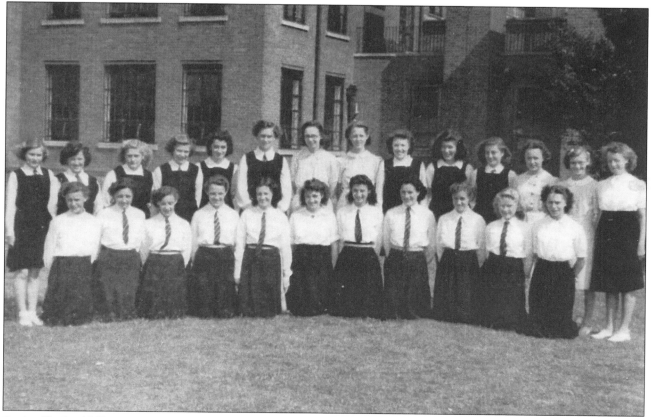

Senior Choir c1949

Winning Netball team. Bronte House 1949

Prize winners

Late 1940s

Netball team c1940s

County Boys' five pack changes

As a result of the defeat by Warwickshire last month, Leicestershire Boys selectors have introduced five newcomers — all forwards—in the side to meet North Midlands at Edgbaston tomorrow (kick-off 2.30).

The selectors have relied on boys from Hinckley and South Wigston, who supply 10 of the 15.

The Leicestershire side is Pratt (Hinckley); Brandreth (Gateway), Moore (Hinckley), Reeves (South Wigston), Jenkins (Ald. Newton's); Boden (Lancaster) or Hunt (Desford), Bolsover (South Wigston); Hall (South Wigston), Sanson (Hinckley), Hunter (Hinckley), Godfrey (Hinckley), Muir (Gateway), Smith (South Wigston), Dunckley (South Wigston), Fox (Hinckley).

News Report c 1950s

The School Orchestra c1950s

Touring Club trip to mid Wales. Easter 1948

*Dramatic group
(date unknown)*

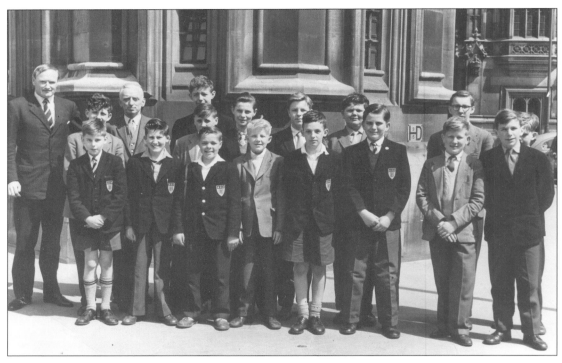

*Sir John Farr, MP
with pupils and
teacher Mr Every
visiting the Palace
of Westminster,
1958*

Mr Nutt 'in the lead'

1st Hockey X1. 1955-56

Autograph Book signatures 1952

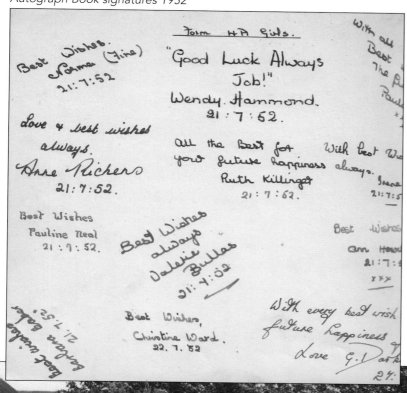

School Captains 1949. Doreen Wall, A
N Other, Lilian Haines, Dorothy Brown

Cast of the Great Bell of Burley 1953

Stratford Memorial Theatre
c1949. Pictured Miss
Walker and Mrs Vrolijk

Nymphs and Shepherds c 1949

Mr Walter Higgins with class. Norman Durham 5th back row

Margaret Hipwell. Leicestershire rounders tournament 1 July 1950

Boys with Masters working on the potato harvesting 1947

June Bull nee Sowden pictured with the Rounders team

Ena Wright centre with the ball. Margaret Triggs and others are pictured

L to R Jenny Gamble, Muriel Bray, Grace Allsop, Lilian Haines, Dorothy Weston, Christine Embrough, Kathleen Embrough

South Wigston Old Boys Rugby Football Club

Back Row L to R
J Wooley. M Bailey. M Forty. M Bown. R Smart. R Cooper. M Wilson. D Hillsdon.
Front row L to R
A Allsopp. R Tollafield. B Smith. N Blick. K Coulson. A Gregory. M Hanney.

Girls with recorders. c1950s

The Choral Speaking Group forms 111A and 11G who took part in area and county music festivals during 1955 and 1956

Happy Faces from the train window c1950s

Gouffre de Padirac. Le lae de la Pluie, exploring a subterranean river system known to exist in the third century

Chapter Five
The Numbers Game
(1968 - 1978)

The autumn term of 1968 began with the new entrants settling in. Work began in earnest. The winter games were on the agenda and very soon the results were being reported. The rugby cup was won by Bosworth House whilst Wistow took the soccer trophy and were also the winners of the cross country event. Belvoir were successful in achieving the most points for netball whilst Bradgate narrowly beat Belvoir by one point for the hockey.

By April the new £25,000 assembly hall and music block was well advanced under construction and was expected to be in use by the end of August. The development was welcomed by pupils and staff alike the scheme having been previously shelved for several years by the Education Authority through Government restrictions on expenditure. The assembly hall measures fifty five feet by fifty feet and is eighteen feet high inside. It was stated to have a capacity for six hundred children. The music block, forty feet by thirty feet, was designed to possess a classroom, an instrument store and three practice rooms. The school had a full set of instruments purchased from the sale of school concerts. The school orchestra would be able to meet in the music block away from other distractions.

The Assembly Hall and Music Block under construction (Leicester Mercury)

At a meeting in April 1969 the Leicestershire County Council Education Committee were looking at a memo from the Director, Mr Stewart Mason regarding Countesthorpe College and the catchment area. The completion of the building plan was expected by August 1970 giving 1,440 new school places. It was estimated that the raising of the school leaving age from 1972 would require a total of 1,700

new places. In turn Upper School places in the area would rise to at least 2,400 in 1977. This meant that some relief to the South Wigston High School would be needed immediately.

Further to that it was thought that by 1974 fourteen year old pupils from South Wigston would also proceed to Countesthorpe. Meanwhile South Wigston would continue to look to Guthlaxton, yet it must be borne in mind that unless the latter could eventually be relieved of South Wigston; the roll at Guthlaxton would build up again to about 1,300. These predicted figures were forecast quite apart from any new housing in the area.

In June 1969 Mr Stewart Mason, presented a report to the Leicestershire County Council Education Committee on the 'Leicestershire Plan' 1957 - 1969 and beyond. Colonel P H Lloyd, Chairman, of the County Council, stated that the Leicestershire County Council had reason to be proud of its record in being the first county to be recognised in a comprehensive system of education.

By 1969 'The Mason Plan' described in his booklet, *'The Leicestershire Experiment and Plan'* covered the whole county. It was the first shire authority to turn comprehensive and was described as Mason's finest achievement.

At the count in August the roll was confirmed as 957 pupils which were allocated accordingly to their respective forms. The First Year Group consisted of 329 pupils, the Second Years, 329, Third Years, 241 and the Fourth Years, 58. The Fourth Years were situated in the former nursery building with Mr Pell and Mrs Freestone and the 'Free Timetable' gave freedom of choice of activities. This was described as 'giving plenty of scope for individual initiative'.

The school log records that three retarded classes were taught by Mr Lingard, Mr Pell and Mr Read. Historically many changes have taken place in the teaching of less able students including the terminology.

After years of school meals being cooked in the kitchens on site, a new cafeteria service was introduced with a choice of meals each day. The 'Order of Entry' varied each day so that all diners had the widest choices one day in three. Sometimes those last into the hall in the third group would **have** to eat what was left. The first few days of this scheme brought praise and satisfaction. Pupils accept that arrangements are fair to all, (stated in the school log!) The kitchen was not large enough to provide meals for those who wanted them. This resulted in some classes being asked to bring sandwiches on certain days.

One of the best achievements of the year was in October when the new music block was open for lessons. A report by Mr Ralph Paddock, music teacher, taken from the Golden Jubilee History of the school sets out in detail the features of the building. In addition to the fine music room there are three practice rooms which are used by not only peripatetic staff for individual lessons and the children at lunchtime for instrument practice, but also for group work as part of the curriculum.

The first school carol concert was held in the new hall. The school choir and orchestra were joined by The Leicester Catholic Choral Union, whose fine singing evoked much admiration. Lunchtime recitals have been a welcome feature with eminent Leicestershire musicians filling the hall to capacity. Recitals varied from violin, piano and guitar works. The Guthlaxton Chamber Choir enthralled the audiences with its technique.

Gilbert and Sullivan's 'Mikado' was the highlight of the year with John Wale, Kim Orton, Marco Roginsky and many children taking part in the production. Playing for three nights forty pounds was raised for the organ fund.

Mr Paddock expressed his sadness that many of the young musicians would be lost to Countesthorpe College. This fact sadly is a consequence of the new education system. However, it must be recognised that a good grounding in all subjects is of the essence.

Mr Paddock had been at the school as the music teacher for the past twelve years and he had actually taught the school's woodwork master, Mr Peter Bradbury, to play the double bass. Mr Bradbury played the violin at the school when he was a pupil there.

Two boys, Peter Bradbury and Brian Bray attended South Wigston High School as pupils who had failed the Eleven Plus Examination and both left South Wigston at fourteen to attend Guthlaxton. Brian Bray achieved twelve GCE O Level certificates and became Head of Mathematics at South Wigston High School and Peter Bradbury

became the Handicrafts Master there too.

A letter in November which began, 'Dear Parent' and signed by the Director of Education, Stewart Mason outlined. 'Secondary School Education in Wigston Magna - South Wigston - Countesthorpe Areas'. The content is summarised here. Referring to the new building of Countesthorpe Secondary School it advised that the numbers of children in the Wigston area was rising. The committee had been undertaking a thorough review of the situation in order to decide which should be the catchment area of the new school and the revised contributory areas for the present schools. The temporary arrangement introduced in 1965 for a large number of pupils living in South Wigston to attend the Abington and Bushloe schools will terminate. The Abington and Bushloe Schools will share a catchment area serving Arnesby, Kilby and the whole of Wigston Magna for children in the eleven to fourteen range.

The Guthlaxton School will take fourteen year olds from the Abington and Bushloe new areas together with those living in South Wigston itself for the time being. Parents will obviously be concerned to know how these new arrangements will be introduced and I will do my best to describe the proposed method as briefly as possible.

New eleven plus high school entrants and fourteen plus upper school entrants in September 1970 will proceed to whichever school is the appropriate one for the district in which they live from that time. Children who live in Countesthorpe and Blaby who, in a year's time, are about to begin their second and third year of secondary education will be moved from Abington/Bushloe or South Wigston, as the case may be, to the high school section of the new school at Countesthorpe. If they did not move then they would have to do so at the upper school stage, so it will be better if all those concerned move in September 1970 as a group and take up their places as the first members of the fine new school at Countesthorpe.

Children living in South Wigston now attending the Abington and Bushloe High Schools will not be moved back to South Wigston High School because they will continue to look at Guthlaxton Upper School.

Children from Countesthorpe, Blaby, Glen Hills and Eyres Monsell who will be starting their fifth year in September 1970 will not be moved out for that year but those of them who want to follow a sixth form course will be offered a place at Countesthorpe from September 1971. It will also be the aim to start the nucleus of a first year sixth form at Countesthorpe from September 1970. We hope that at that time the young people who wish to follow a sixth form course will not be deterred by the prospect of changing schools but will seize enthusiastically the opportunity of being the first members of a brand new sixth form at Countesthorpe.

The committee realise that there may be parents who may regret that an association with a particular school is to be terminated but they trust that parents and pupils alike will respond to the excellent opportunities offered at Countesthorpe and after a short time look upon that school as 'theirs'. The changes proposed are inevitable in the face of rising numbers if we are to prevent serious overcrowding in the Wigston schools, bearing in mind that still further growth is to come from the considerable amount of new housing under construction or planned.

There may be a limited number of cases where the proposed new arrangements would have the effect of separating brothers and sisters. The Committee will give sympathetic consideration to individual applications for brothers and sisters to be together as far as possible provided that this would not lead to difficulties at the school selected. A large number of applications for exemption could not be entertained for this would perpetuate overcrowding.

It will be seen from the information given in this letter that for the time being the Education Authority is still providing secondary education for Eyres Monsell pupils who live in the City of Leicester. When the City of Leicester Education Authority is able to make its own provision for Eyres Monsell pupils a further change will be made on our side and fourteen year old pupils living in South Wigston will then go to the Countesthorpe Upper School and not Guthlaxton. It cannot yet be said when this change will be made as this depends on building programmes in the City.

When this further change is made it will mean that South Wigston High School will send all of its pupils to Countesthorpe whilst Guthlaxton Upper School will take its pupils only from Abington and Bushloe so that each group of high and upper schools will be working on a self-contained basis. Nearer the time of the further change the Committee will investigate closely the question of transport from South Wigston to Countesthorpe. They will also review the possibility of considering marginal addresses for free transport.

Mr Mason went on to introduce the Headmaster of the new school at Countesthorpe, Mr I McMullen. BA to the parents. Apart from military service during the 1939/1945 war, Mr McMullen had spent his working life in education. His post from 1958 to 1965 was as the Head of Thomas Bennett Comprehensive School, Crawley, Sussex. A wide experience in other educational fields Mr McMullen served as a member of Her Majesty's Inspectorate, a Principal Lecturer in a College of Education, the Director of the Nuffield Resources for Learning Project and Consultant to the Organisation for Economic and Cultural Development in Paris.

Mr McMullen asks that parents can be reassured on the matter of uniforms; the school will not require a new one to be bought specially upon the opening.

The hope that parents would join in the spirit and enthusiasm which will surround the opening and development of the new school was expressed. Those pupils not involved in its establishment will draw their own benefit from the other consequential rearrangements and the relief which the new school will bring to the accommodation at the others.

In all cases allocation to High and Upper Schools depends on the home address.

On 25 and 26 November 1969 the school closed due to the National Union Of Teachers Strike. On 6 December a strike was called by the National Association of Teachers and the N.U.T. On 9 December another day of action took place with a further N.U.T. strike.

Mr Horst Briel left South Wigston High School at Christmas to take up an appointment as Lecturer at a College of Education in Leeds.

The New Year term began on the 6 January 1970. A month later on 13 February, the Headmaster Mr Rutherford attended a reception at County Hall to meet the Education Secretary, Edward Short MP.,

A very significant change occurred in February at the school. An unusually high rate of third years were in attendance. It was announced that this age group in future were to be transferred to the upper school system. The outcome of this meant that the fourth year classes would be dropped. Consequently the part time teacher of commerce, Mrs Clark, left her post as the subject was due to end. By July seven staff were leaving the school as the numbers on the roll were falling. Four hundred pupils were transferring to the new school at Countesthorpe. There were no new appointments for the next term planned.

One of the seven staff who left the school was Mr Aubrey Burl. His new post was as Principal Lecturer in Prehistory at Hull College of Higher Education. On his retirement in 1980 he was regarded as an authority on stone circles in Britain, Ireland and Brittany. A prolific writer Mr Burl's books include *'A Guide to The Stone Circles of Britain, Ireland and Brittany'*, *'The Stonehenge People'* and a biography of the Roman poet, *'Catullus'*. Mr Burl has made two lecture tours in America.

A sub-committee of the Governors and staff met in March 1970 to discuss the sum of money left to the school by the terms of Miss Edna Walker's will of 1966. It was in September 1971 the school purchased a sound amplifier with twin speakers housed in a console made in the handicraft department.

Government ministers changed in mid-June. Mrs Margaret Thatcher became the Secretary of State for Education and Science replacing Edward Short. Mrs Thatcher's innovations in the post are notable. Establishing a review of Remedial Education led Baroness Warnock to investigate the structure of education for Special Educational Needs children. Research on education for children in main stream schools caused much debate.

The 1970 Education Act ended the long standing practice of a small minority of children being classified as ineducable. The Act put a stop to the arrangements for 'classifying children suffering from a disability of mind as children unsuitable for education at school'.

It also took away the power of health authorities to provide training for these children and from 1971, some twenty four thousand children from junior training centres and special care units across England, along with eight thousand in one hundred hospitals became entitled to education.

This Act was a hugely significant acknowledgement by Parliament towards the last, small minority of the population who for generations had been denied access to a basic education. For the first time in the United Kingdom's history, 100% of school age children were now entitled to an education.

Mr Tom Pell organised a school camp activity holiday in Guernsey for one hundred pupils in July. Pupils shared sleeping quarters in large ridge tents. Parents and relatives were encouraged to apply to join the party making it a 'family camp'. This idea aimed to promote good Parent/Teacher relationships. Trips were taken to many of the islands and towns with rambles round the coastline and bays.

In August there were no longer any pupils coming from Blaby to South Wigston. The school was taking pupils from South Wigston, Glen Hills and Rolleston Junior Schools. The latter being in the Leicester City Borough. There were eleven classes in the first year and eight in the second and third years. The school closed for the Bank Holiday on the last day of August. On the following day in September, which began the autumn term; many children were absent from school as they were still on holiday with their parents.

Ann Mellor nee Rawlinson started at South Wigston High School in August 1970 as a Laboratory Assistant. She was just sixteen years old. Ann recalls that there were five science laboratories in the school and Mr Ron Baker's was situated in the former Boys' section. There were three laboratories in the old Girls' section of the school. In addition, two small preparation rooms existed one at each end of the building. Ann said that she used to wear out a pair of shoes a month walking from one end of the school to the other.

Ann followed in the footsteps of her parents as they both attended and met at the school. Her mother Margaret Mary Fisher was a former Head Girl and Captain of Nightingale House and her father was Dennis Rawlinson. Her grandfather was the local butcher situated on the corner of Countesthorpe Road. Many school children will remember Mr A J Rawlinson as they passed the shop every day on the way to and from school. It was a popular calling point as the shop sold sweets and penny iced lollypops. Others remember an array of delicious cakes baked on the premises. Dennis was also a very good drummer and with two former pupils of South Wigston School, Fred Hipwell and Ivor Kenney; they entertained publicly for many years. Ivor

Kenney was a well known pianist and Fred Hipwell had an extensive career as a musician playing first the accordion as a young boy then following on with the flute, the saxophone and the piano. Many past pupils of South Wigston Secondary Modern School for Girls' and Boys' recall the times spent at the Palais de Dance on Humberstone Gate in Leicester where the Ivor Kenney Dance Band helped them dance the night away.

Dennis Rawlinson

Fred Hipwell with his accordion, Dennis Rawlinson drums

As a laboratory assistant Ann was able to acquire many of the specimens needed for school experiments from her grandfather's shop. She collected lungs, hearts and eyeballs. The children discovered that Ann did not like stick insects so they would collect them and place them on her trolley. On one occasion they locked her in a classroom which forced her to climb out of a window to get back in through the front door.

Ann remembers if she ate with the children at lunch time she was given free school meals.

Ann recalls helping to run a disco at lunch times and in the evenings the youth club, 'Andromeda' in the garden hut with a police presence!

Joining in some of the school trips took Ann on one occasion to Dovedale. On route they encountered a very bad thunder storm with the obvious addition of lightning. Ann recalls that one or two of the girls became hysterical.

A camping trip to Guernsey was also enjoyed. The boys tents were situated on one side of the field with the girls tents on the opposite side. A Land Rover with spotlight was placed in the middle to make sure that there was no tent swapping.

Walking in Guernsey was very pleasant and Ann recalls the staff who accompanied the party. Mr Chris Lingard, Jenny Harrold and her husband and Mr Tom Pell.

Ann left South Wigston after two and a half years but says that she has never forgotten the school. She made good friends there and is still in touch with Jenny Harrold who moved to Cornwall.

Mrs Marion Baker returned in 1970 to South Wigston and Countesthorpe College to do supply teaching part-time eventually working full-time at South Wigston. Over the years she taught English, French and humanities. Mrs Baker recalls the year assemblies in the new hall when year heads, form teachers and their forms would take assemblies. The school was divided into two bands, A and B with weekly assemblies taken mainly by the Headmaster.

Mrs Baker recalls some enjoyable trips out of school with pupils. They visited The Roman Jury Wall Museum, The Guildhall, Leicester Cathedral and the William Carey House. William Carey was a Baptist Minister in Leicester and a missionary in India.

Life at school continued until the Christmas holiday.

In 1971 a County Education Scheme was introduced which allowed teachers to go into industry to see what 'life was like on the outside'. Mr Lingard was seconded for two weeks into the Police Service. He found the experience very interesting and enjoyable. During his time there he was taken out in the patrol cars and began to understand how the policemen themselves felt. Mr Lingard describes the duty of checking the speed limit on vehicles.

Travelling behind a speeding lorry they observed the driver reducing speed. By use of his mirrors he realised that he was being followed by a police car.

It was explained to Mr Lingard that policemen are not there to harrass the public but to enforce the law. Convinced that the driver was aware of the law as he conformed on observing their following vehicle, the officer at the time, left him to continue his journey.

The duty of informing family members of a fatality is something that Mr Lingard was told they never get used to. One officer was detailed to break the news to a family who tragically had lost two sons.

After the two week period it was evident that police officers were quite human and approachable.

Mr Ron Baker was seconded to the G.E.C Works at Whetstone for one week. The week was to give Mr Baker an insight into electrical engineering with a view to assisting the boys back at school. There were many career opportunities with the company.

By April more staff were leaving the school including Mr David Nutt who became Vice Principal of Roundhills College, Thurmaston.

In June 1971 the Leicestershire County Council Education Committee reported at their meeting that this would be the last meeting to be attended by Mr Stewart Mason CBE before retiring. His service had spanned nearly a quarter of a century.

The Chairman spoke of Mr Mason's qualities as Director of Education and in particular in connection with the introduction of the Leicestershire Plan with the abolition of the Eleven Plus Examination. Mr Mason's personal involvement with the County Schools Orchestra and County School of Music, the County Art Collection and his interest in the less able

child were also praised.

Mr Andrew Fairbairn succeeded Mr Stewart Mason as Director of Education and Mr A J Davis, was appointed as his Deputy. Enthusiastic about education and music Mr Fairbairn has been described as one of the founding fathers of the comprehensive system.

In August there were 780 pupils on the roll. All of the fourth years form Parklands School at South Wigston, Glen Hills and Rolleston schools now attended. The staff consisted of the Head, thirty three full time staff and five part time.

At the Christmas celebrations that year, teacher Miss Gladys Darkins, who was also a past pupil of the school, directed the very successful production of 'Tom Sawyer'. £222.00, food and clothing was donated to The Family Service Unit.

At the start of the new term January 1972 there were ninety nine absentees from the Eyres Monsell Estate. They returned on the following day. Letters were sent to all parents.

Problems occurred again for the school a few days later in the form of the coal miners strike. The school became very short of fuel. The promise of a special delivery from the County's stock pile was thought to tide them over for approximately one week. By early February the supply was exhausted and pupils were given two days off. The strike lasted for seven weeks.

Mr Andrew Napier Fairbairn MC

The winning team back row left to right, Julie Smith, Pat Moore, Alison Pole, Susan Delves. Front Row. Jenny Dunmore, Susan Russell, Jenny Bowles

South Wigston High School '5' A Side winners 1973. Back Row Mr Chris Lingard. School Football Team Manager Coach. Second Row. L to R Steve Brady, Richard Groom, Anthony Ballard, Chris Arnold, David Williams, David Barratt. Front Row. L to R. Alan Birchenell (Leicester City Football Club) John Culley (Captain) Steve Earle (Leicester City Football Club)

For the first time the Mid-Leicestershire under fourteen netball tournament was won by the South Wigston High School Girls' team. The final was played at Manor High School, Oadby, and the South Wigston girls beat Roundhill 22-20.

In April 1972 a party of twenty girls visited London for the day to look around the expensive stores. The evening was spent at the Prince of Wales Theatre to see Sacha Distel. Olivia Newton John, Ted Rogers and Stefan Grapelli.

Anthony Ballard attended South Wigston High School 1971-1974 between the age of eleven years to fourteen. He has many sporting memories and although the school had always had a strong rugby tradition, football had become popular also. Written by Mr Chris Lingard, Anthony is proud to have been included in the article below as one of:

The Ton Up Boys

'This year the 2nd Year Soccer Team have earned the title. The chase for records was on from the start of this season and they duly came. One hundred goals in a season was their target and so set a new school record. The record came and they went on to set a target of one hundred and thirty goals which must stand as a record for some time to come.

The most dramatic game was against Abington School. At the start of this game the team had a record of ninety four goals. This game was important as we had lost by seven goals to six early in the season and there was a chance of reaching the hundred. As the goals came the tension mounted and with ten minutes to go it nearly reached breaking point as the score stood at five-one in our favour. With six minutes to go John Cully netted a beautiful goal which released all the pent up emotion and the celebrations held up play for a few minutes. At last with that sixth goal the magic figure had been reached. Our thanks go to the First Year team who helped give this game its atmosphere.

Once again this season the emphasis has been on attack and still the team find it difficult to realise that defence is as important. The record shows that they are getting caught all too often without a sound defence. David Hale has done his best and played an excellent season but too many of the other defenders are committing themselves to attack too often. If we can solve our defensive problems and give David the support he must have, then this can be a very good team. The forward line have all played their part from the quiet neat skills of John Cully through the highly competitive play of Andrew Greaves to the real forceful play of Graham Ruck. Graham has used his size well and although not the highest goal scorer he has created the chances for the smaller much lighter Andrew and John to become the top goal scorers.

Mention has been made of some players but it

must be stressed that this has been very much of a team game. Individual skills have blended together into a powerful scoring machine. Two more players must be mentioned. Philip Capell came into the First Year team from the reserves and has now become the most improved player in the side. What can we say about Anthony Ballard? In two seasons he has missed only one game and although he will not become the World's No.1 goalkeeper, Anthony is reliable. 'Little Tubby Ballard', has taken all the insults, abuse, etc, and still turns up again next week. His biggest fault is not being consistent enough and after one game of being threatened with the axe he plays a brilliant game.

Next season with a sounder defence I think we will give any team in the area a run for their money and maybe break some more records or even win a cup.

Played 21   Won 15   Drawn 2   Lost 4
Goals for 130   Against 63

The following boys have played. Anthony Ballard, Paul O'Beirne, Michael Simmons, Stephen Gant, David Hale, Philip Capell, Russell Morris, Graham Ruck, Andrew Greaves, John Cully, Terry Whitmore, Christopher Arnold, Gary Youmans, Peter Mort, Timothy Harrison, Ricky Atton, Colin Palmer.

Half Colours awarded to: Anthony Ballard and Philip Capell

Full Colours awarded to: David Hale, Graham Ruck, Andrew Greaves, John Cully

Graham Ruck played for the Mid Leicestershire Under 13 Team.

Rugby was as important as ever as the following demonstrates:

RUGBY REPORT 1972-1973
'During the season of 1972-1973 we saw rugby of varying quality. The under fourteen XV with some outstanding players seem to play according to the weather, or perhaps the moon. They recorded some excellent victories, five times scoring over forty points in a match. On other occasions however, roles were reversed and heavy defeats resulted. Whenever the under fourteens played one could expect a fast open game with plenty of points scored.

The under thirteen XV started off the season showing promise winning their first five matches. They then seemed to meet teams containing much bigger boys and results went against them. To their credit the under thirteens battled through this sticky period and when the Spring came the results improved. I hope before next season the South Wigston midgets start to grow.

The future looks bright for the under twelve XV a team with immense promise. The season was completed with only two defeats and ten victories. They reached the semi final of The County Under 12 Cup and have proved themselves an outstanding all round side.

Rugby wise 1972-1973 was a good year, we look forward to the next season and for this year we congratulate the following boys on representing the school.

UNDER 14 XV.
D Eabry, K Sales, M Wyman, R Riley, M Thistlethwaite, C Burrows, M Baker, P Barradell, L Harris, K Hill, I Stripp, G Holmes, K Howsin, S Osadosuk, P Knight, G Henson, W Gibson, D Loomes, H Carter.

UNDER 13 XV
P Bale, L Robinson, P Capel, D Hale, M Worn, P Foster, L Plumb, J Higgs, T Harding, S Halford, M Hughes, G Chamberlain, A Pickering, N Dean, M Alesky, A Barratt, M Penlington, P Gibson, M Wright, K Tams, J Harrison, W Tipton, C Minshull

UNDER 12 XV
K Eames, N Spence, P Starmer, D Mayes, J Pidd, I Dodson, R Johnson, H Palmer, P Leutchford, G Bird, K Hull, A Hopper, A Gamble, A Lee, M Wilson, R Welford, I Gibson, A Nicholson, C Alletson, P Clowes, S Spilsbury, R Peardon.

Outstanding Achievements

Stephanie Heircock. Two Bronze and one Silver County Cross Country Medals. Member of Leicester Corinthians Athletic Club. Ran in the All England Cross Country Championships.

Angela Hext. Member of Leicester Corinthians Athletic Club. Discus and Shot. Selected to compete in the All England Athletic Championships in July 1973.

Kevin Howsin. *Member of Leicester Corinthians Athletic Club. Hurdles. Outstanding competitor in Long Jump, Triple Jump and Javelin also. Selected for the All England Athletic Championships in July 1973.*

David McMillan. *Selected for the All England Gymnastic Squad. Training with the under fourteen team.*

Samuel de Soto entered the school 1972-1975. The form teacher was Mr Noel Brannan who taught pottery. Samuel's memories are vivid of Mr Rose known to the pupils as 'Bud Rose' who taught metalwork. Samuel remembers creating a model of a Spitfire on one occasion using a mould which had been made by Mr Rose who would warn the class 'not iron filings in my tea please'. Mr Rose also made a steam train for children in Abbey Park, Leicester.

Mr Rose and his son

Mrs Rose with their daughters in Abbey Park on the engine designed by Mr Rose

Mr Rose at work

Mr J Griffiths, the Welsh maths teacher is recalled as very strict. Mr R.Oakes taught PE and was assisted by Mr Spirrett believed to be involved in Amateur League Athletics and a javelin expert. Samuel recalls Mr Wild as extremely strict.

Cross country running was not popular with all boys. On leaving the school to run approximately three miles, the circuit took them over the fields, along the canal towpath and back to school. A plan was often put into operation by a few. On reaching the entrance to the bridle path by Crow Mills, the viaduct bridge became their saviour and escape. The discovery of an inspection hatch, reached by shinning up an iron step ladder and removing an iron ring; the group spent many an hour inside the top of the viaduct enjoying the view of the countryside and the towpath. Infamously smoking their cigarettes which were concealed in their socks, apparently they were never detected. The 'look out' could easily spot the returning runners on the towpath. Shinning down the iron ladder once more to tag on behind the runners was easy.

The Viaduct, Countesthorpe Road, South Wigston

On the last day of January 1973 the Leicestershire County Council minutes were recording on a report by the Director of Education, Mr Andrew Fairbairn, 'A ten year plan for Education'. It reads that 'The Authority has now declared its policy on four year High Schools as follows:

i) that a firm policy decision be taken by the Authority to establish Four Year High Schools throughout the County as and when local circumstances permit.

ii) that accordingly the Director be asked to advise the Committee immediately favourable conditions arise in the area as envisaged in (i) above

(iii) That the Four Year High Schools shall, in the first instance shall be for pupils of ten to fourteen years'.

The Education Committee has now accepted as a policy the introduction as and when possible of Four Year High Schools.

New High Schools are being built to very different concepts from those who began life as Secondary Modern Schools and all of the latter are likely to require modification to their buildings.

Proposals from the Schools Council are already being considered for a single examination at sixteen plus which will reform the O Level GCE and CSE examinations and it seems quite probable that the new examination will be firmly established by the end of the decade.

In 1973 the School leaving age was raised to sixteen.

A very sad day was reported in the School Log on 2 July 1973. Miss Molly Vann BA died after a long illness. She had been absent from school since January.

On 31 December Mr Rutherford officially retired after twenty one years as Headmaster. Mr S C Reid who had worked at the school for sixteen years also retired. Mr Leslie Wild acted as Headmaster from the beginning of the term January 1974 until Mr Graham Norris arrived in post.

Mr Graham Norris was appointed to the Headship of South Wigston High School on 14 December 1973 taking up his post in April 1974. Mr Norris began his teaching career at the Rushden School for Boys in Northamptonshire where he also was responsible for a two hundred strong youth club. Continuing as Deputy Head of Anstey Martin High School, Mr Norris was further appointed to the Headship of the Faculty of Humanities at The FitzWimarc School in Rayleigh, Essex.

Mr Graham Bowen Norris

On his arrival at South Wigston High School the Chairman of the Governors was Mr Curtis Weston and the clerk was Mr Harry Broadhead. At the time there were only eight hundred pupils on the roll with ages ranging between eleven and fourteen. There were three feeder Primary Schools, Glenhills in Glen Parva, Parklands and Fairfield in South Wigston. Children transferred to Guthlaxton at the age of fourteen and those from Glen Parva to Countesthorpe College. Nevertheless, Mr Norris writes; 'Parental choice resulted in some Glen Parva children going to Guthlaxton and a number of South Wigston pupils moving to Countesthorpe College'.

A major part of Mr Norris's role was to build relationships with the local community and parents and staff with a view to forming a properly constituted Parent Teacher Association. This was finally achieved in the autumn of 1974.

Developing continental links with Europe was helped as a result of modern languages, French and German being taught. Exchange visits to France and Germany of usually a week's duration were arranged. In May, a party of German children from Jollenbeck School in Bielefield were welcomed at a Civic Reception by Councillor Fred Bennett who was also a Governor of South Wigston High School. A dinner at Kibworth Lodge to entertain the visitors was also given by the staff of the school. The thirty two German children stayed with the families of the pupils, some of which had visited Germany over the past two years. Mr Tom Pell, schoolmaster at South Wigston was credited with much of the success of the schools links. During their stay the Germans visited Coventry, Dovedale, Warwick and Stratford Upon Avon. Mr Norris the Headmaster was presented with a memorial plaque and the Mayor of Oadby and Wigston gave each of the children a badge depicting the City of Leicester coat of arms. The Mayor spoke of South Wigston High School's fine sporting tradition in particular mentioning rugby where the school had produced several internationals. Mr E H Sandiford, Chief Engineer of the Borough, a fluent German linguist, was in attendance.

Mr Norris described the German visit as a good example of staff and parents working together. Money to entertain the visitors had been raised by the pupils, parents and staff of South Wigston High School.

Two days later Mr Norris was on his way to Dieppe with a party of photographers and linguists. In mid-June he was on his way to a visit to the children's home in Mablethorpe where the school band gave a concert at the Seaview Theatre.

Sports Day was celebrated in June with Mr Curtis Weston presenting the prizes. The fire alarm was deliberately set off in the boiler room which after a long investigation the culprits were caught and dealt with.

June 28th ended the term with a bomb hoax.

On 17 August the news of the death of Mr S C Reed was met with sadness. Head of the Remedial Department, Mr Reed died after a long illness and was a great loss to the school. He was going to be sorely missed by staff and pupils alike.

Throughout September in the new autumn term an army of County Education Advisers invaded the school. These were, Mr R Bibby, Assistant Director, Mr Maurice Stevens, Religious Education, Miss Cartwright, Physical Education, Mr Rowley, Schools Pottery, Mrs N Perrins, Domestic Science, Mrs Barradell, Schools Welfare and Social Worker, Mr Laxton, Design, Mr G D Davies, Principal Music Adviser, Mr McGregor, Music, Mr Perry, Science, Mrs Barradell and Mr Waterman, Psychological Service, Mr R P Edwards, Library Adviser and Mr Rawson with Mrs Vaisey, two Church Wardens.

Mr David Smith and Mr Duncan Sidwell, Senior Modern Languages Advisers, visited on a regular basis to guide the development of new techniques in modern language teaching. A particular pleasing and motivating aspect of their visits was that of actually teaching groups of pupils for extended periods and running workshops for modern language teachers. Links with the University School of Education became well established during this period and some excellent graduates, who had done their teaching practice at South Wigston were appointed to the permanent staff.

A party of twenty children visited Streatley Youth Hostel in October accompanied by Mrs Bull, Mr Kelly and Mr Parnell. They spent the weekend enjoying the chalk downlands of Berkshire, the Chiltern Hills and the valleys of the River Thames and Kennet.

Mr Lingard left the school in 1974 to take up a new appointment at Manor Brook School in Leicestershire. The school worked with children aged five to sixteen years with emotional and behavioural problems

After the Christmas celebrations and a concert for South Wigston elderly people the term ended.

The new term began January 1975 and a party of first years were taken to the Haymarket Theatre in Leicester to see 'The Owl and the Pussycat'. Two days later the Police Forensic Team were investigating a break in at the school. The staff room had been ransacked and the science laboratory broken into.

On a February evening Mr Booth and Mrs Swannell organised a disco with the help of a pupil committee.

Until Easter the school carried out its normal functions with many visitors arriving at the school.

In May and June two further school trips were arranged. The first to the Peak District in Derbyshire. From Ravenstor Hostel in Millers Dale the party visited Thor's Cave in the Manifold Valley. In addition Chatsworth House and the plague village of Eyam, Peak Cavern in Castleton, were also enjoyed.

The second trip took in Cheshire, Lancashire and Staffordshire. On a very hot weekend they stayed in a hostel and visited Chester followed by a military tattoo. The Red Devils, Parachute team and the Blue Eagles was described as wonderful. The following day the party visited the Barton Swing Bridge which takes the Leeds and Liverpool Canal over the Manchester Ship Canal. This was followed by viewing the Jodrell Bank Radio Telescope and a moated manor house called Little Moreton Hall. Here was excitement for one boy who found a secret room. Ending the tour the Hill of Mow Cop was climbed to see the building called The Old Man of Mow.

On 18 June Mr Paddock escorted twenty nine children to Kneller Hall near Twickenham, home of the Military School of Music.

On 2 July Miss Norah White, Senior Mistress, celebrated her retirement after thirty eight years service to the school. Mrs Davies, Cook Supervisor also retired after thirty years. The evening was enjoyed with a cheese and wine party.

The autumn term began again with various meetings again taking place. The Heads of the Remedial English and Mathematics Departments met to discuss the new intake.

Mr Norris attended the Brighton Conference and the following week the Assistant Director of Education was again at the school to discuss catchment areas and capacity. By the end of September the Director of Education was at the school to discuss Secondary School Reorganisation with further meetings at County Hall.

'Round and about with Stroller' in the *Oadby and Wigston Advertiser* the September headlines were highlighting the busy programme by the South Wigston High School's recently formed Parent Teacher Association. The Association whose Secretary was Mr Alan Maccabee of Glen Parva was embarking on a fund raising programme to raise funds for the school's six hundred pupils. A fashion show was planned and it was hoped to raise money to support children in their swimming lessons at the Wigston baths, school camps and trips. With economies being observed by the Education Department Mr Maccabee pointed out that he aimed to make the school a social centre in the evenings for parents. The thirteen committee members which included parent governors and teachers had the full support of Mr Graham Norris, Headmaster.

A meeting at the school in October approved the draft constitution of the Parent Teacher Association and the Steering Committee was elected for a full year of office. The first official function was held in November when a hundred parents, teachers and friends of the school enjoyed a Halloween dance. Thirty pounds was raised for school funds.

In November the *'Oadby and Wigston Advertiser'* reported that Mr Norris at South Wigston High School. prided himself on the individualistic learning of the schoolchildren. It stated that, with its basic 'common core curriculum' South Wigston High School exemplified the success of the current comprehensive school system. An example of the new way of learning was demonstrated in the science department where pupils can select from listed experiments a project to carry out with team mates under supervision. Mr Baker explained that the department taught combined sciences in the first two years followed by physics, chemistry and biology in the third year. At the time of the report Miss Burbidge was teaching electricity with pupils occupied in setting circuits. Mr Fagg had been teaching pupils in measuring work, assessing amounts of energy needed. Mr Rajanikani Dawada

Miss Jean Burbidge demonstrates electrical circuits to Dawn Perkins left and Deborah Atkinson
(Leicester Mercury)

from Uganda and two laboratory assistants, Mrs Jennifer Lymn and Mrs Maureen Hinman completed the team.

A party of eighty six children and three staff left for Dieppe at this time returning after one week whilst investigations were under way into the possibility of a Pelican crossing being installed outside the school gates. Later in November a display was given by the Royal Marines.

A Christmas concert ended the season and a cheque for £280.00 was presented to the Leicester Family Service Unit.

The New Year of 1976 more sad news was reported. On 18 January, Miss Valerie Cooper, an English teacher died. Valerie was only twenty five years old. Mr Norris and Mr N Davies attended the funeral at Hull.

March 1976 saw Mr Chapman of the County Surveyor's Department visiting the school with a view to excavation of part of the school field for a drainage channel. Further meetings occurred regarding the continuing question of a Pelican crossing at the school. From the beginning of this campaign the Pelican crossing would take twelve years to achieve.

At the Methodist Church in South Wigston the audience was entertained by the school choir and handbell ringers.

In April the Physical Education Department presented an evening of entertainment entitled 'Music on the Move'.

The school closed for the day on 6 May in order to be used for a polling station.

A very successful fete was held at the school in June and a grand total of £350.00 was raised.

Miss May Harris and Mr Leslie Wild receiving retirement gifts from Mr Andrew Fairbairn MC Director of Education 1976

Parents, children, staff and Governors attended.

On 25 June a retirement dinner at the Post House Hotel was enjoyed to mark Mr Leslie Wild's retirement from the school after thirty eight years. Mr Andrew Fairbairn, Director of Education was in attendance. Mr Fairbairn made a surprise presentation of a typewriter to Mr Wild to mark his retirement as Deputy Headmaster. Also retiring was Miss May Harris after sixteen years service. Mr Fairbairn presented her with a cheque for £50.00.

A few days later a summer concert was held in memory of Miss Valerie Cooper who died in January.

On the last day of the summer term at Assembly the children made a presentation to Mr Wild and Miss Harris.

As the autumn term began the importance of maintenance at the school was uppermost with visits from Mr Evans of the County Architects Department to check the heating system. Also Mr Goss attended, Professional Assistant Development Branch to check the Fire Precaution Minor Works Programme. This was followed up by a Health Education Evening when one hundred and three parents attended.

First Year curriculum meetings had taken place over the weeks and a Primary Nuffield French Project was discussed with Mr David Smith, the County Modern Language Adviser.

In October a visit was made to the school by the composer, Douglas Young and the following evening the Wigston Band were in concert with the school choir. Evening discos had been enjoyed earlier by a number of children

In December Mr Norris addressed the staff on the subject, 'The Teacher and the Law'.

Celebrating the Christmas spirit 'Carols by Candlelight' was enjoyed by all and forty children accompanied by Mrs Jackson and Mrs Kendall made a visit to Olympia.

The Spring Term of 1977 began with a blizzard. On the second day the school bus failed to arrive and children were stranded in school until they were collected by their parents.

By March 'Islands and Journeys' was performed in the presence of the Director of Education and his wife, Mr and Mrs Andrew Fairbairn. The composition was written by Douglas Young, composer in residence. The 'islands' refer to geographical locations and to the groups of instrumentalists employed to evoke the sounds of trains in and out of tunnels, aeroplanes taking off and landing, storms, a volcano in action when molten lava meets the sea and a forest fire.

In May, a music course for ninety teachers based on Douglas Young's 'Islands and Journeys' was earmarked.

The school closed for one day in support of a National Union of Public Employees, 'NUPE' strike and for one other day for the County Council Elections to take place.

In May a site meeting was held to discuss the removal of blue asbestos lagging from the central heating pipes. This was to precede the installation of a new gas fired system.

Later that month Mr Norris attended a National Association of Head Teachers Conference, NATH, at Hind Leys College, Shepshed. The guest of honour was Mrs Shirley Williams, Secretary of State for Education and Science.

A careers evening for pupils and parents was hosted at the school with a view to offering advice to school leavers. Major employers were in attendance to form a discussion panel.

Once again the June fete was a resounding success regarding fund raising even though the rain spoiled the proceedings. With the grand total of £585.00 raised everyone's hard work was rewarded.

The term ended with more visits by County Education Advisers one of which was Mr Bill Stockdale, the Remedial Adviser. Later a gathering of High School and Upper School Head Teachers took place at Beaumanor Hall in the presence of Mr Andrew Fairbairn, Director of Education.

September and October were as usual months for

many meetings of staff and visitors. Parents evenings were arranged called, 'Getting to Know You' and Mr Oliffe, Head of Remedial and Diagnostics Department talked of the new intake's reading and numeracy ages.

Mrs Baker writes that in the autumn term of 1977 despite being very ill with peritonitis Mr Baker continued to organise the trips to Weiskirchen until the summer of 1982.

A party of German School Head Teachers visited the school in October and in November a European Exhibition was held as part of the celebrations for European Week. With Mr Norris three pupils, Adrian Dilks, Kerrie Hunt and Perdita Caswell attended the European Flag of Honour Ceremony at County Hall. The flag was presented to Leicestershire. A dinner in the evening was attended by Dr. Jutta Grutzner the Cultural Attache of the German Embassy.

The exhibition in school depicts work done by pupils on their previous visits to Weiskirchen in the Saarland area of Germany and Dieppe. Also displayed were nineteenth and twentieth century German paintings. Mr Noel Brannan, teacher of art and European studies at South Wigston had included German wood carving and German jewellery to the display.

Again the year ended with carols by candlelight.

January 1978 once again was filled with various meetings with the Headmaster including liaison meetings with fellow Heads of the local schools. The first Parent Teacher Association Health Evening took place.

Later in January discussions were held regarding converting a redundant cloakroom into a community room and a few days later Home Economics and Design Advisers had meetings with staff to draw up plans for the new Design Project.

The many visits to the school ended just before half term with Mr Derek Ogden, Head of the Statistical Research Department which involved the study and projections of numbers on rolls; and Mr Colin Selby, Her Majesty's Inspector of Schools.

It is significant to note here that twenty years on, (2008) Mr Derek Ogden is still very much part of the school's life in his role as Clerk to the Governors.

March of the new term saw Mr Norris acting as a tutor on an in- service training course for Heads of third years.

The Chairman of the Governors Mr Curtis

Mr Derek Ogden. Clerk to the Governors 2008

Weston and his wife celebrated their Golden Wedding in early April and the chief guest was Colonel Andrew Martin.

Later that month ATV made contact regarding the boy impersonator, Paul Harkins, who had previously participated in Chris Tarrant's programme 'Tis Was'.

A party of science teachers from King Richard 111 School visited South Wigston High School in May to observe the teaching methodology in the Science Department.

A party of pupils accompanied by staff from the Music Department enjoyed visiting the Boosey and Hawkes factory in London.

Mr A J Davis, Deputy Director of Education attended the summer concert. The orchestra was conducted by Mrs Ann Gosling and the handbell ringers by Mr Gordon Oliffe.

12 June began the Activities Week. This was a week when the normal timetable was suspended. A party of forty children accompanied by four staff members visited Weiskirchen once again in Germany. Others enjoyed an evening at Beaumanor Hall where they saw a demonstration of percussion and heard a talk given by James Blades the famous percussionist. Jimmy Blades was famed as the man who banged the gong at the beginning of J Arthur Rank Films.

A week later two Modern Language Advisers, David Smith and Sam Muir, spent the week teaching in the school.

The Warnock Report on Special Education in 1978 in England, Scotland and Wales was the biggest ever investigation into special education in these countries. For the first time it put the issue of integration of disabled children in ordinary schools on to a national agenda. The report created a turning point in public and professional opinion, saying that parents of disabled children had vital information about their offspring that must be incorporated and used in the assessment, placement and educational process.

Looking back Mr Norris put his thoughts into words when he wrote the following, *'the success of a High School in The Leicestershire Plan would be assessed according to the rate of transfer of pupils to the Upper School. I suppose therefore that we can regard ourselves as being reasonably successful. I am not sure that the school is better. It is our experience that the higher the rate of transfer is, the harder is the core that remains. Our Fourth year may be smaller but the pupils in it, often socially deprived and lacking parental backing very much miss the beneficial influence of the rest of their age group. Young people learn more from one another than from their elders. Once the rate of transfer exceeds the rate of 55% all should be compulsorily transferred so that a recalcitrant remnant is not formed. I foresaw this possibility some years ago and expected that we should just manage to avoid problems at South Wigston because the raising of the school leaving age would bring about a complete transfer at fourteen plus and so give the 'weaker' pupils the continued support of their fellows. Because of the way we are organised in Leicestershire the deferment of the raising of the school leaving age may well have unfortunate results in some cases. I do not wish to convey the idea that, because we have been 'successful' at fourteen plus, the Fourth year is composed of layabouts and hoodlums.*

Realising that our pupils will be out at work a year earlier than many others we have tried to organise courses to enable them to mature one year earlier than would otherwise be the case. Working groups are smaller usually twelve to fifteen, and the most experienced teachers are in charge. With just a few notorious exceptions we have managed very well in our Fourth year.

Between 1960 and 1967 we had one class in each year for about twelve really backward pupils. The other pupils were divided into two bands - half being academic with good or reasonable GCE prospects, and the other half non - academic looking more towards CSE or no exam at all. In the first year there was some measure of transfer between the bands but not much in the second year.

The academic Band (A) usually for some times five classes was streamed and the non-academic (B), unstreamed (four or three classes). Generally Band A was taught by specialists and Band B by form teachers some of whom used modern class organisation with individual learning, rather than class teaching patterns, and subject integration at times. This (B) Band idea eliminated (C) forms of low morale. The 'A' Band always had classes of thirty plus and the 'B' Band classes of twenty five plus and we feel confident that by the time decisions had to be taken in the third year about Guthlaxton courses, pupils and parents, could do so without much anxiety and misgiving.

In 1967 we unstreamed the first year except for a very small retarded class and arranged sets in English, History, Geography, French, Science and Maths, all with specialist teaching. It is interesting to note that of two hundred and fifty pupils only seven were in the top set for everything and only six in the lowest set. As we could not set eight classes simultaneously they were divided into two bands of four each. This setting has meant, of course, simultaneous teaching of one subject to four classes and as subject rooms have been grouped together whenever possible there have been team teaching experiments in some departments. Although there is close understanding between different departments there has been no crossing of subject boundaries. These arrangements have continued into the second year.

In 1968 we admitted ten first year classes plus a remedial class. As we were unable to split these into two bands because of staffing and timetabling difficulties, we have grouped two, three or four classes together for most subjects so that if Heads of Department agreed there could be setting in each subject within the groups of classes. As classes were by no means as homogeneous as they would be in a rigidly streamed school, simultaneous class teaching is not really possible. Pupils are increasingly being put on to work cards or individual projects, going at their own pace. In order to make this method possible we have acquired in the last year or two three overhead projectors, various copying, printing and duplicating machines, tape recorders, strip projectors, ear phones etcetera and they are all being well used. Partly to avoid loss of time moving about our large site between lessons and to allow more time at lessons once they begin, we have as often as possible put double or treble periods in the timetable. If one uses modern gadgets, (and we do very effectively) it is silly to spend the first ten minutes of forty setting them up and the last ten putting them away.

Looking back over ten years there has been a silent educational revolution. This has not been forced upon us by outsiders, nor can it be ascribed entirely to the Leicestershire Plan, although doubtless freedom from the pressure of external examinations has had a liberating effect. Nor is it the newcomers to the staff who have brought all the new ideas. It has come from the Heads of Departments who have been anxious to further comprehensive education in Leicestershire, giving each pupil the maximum opportunity to develop.

With this organisation we can by the end of the second year judge fairly well how pupils are likely to fare in the rest of the secondary course and are Third year work is more closely geared to Guthlaxton requirements and in parallel to the work in the other contributory High Schools. This is brought about by much joint consultation between High and Upper School staffs. We ask the Upper School to give us a frank assessment of our pupils in various subjects so that we can know where we fall short of reasonable standards and do something about it.

It may be that in my catchment area parents, even of obviously clever children, are tame and uncomplaining. It is a fact that over the years there have been very few who oppose comprehensive education or disagree with our methods. Their children have done well here and continue to do well at Guthlaxton. Our pupils who have removed to other areas and who have been recommended for 'grammar' schools by us have always been found places.

Incidentally, I have on the staff two 'old boys' both of whom came to the schools as Eleven Plus failures and who transferred to Guthlaxton at Fourteen Plus. One of them, Brian Bray, who hit the national headlines when he got his twelfth O Level at Guthlaxton is now our Head of Mathematics; the other Peter Bradbury is a first class handicrafts master. I think that the Leicestershire Plan is marvellous - or is it just comprehensive education that is marvellous? I have a quite unprovable 'hunch' that changing schools at fourteen plus gives a boy a much greater boost than merely moving from one year to another. I am not so sure about girls. They seem less adventurous than boys and reluctant 'to have a go at a new experience'.

Mrs Baker recalls that the A and B band system at South Wigston ended in 1978. The summer term ended on the last day of June.

Chapter Six
Enter The Ten Year Olds
(1978 - 1988)

The fifth decade in the school's history, commenced on 30 August 1978. The Headmaster's Log Book records that, at a pre-school staff meeting the previous day, newly appointed members of staff included:

Mrs E.Larkin   Head of Resources
Mrs S.Humby   English
Miss J.Smith   English
Mr P.Norton   Mathematics and Science
Miss N.Fisher   French
Mrs J.Murrell   French

On 29 September 1978 a dinner was held at Beaumanor Hall, Woodhouse, Leicestershire to celebrate twenty one years of the Leicestershire Plan. The Headmaster, Mr Graham Norris was responsible for the organisation of this prestigious event where the guests of honour were the Director of Education, Mr Andrew Fairbairn MC and his illustrious predecessor, Mr Stewart Mason CBE, the architect of the Leicestershire Plan, still referred to widely as the 'Mason Plan'.

Stewart Carlton Mason photographed at the celebratory dinner

The season of goodwill brought a series of problems in its wake. Extensive damage was caused to the school premises, over the Christmas and New Year closures, as a result of fire and flooding. On Christmas Day 1978 the Head Caretaker discovered

Musical accompaniment provided by a quartet consisting of Mrs Anne Gosling, Head of Music, South Wigston High School, the lead violinist on the left, and three peripatetic teachers

an intensive fire in Laboratory 16. The fire caused severe damage and three days later an external woodstore was completely destroyed in a second fire. In this instance it was thought to be the work of an intruder.

An entry in the Headmaster's Log Book recorded that there was widespread frost on 30 December followed by three to four inches of snow the following day and further severe frost (-8° centigrade). The main water pipes burst in five places above the Boys' gymnasium, on 2 January 1979, flooding the gym, dining hall and resources area. Despite all of these difficulties plus the maths huts being out of commission, due to a lack of fuel, the school reopened as planned on 4 January. Four days later the water pipes in the maths huts burst to add to the catalogue of disasters during an exceptionally severe winter period.

The school was saddened to receive the news of the death of the former Deputy Headmaster Mr Orson James Kind on 2 April 1979. He had retired in July 1951 and during the twenty-eight years of his retirement, he had regularly been seen by many of his former pupils and teaching colleagues watching county cricket matches at Grace Road, Leicester; the home of Leicestershire County Cricket Club. A real lover of the game he had also served as the Vice-

President of Blaby Road Methodist Church Cricket Club, South Wigston.

The death of Mr Kind severed another link in the chain with Bassett Street and the Blaby Road Intermediate Schools where he had taught with distinction and had fired the imagination of many schoolboys with his unique and fascinating teaching of science using a range of experimental modules.

The school's high tradition in musical achievement reached a further peak on 3 April 1979 when the handbell ringers played in front of a large audience at Leicester's de Montfort Hall. The pupils had been taught by Mr Gordon Oliffe, the Head of the school's Remedial and Diagnostic Department and they consisted of boys from his class. They performed an original composition by the British composer Douglas Young with the Leicestershire Schools' Symphony Orchestra.

Douglas Young won the composition scholarship to the Royal School of Music, London (1966-70) and continued postgraduate studies with Milner and Pousseur. He won the Karl Ranke Prize for orchestral composition in 1970 by which time he was working professionally as a freelance composer.

He was the composer in residence at Guthlaxton College for the High Schools in the Wigston area. He spent a good deal of time at the schools and in particular, at South Wigston High School preparing the pupils for this prestigious musical occasion. The entire concert was filmed by BBC Television and excerpts were shown on the Nationwide programme on 21 May 1979.

Lorraine Ellen Yates, nee Davis, commenced as a pupil at the school in 1979. She was the daughter of Lance Davis and a niece of Roy and Keith Davis all of whom had attended the school following their arrival in the United Kingdom, from Australia, immediately before the outbreak of the Second World War.

One of her vivid memories was attending the 'French Club' which was held at the school, during lunch time, once a week. French traditions, food and use of the language all featured at the club.

Lorraine left South Wigston High School to go to Guthlaxton College in 1983. After completing her education at Guthlaxton, when aged 16 years, she worked for the Midland Bank (later HSBC), firstly at the Blaby branch and then at the Granby Street branch in Leicester, where one of her colleagues was

Lorraine Ellen Yates, nee Davis pictured in 2006

Martin Johnson the Leicester Tigers star who went on to captain the successful England Rugby team when they defeated Australia 20 - 17 in the 2003 World Cup Final.

After working for the bank for 19 years, Lorraine left in 2004 when she had her first child and now has three children.

Eleven Belgian Head Teachers made a second visit to the school on 2 November 1979. The occasion was notable in the sense that the visitors brought with them a copy of the South Wigston High School induction booklet which had been translated into the Belgian language and introduced into the Pope Piux XIX School in Antwerp where it was being successfully used by new pupils.

Gardens, trees and playing fields had always featured prominently in the life of the school and their importance was borne out in the spring of 1980. On 7 February, BBC Radio Leicester broadcast their 'Down to Earth' programme from the school. Before the month was out the Headmaster was visited by Mr Summerfield, an Assistant Director of Education, from County Hall, in order to show the Head the plans for the proposed development of the school's playing fields. Mr Norris pointed out that the land, earmarked for sale, included two of the best rugby pitches in Leicestershire! Despite the protestations of the Headmaster the Leicestershire County Council went ahead and the result was the

Part of the 1980s Pippins housing development
built on the playing fields

encroachment of a private housing development
built on the lower section of the playing fields
adjacent to the Grand Union Canal. The revered
rugby pitches were lost for ever.

The ravages of Dutch Elm Disease took its toll
on some of the fine trees in the school grounds. On
20 March 1980 a number of young trees were
planted by the pupils and technical services staff as
replacements for the Elms lost to the disease. The
children raised over £100 to help to pay for the
replacement trees.

During the spring term of 1980 a presentation
called 'Smirk' - an adaptation of Charles Dicken's
Nicholas Nickleby was performed by pupils studying
music and drama. Two performances were given and
one of the clarinet players was Gail Herbert. She
lived at Glen Parva and over the years followed the
pattern of many families having several members
attending the school. Five members were pupils of
the school, Gail's mother Valerie nee Mathers,
attended in the 1950s to be followed by her four
children, Mark, Gail, Jane and Jeremy.

A further change in the Headship of the school
became apparent when it was announced, on 30 June
1980, that Mr Graham Norris had been appointed to
become the new Principal of Guthlaxton College,
Wigston in succession to the Reverend Arthur
Watthey. The appointment was to take effect from
April 1981.

A notable visit by the South Wigston High School
Orchestra to Weiskirchen situated in the Saarland in
Western Germany took place between 31 May and
6 June 1980. A report of the visit was prepared by
Mrs Anne Gosling, the school's Head of Music who
recorded, in engaging detail, the events of a
memorable week spent in the Rhineland. Clearly, the
musical tradition of the school continued to be

nurtured and developed as Anne Gosling's account
of the visit reveals:

Orchestra Course in Weiskirchen, 31st May - 6th June 1980

*Following the success of the first three day orchestra
course in Tur Langton, it seemed appropriate if a
little ambitious, to extend our horizons and attempt
a similar course abroad in Germany. There had been
several very successful visits to Weiskirchen in the
Saarland by South Wigston High School and this
year we hoped to shift the emphasis to music by
sharing several informal concerts with the local
German Secondary schools. Any apprehension on
the part of the musicians (and staff!) was very soon
dispelled following our first concert and the week
gathered momentum rapidly. We still sometimes
muse in awe at the warmth of the receptions,
enthusiasm of the audiences and friendliness of our
host families. The only real problem seemed to be a
shortage of encore pieces!*

*Our itinerary, on reflection, seems daunting!
Three concerts in five days – one day's sightseeing
down the Rhine Valley – visits to the towns of
Saarbrucken and Neunkirchen, as well as time spent
in our local village, two excursions to the finely
equipped local swimming pool and a fascinating
afternoon spent at the Bell Foundry.*

*Weiskirchen, although no more than a village,
offered us much insight into typical German lifestyle
and we learnt much about their everyday working
pattern from our walks. Of course, the scenery of the
Rhineland lived up to the tourists' guides and was
truly 'breath-taking and spectacular' as it is so often
described. We felt fulfilled and exhausted at the end
of our day, having absorbed this busy river with its
surrounding rolling vineyards, noble castles and
frenetic trading traffic. Imagine our joy at stumbling
over a Beer Festival at Boppard, and an
inexhaustible repertoire of Sousa and Strauss
marches! The Bell Foundry visit was yet another
occasion when our musical links became a three-
way dialogue developed between the foundry guide,
the translator and the children! It would be difficult
to assess who learnt the most that afternoon!*

*After only a few hours in the Centre we had
begun to formulate a routine, and as our practices
were vital to the musical success of the week, we
soon established a timetable making use of the very
excellent facilities there. Herr Glauben (the warden)*

warmed noticeably during our invasion and his reaction ranged from guarded reserve and tolerance to enthusiasm and delight! It was gratifying that he was so complimentary about the children's behaviour and approach to their daily duties. The children responded in turn by making intelligent use of the table-tennis, football and other games facilities.

Although the week was full of exciting and rewarding experiences, few of us would question that it was highlighted by the three concerts we gave in German schools of the Saarland. Our audiences were more than enthusiastic and showered the children generously with gifts and delicious gastronomic delights. They were proud to escort our youngsters around their home towns and our children in turn revelled in the opportunities offered and undoubtedly returned enriched to England.

South Wigston High School orchestra may not have equalled the B.B.C. Symphony on tour, but in the best eclectic manner we beat them in resourcefulness! Although we left Leicester with 14 string and 20 wind players, this also included much 'doubling' as recorder and guitar players, soloists and singers emerged.

We offered programmes ranging from Classical String Quartets and Wind Ensembles to Baroque music in the Recorder Ensemble and light Pop in the orchestral pieces (from 'Z cars' to 'El Condor Pasa'). By taking our own translations of programmes and an Introduction to our school and its orchestra, we found the children and staff of the German schools quick to warm to us.

We ended our work at Dudweiler School and the final day was a more than fitting close! We played in an enormous Concert Hall (that could only be likened to a Roman Ampitheatre) to an audience of nearly 1000 and followed this by a champagne reception. The weather was radiantly hot and we celebrated the end of a rewarding and enjoyable week by swimming in the nearby lakeside yachting marina!

Anne Gosling 1980

The Academic Year 1980-81 commenced on 27 August 1980 with 644 pupils on the roll. Several new members of staff were welcomed to the school and at 3.35pm, on the first day of the autumn term, the customary tea party for newly appointed staff took place.

A further change in the composition of the senior staff occurred on 14 November when it was announced that Mrs Carole Jackson, Deputy Head Teacher had been appointed to the Headship of Limehurst Girls' High School at Loughborough, Leicestershire.

Pupils and staff had remained in suspense for over seven months pondering and speculating who was to be the new Headmaster in succession to Mr Norris. On 6 February 1981 the candidates for the Headship attended the school for a pre-interview visit. One can imagine the unofficial assessment of the candidates being carried out under the gaze of hundreds of pairs of prying eyes as their every step was followed, evaluated and discussed by the pupils.

Three days later, on 9 February, Mr Eric Bothamley, Senior Master at Leysland High School, Countesthorpe, Leicestershire was appointed as the new Headmaster of South Wigston High School. The appointment was to take effect from the commencement of the summer term 1981.

Born in Gedney, South Lincolnshire in 1942, Mr Bothamley attended school in Spalding. He obtained his qualification at the Teacher Training College at Scraptoft, Leicester prior to taking up his first appointment at Ilford, Essex where he taught mathematics and physics and became Head of the Maths Department.

He then obtained a position at Rothwell in Northamptonshire before coming to Leicester to the newly-built Leysland High School, situated adjacent to the controversial Countesthorpe College, where he was to spend the next eight years.

School numbers were dropping by this time due to fewer children having been born in the South Wigston area and other parts of the county during the previous decade. The seriousness of the problem was reflected, in the setting-up, by the Leicestershire County Council Education Committee of a 'Falling Rolls Working Party' which met on a regular basis and was attended by the Headmaster as the representative of South Wigston High School.

Early 1981 was marked by the 'comings and goings' at senior level in the school hierarchy. Firstly, on 25 February, Mrs Ann Hinchliffe, a tutor from Brookvale High School, Groby, Leicestershire was appointed to the Deputy Headship. Then came the departure of the Headmaster. Mr Norris said 'farewell' to the pupils and staff on 10 April upon leaving to take up his appointment as Principal of Guthlaxton College with effect from 27 April 1981.

Graham Norris was appropriately honoured and serenaded before leaving the school on the evening of 25 April with a music medley "Eine Kleine Norrismusik" presented by the pupils. The programme, for the concert, contained the following tribute, on behalf of the Music Department by Ann Gosling:

Eine Kleine Norrismusik

This evening's musical "pot-pourri" is presented by way of a tribute and vote of thanks to Graham Norris. Whilst the Music Department is by no means the only area in school which has expanded and flourished in the last 6 years, we feel particularly indebted for the support and guidance he has given to our work. (Tchaikovsky was not alone in his dependence upon his patron for encouragement and survival!)

Several generations of South Wigston High School musicians are combining this evening in mixed mood of sadness and optimism as we share with Graham Norris our feelings of "ever onward". Perhaps these words of James Russell Lowell are appropriate as our final dedication:

"New occasions teach new duties;
time makes ancient good uncouth;
They must upward still and onward,
Who would keep abreast of Truth".

Anne Gosling
March 1981

The programme consisted of items performed by the Madrigal Group, the Handbell Ringers, the Clarinet Trio and the Brass Group.

Mr Norris had been at the helm at South Wigston High School for exactly seven years. During and following his years at South Wigston, Graham Norris served on the Board of Visitors at Glen Parva Young Offenders Centre. For fourteen years he was a member and Chairman of the Board representing Board members of The Parole Committee and chairing Adjudication Panels. Representation on various committees and governing bodies gave him a wider understanding of the workings of the Leicestershire County Education Committee and the opportunity to build personal contact with the people who would support the development of the school.

Several boys from the school became local heroes when they rescued a six-year old boy from drowning in floodwater. The *Oadby and Wigston News* (1 May 1981) reported that quick thinking by the pupils saved the life of Shaun Halford who had been attracted by the floods at Crow Mills, South Wigston and had fallen into the surging torrent.

The three boys concerned were Andrew Lewin (12) of Arnold Avenue and his friends Scott Merrican (12) of Kirkdale Road, South Wigston and Phillip Allen (14) who responded to the boy's cries when he was sucked into a brick culvert and disappeared. They immediately rushed to the other side of the culvert which fed into the River Sense. Shaun managed to keep afloat by virtue of his anorak, the hood of which was grabbed by Andrew and Scott managed to pull him out of the water.

(Leicester Mercury)

Crow Mills Bridge, Countesthorpe Road, South Wigston

The boys then took the fortunate young Shaun home to his worried parents in Lansdowne Grove who had been out searching in the local vicinity for him. The reason for the presence of the boys at Crow Mills was a noble one, they had gone there to see if they could assist in pushing out cars which had become stranded in the floodwater.

The commencement of the summer term 1981 was marked by the arrival of the new Headmaster, Mr Eric Duncan Bothamley. Although there were 640 pupils on the registers, at the time, the worrying demographic downturn resulted in projections of pupils at South Wigston High School ultimately falling to an unsustainable level of 320 children. Clearly Mr Bothamley had a major problem to face at the commencement of his Headship.

At the meeting of the County Education Committee, on 28 July 1981, Mr Andrew Fairbairn, the Director of Education presented a report to his committee entitled: The Education Act 1980: Admissions to Schools.

The 1980 Act was piloted through the House of Commons by Mark (later Lord) Carlisle, the Secretary of State for Education and Science in Margaret Thatcher's first administration. The legislation contained some new ideas in the field of education.

The principal provisions of the Act covered seven major areas of the education service:

School Government
Admission to Schools
School Attendance Orders
Establishment, Discontinuance
and Alteration of Schools
Awards and Grants
School Meals
Nursery Education

Andrew Fairbairn informed his Committee: "The Education Act 1980 will undoubtedly come to be seen as one of the most important and far reaching pieces of Government legislation about education since the Education Act 1944."

Under Section 6 of the Act - Admission to Schools, all Education Authorities were required to make arrangements for enabling parents of children in their area to express a preference as to the school they wished their children to attend and for parents to give reasons for their preferences. Thus a major area of change – parental preferences, affecting the admission of pupils to primary and secondary schools, was now the way forward.

Once again South Wigston High School would be called upon to face new challenges in the wake of the legislation. The complexities and logistics associated with changing catchment areas were well-known to the school but parental preferences in relation to the allocation of school places represented a significant new development.

The Act also clarified the designation of School Governors. Under the Education Act 1944 they were known as Managers but in practise they were designated as Managers or Governors in various parts of the country. The 1980 Act stipulated that henceforth Governors should be the term used throughout England and Wales. This had, in fact, been the case at South Wigston for a number of years.

At the conclusion of the summer term 1981, Mr Ronald Griffiths, the conscientious and well-respected French teacher retired after spending a quarter of a century at the school. His time at South Wigston High School spanned the period September 1956 to August 1981. His expressions of gratitude, upon leaving, clearly indicated the feelings of a master who had derived ultimate job satisfaction and a real sense of pleasure in the companionship of his colleagues at all levels:

"My sincere thanks to all who have been so kind and friendly over the years – our dinner ladies, caretakers, secretaries, resources ladies, fellow teachers and Heads and also the families whom I have got to know in that time. Thanks for making mine an interesting and rewarding job and helping me to get on with it."

The ravages of winter came early in 1981 when, on 14 December, the Head Caretaker, Mr Atkins reported that water from burst pipes had flooded the art room, the top corridor of the west side and the adjacent staircases.

As two major staircases and seven classrooms were out of use it was necessary for the school to close for one day. The staff attended as usual and supervised and served hot lunches to all pupils who hadn't heard the message on the local radio, that the school was closed and had turned up as usual. By lunch time the caretaking, teaching and ground staff had moved all items of stock and cleared and dried the floors. At 2.00pm the library ceiling collapsed, however the stock of books and furniture were quickly removed. Although the floor was ankle-deep in water remarkably only five books were damaged.

'Open Evenings' at the school were considered to be important and one such evening, held in April 1982, featured in the *Leicester Mercury* (23.4.1982).

The thorny question of a falling roll and the long-term future of the school was addressed by Mr Bothamley early in 1982. An article in the *Oadby and Wigston News* in the spring had appeared under the heading 'Four Plus/Ten Plus' and had reported that: 'The idea of sending 4 year olds to Primary Schools and 10 year olds to High Schools in Oadby and Wigston was devised in 1980 because of falling rolls'.

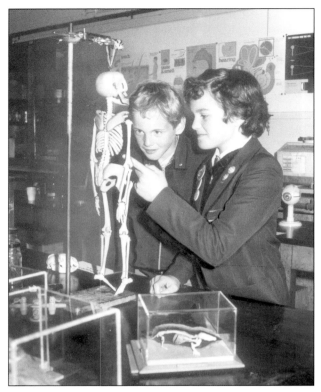

Dawn Adams of 70 Little Glen Road, Glen Parva a pupil of South Wigston High School showing her brother Matthew one of the projects in the laboratory during the school's open evening. Matthew is leaving his own school soon and will be joining his sister at South Wigston High. (Leicester Mercury)

On 6 May 1982 the Headmaster wrote to all parents. In his letter he detailed succinctly the case for change.

Headmaster: South Wigston High School
E D Bothamley   St. Thomas' Road
                          South Wigston

                          6 May 1982

Four plus, ten plus (School re-organisation)

You must have read about school re-organisation in the local press? This year in Oadby pupils will go to their High Schools at 10 years +, that is after three years in the Junior section of the Primary School. In addition to this, other parents will have the chance to start their children at Primary School earlier, at 4 years +.

It is planned that this scheme could be introduced into the Wigston area next year, that is to say, Autumn Term 1983.

*This is only part of a long standing plan for reorganising **all** County High Schools and Primary Schools as and when it is possible to do so.*

Why is it possible to reorganise the South Wigston area now? Because we have fewer pupils in

our schools, for during the past twelve years or so in this area, fewer children have been born. This means that there is now room in this High School for an extra year without expensive extra buildings.

It is argued that children are maturing early, and would benefit from starting specialised education in a High School a year earlier. There are many facilities here that most Primary Schools cannot provide, e.g. Science Labs, French Rooms, Computers, Gymnasia, Music Block, Orchestra and Craft Rooms.

A reorganised High School would have a year base staffed by teachers trained to teach top Primary children. Here the youngsters would do Maths, English and Humanities in their own classrooms so that they would only have to move around the school about half as much as the older children. At South Wigston High School we are specially lucky because we have two playgrounds and two dining halls. These would enable us to make sure that young ten year olds were not overawed by their thirteen year old brothers and sisters !

I am explaining this to you all in some detail because later in the term the Director and his officers will be meeting with parents of Primary School children to explain the system to them. Regrettably money is very tight these days and circumstances are not ideal. In three years time if we don't reorganise there will only be enough children 11-13 years old in Wigston to nicely fill two high schools. In those circumstances it would be a considerable saving to shut down one High School completely. As we have the oldest building, and are the only high school not on the Guthlaxton Campus, we at South Wigston High School naturally feel extremely vulnerable.

All of my staff believe in the four year high school. All of them would like reorganisation to be discussed, argued and won on its educational merits alone. However we cannot forget that if we don't get 10+ reorganisation the fifty years of excellent education at South Wigston High School may soon be just a fond memory and another part of our vanishing heritage.

E.D.Bothamley

Christine Kenny, who initially taught General Subjects and later Special Needs Children recalls that the school was under threat of closure unless 10+ was brought in. All of the staff attended a meeting at Guthlaxton College and it was a very unsettling time for everyone concerned.

Following consultation at the Wigston Schools on "thinner" registers a further article appeared in the *Oadby and Wigston News* on 6 July 1982 headed 'Now Wigston Schools Join Classroom Revolution'. The front-page item described how, following consultation meetings, the Governors were very supportive provided the resources could be made available.

It was at this point, that the Leicestershire County Council Education Committee gave approval for the Wigston scheme to go ahead. A report by the Director of Education, Mr Andrew Fairbairn, to his Committee, stated that the overwhelming view to emerge from a series of public meetings on the subject was that people felt that the Four Plus/Ten Plus scheme should be introduced in the Wigston area. The planned changes were scheduled to be introduced from the autumn term of 1983 onwards.

In the case of South Wigston High School although it was hoped the new scheme would commence in August 1983, significant alterations to the building were required in order to create the new Base for Ten + pupils as envisaged by the Headmaster and his staff. In the event it would be the beginning of the Academic Year 1984-85 before the plan could be implemented.

In November 1982 all First Year pupils went on a residential trip to Quorn Hall, Leicestershire, this scheme had a major impact on the life of school for two weeks. Mr Michael Booth, mathematics teacher was responsible for this pioneering venture. In a short report in *South Wigston High School: The First Fifty Years* mention was made that: "The scheme even merited a mention in the local press! More importantly the idea roused interest in the educational world. An exhibition of work our pupils did there is currently on show at Beaumanor Hall, Woodhouse. We have also received several requests from teachers at other schools to copy the lessons and worksheets our staff devised and wrote prior to the visit." Thanks were recorded to Mr Booth for his innovative work.

On Valentine's Day 1983 Mr Edward Thomas,

acting Deputy Headmaster and his wife Margaret endured what must have seemed like the least romantic day of their marriage. Ted had to drive, through the snow to Dover en route to an art college in Normandy whilst his wife had to cope with a lack of central heating, due to a defective boiler in addition to the care of their three sons.

Mr Thomas had been given a year's sabbatical as a result of a scheme introduced by Prime Minister Margaret Thatcher known as 'Teachers' Renewal'. Andrew Fairbairn saw it as an inspirational idea and the Deputy Head was on his way. Whilst in France he sketched the Manoir d'Ango near to Dieppe which in due course he showed to the Director of Education who was suitably impressed with his work.

The sketch by Mr Thomas of the Manoir d'Ango

On 24 February 1983 the Governors, staff and pupils received, with great sadness the news of the death of Mr Robert Curtis Weston who had been Chairman of the Governors from 1957 until November 1982.

'Curtis', as he was known to all his friends, was a native of South Wigston who had served as a corporal in the Seaforth Highlanders on the Western Front in the First World War and as a sergeant in the Home Guard in the Second World War. He developed a successful building and undertaking business in the locality and entered the local political scene in 1947 when he was elected as a Liberal councillor for the Bassett Ward in South Wigston. During a thirty year period he was the Chairman of the former Wigston Urban District Council in 1955-56 and again in 1964-65. He became a County Councillor in 1955 and was created an Alderman in 1970.

Curtis Weston proudly marching in a Remembrance Day Parade in South Wigston

His involvement in local affairs and his service with many organisations was legendary and he had a keen interest in Social Services and Education which occupied a great deal of his time following his election to the Leicestershire County Council. Local schools owed much to his enthusiastic commitment and his renowned personal touch with pupils for whom he made time to stop and speak to. He had been a Governor of five schools in Wigston and South Wigston and had only retired as the Chairman of the Governors of South Wigston High School on his admission to hospital three weeks before his death at the age of eighty four years.

Curtis Weston had been a great servant to the community of South Wigston and had made an outstanding contribution to the work of the school and to education generally.

The sadness, throughout the school, was compounded with an announcement at a Governors' Meeting, held on 9 June 1983 by the new Chairperson Mrs Primrose Wray that the deaths had occurred of Mr Ronald Baker, Head of Science and the former Headmaster Mr Mark Rutherford. The Governors observed a minute's silence in remembrance.

Sadly, Mr Baker's health had deteriorated and he died suddenly on 6 March 1983. The following year on 27 June 1984 their son Daniel was killed in a motorway accident. Mrs Baker and her other son Ian

still grieving for the loss of Mr Baker were devastated. Mrs Baker paid tribute to the outstanding support, care and kindness she received, during the heartbreaking years from the Headmaster, Mr Bothamley, the staff especially close friends in the Humanities Department, Mrs Larkin and Mrs Kenney also the pupils and their parents. The 'family' at South Wigston High School sought to show their respect for a popular teacher who had died prematurely and their love and concern for Mrs Baker in the noblest traditions of a caring school.

The passing of the school's longest serving Headmaster also caused sorrow amongst teaching staff and former pupils. In a tribute to Mark Rutherford in the *Oadby and Wigston News* (3 June 1983) mention was made of his deep involvement, during his Headship 1952-1974 in the Mason Plan – the reorganisation of secondary education which was the forerunner of comprehensive education. The report also stated: "He was a long-serving member of the Leicester Society of Friends (Quakers), was actively involved in several community groups and was Secretary of the Leicestershire Head Teachers' Association for a number of years."

The long-awaited commencement of the preparations for the Four Plus/Ten Plus reorganisation finally got underway. The school records show that on 12 December 1983 it was reported that: "Work will start early next term on adaptations for the 10+ Base, new Science and new Design facilities. This will mean some inconvenience because of workmen on the premises."

Teacher Christine Kenney recalls that part of the school was converted to a 10+ Base (open plan) to bridge the change from Junior to Senior School.

A great deal of advance preparation, by the teaching staff, was called for and the necessary building work caused degrees of disruption throughout the school. Finally South Wigston High School was geared to take pupils from 10 to 14 years of age.

An article appeared in the *Leicester Mercury* (31 August 1984) which explained that the Four Plus/Ten Plus education scheme: "Swing into action in South Wigston this week - but only gradually for the four year olds. 180 ten year old children commenced their secondary education at South Wigston High School on the first day of term and

It was a smooth start for the 180 ten year olds at South Wigston High School some of whom are pictured here with a teacher Mr Brian Riorden (Leicester Mercury)

they were accommodated in existing buildings which had been specially adapted for the newcomers."

A photograph of some of the first ten year olds to attend the school appeared in the *Leicester Mercury*.

A splendid account of the setting-up of the Ten Plus Base was provided by Jane Collins and appeared in *South Wigston High School: The First 50 Years*. It is reproduced here in view of its fascinating contents and its historical significance.

Ten Plus

By the time the first ten-year olds made their appearance at South Wigston in September 1984, many gains for the school were already obvious. The large open-plan area had been re-decorated in a bright and cheerful style with fire-engine red paintwork and candy-stripe curtains to match. The former stark secondary modern corridors were conspicuously absent and the new wall-to-wall carpet and lowered ceilings had radically changed the atmosphere. The nearly 200 blue-blazered pupils who arrived quickly brought the place to life with a buzz of energy and enthusiasm. The team of Base teachers brought dedication and a sense of purpose in equal measure. The Base Team were for the most part newly-appointed, with the important exception

of two senior members of staff who shared with the new Head of 10+ the joint leadership of the Base, and a Special Needs Teacher soon to take an "ordinary" class of her own. The Base acknowledges both good primary and secondary practice; 10+ pupils spend half their week in the Base and are taught by their Form Tutor. Their work is organised as an integrated day. The 11+ pupils return to the Base for half of their week and meet their former Form Tutors now as specialist teachers of English, maths and humanities. At any time either the whole of the 10+ Year or 11+ Year is in the Base. The teaching is well-paced and lively. Parents had been told that those who came to the High School at ten would be advantaged by learning in an environment which gave them the security of a primary school but also specialist teaching in some areas. There is no doubt that the benefits for these pupils, but also for the school as a whole, have been incremental in nature, and extend now to every area.

Jane Collins

The teaching of the new younger pupils in an environment which gave them the security of a primary school together with some specialised subject learning, was of real benefit to them and confirmed the rationale defined by the Headmaster

Ten Plus pupils working in the newly-created Base

in his letter to all of the parents involved.

Having overseen the introduction of the Four Plus/Ten Plus schools reorganisation in Leicestershire, Andrew Fairbairn the Director of Education retired on 31 August 1984. He served Leicestershire County Council for twenty three years of which the final thirteen years (1971-1984) he was the Director of Education. He introduced many initiatives which put Leicestershire firmly on the educational map nationally.

A firm advocate of the abandonment of the 11 plus examination, because of his concern for children who were caused distress by the selection process, he successfully implemented the introduction of the High Schools and Upper Schools system throughout Leicestershire. The very ethos of South Wigston High School owed much to the outgoing Director of Education.

A passionate music lover, Andrew Fairbairn was always supportive of developing the talents of pupils and endeavouring to ensure that the Leicestershire schools had sufficient financial resources for all pupils to have instrumental lessons. Walter Higgins in his autobiography *Well Wunted: A Leicestershire Lifetime* described his old boss as being: "An approachable man and most people found it easy to relax in his presence."

Andrew Fairbairn was succeeded as Director of Education for Leicestershire by Keith Wood-Allum, the Deputy County Education Officer for Northamptonshire who had previously served with the Lancashire and Derbyshire Education Authorities.

During the weekend 16-17 March 1985 burglars broke into the school and stole equipment worth £1,300. A report in the *Oadby and Wigston News* (22 March 1985) appeared under the heading "Head sickened by Burglary". Mr Bothamley gave details of the theft of two video recorders each worth £500, fifteen blank video tapes and a coloured television set. He stated that it was clear that the raiders knew exactly what they wanted and where to find it. They had gone prepared with a mallet and chisel and had chiselled around the back of an upstairs storeroom to get at the equipment.

The thieves also tried to steal computers but fortunately they had been locked in steel cabinets. The Headmaster said: "The thefts will cause some disruption to classes which rely on video programmes but it is particularly sickening that all the hard work of fund-raising by teachers and parents has been wiped out."

Nearby Guthlaxton College, in Wigston Magna, was also burgled during the same weekend. A television set and a video recorder altogether worth £800 were stolen. The thefts illustrated the targeting of school premises, by thieves, as the use of technological equipment became more widely used in the teaching of pupils.

Rugby football continued to be immensely popular at the school. In March 1985 the under 13 team reached the final of the Leicestershire Schools Championship. The following report of the match appeared in the *Oadby and Wigston News* (29 March 1985).

"Conversions count in Boys' Rugby Final"
South Wigston High School was defeated 40 - 20 by Hastings High School, Burbage in the final of the County Rugby Championship last week. Hastings scored seven tries six of which were converted, South Wigston scored five tries but none were converted."

Despite losing the under 13 Final, the school was successful during March 1985 in two other rugby competitions. Victory was secured in an eight team tournament at Lancaster Boys' School, Leicester

South Wigston High School Under 13 Team who represented the school in the County Final (Leicester Mercury)
Back row (left to right) Stuart Bozzini, Gary Siddon, Stuart Harding, Matthew Quinn, Paul Smith, Richard Johnson,
Jason Grant and Peter Atkins Front row (left to right) Carl Elsworthy, John Hassall, Dean Loach, Mark Palmer, Captain,
Robert Owen, David Gifford, Darren Lee and Nicky Morton

when South Wigston High School defeated Bushloe High School, Wigston Magna by 6 - 3 in the final.

In addition the school's first year team won the under 11 rugby tournament which took place at the Oadby/Wyggs ground by beating Manor High School, Oadby, Gartree High School, Oadby and Stokes Junior School, Blaby.

Success was also achieved off the sports field and in the area of technological learning. The school's representatives were the proud winners of the Leicestershire Schools' Technological Challenge Shield. The presentation of the award was reported in the *Leicester Mercury* (3 July 1985) together with a photograph to mark the event.

The shield was presented at the school's prize day, held the previous week, and Councillor Hughes also presented Special Merit Awards to Elizabeth Wright and Simon Arthar, both aged fourteen years.

Memories of the school in the 1980's are provided by Leon Taylor 1984-88. Cross country running on a cold winter's day around the area of the Grand Union Canal and Crow Mills are vividly recalled.

Also, playing football in the school yard with a plastic air-flow ball, a necessary precaution to minimise the risk of breaking classroom windows, however, 'kids would stuff them full of paper to make them heavier!'

Two wonderful school holidays are recalled. Firstly, in his second year, Leon and his fellow pupils spent a memorable time at a holiday camp in Cornwall, where they were involved in a range of activities including, fencing, abseiling and archery.

A second holiday took place in France in his final

Winners of the Leicestershire Schools' Technological Shield (Leicester Mercury) The winners holding their award: (left to right) Ruth Blackwell, Tim Osbourne, Simon Arthar and Paul Halley. On the left is the Headmaster, Mr Eric Bothamley. Presenting the prize was the Mayor of Oadby & Wigston, Councillor Roy Hughes

Vice's Bridge (No 93) on the Grand Union Canal at the rear of the school playing fields

year where canoeing and windsurfing, "while trying to balance on the board" were experienced. Leon painfully recalls a visit to a water park whilst in France, where he spent too long without his shirt on in the hot sunshine for which he suffered a badly burnt back.

An important development relating to the school and the safety of its pupils was featured in 'South Wigston High School: The First 50 Years'. The article read as follows:

26th June 1986
Mrs Featherby, with the help of the rest of the Parent Teacher Association, has masterminded our plans for a 'Pelican Crossing' outside school. We hope that the August County Council Meeting will grant the necessary authority for the work to go ahead.

The campaign proved to be successful and the crossing was installed in the Spring of 1987.

By the end of the Academic Year 1986-87 the number of pupils attending the school had risen dramatically. The creation of an extra year, as a result of the 10+ factor; had resulted in the school becoming full to overflowing. It was anticipated in June 1987 that the number on the roll for the following year would be 778. If that projection proved to be correct it would result in the school becoming the largest High School in Leicestershire in terms of pupil numbers.

There was a pressing need for an additional classroom, also the school library was quite inadequate in meeting the requirements of such a large number of pupils seeking library facilities. The decision was taken to convert one of the two dining halls into a library/resources area thus releasing the existing library to provide an additional classroom. Work on the new library commenced on 10 March 1988, the sum of £1500 which had been privately

raised was earmarked to be spent on the project.

During 1987 Kenneth Baker the Secretary of State for Education and Science in Margaret Thatcher's administration issued a pamphlet entitled *Working Together For A Better Future* in which he stated: 'If they are to look forward to a better future, our young people need to be better educated and trained for adult life. They must have a wide range of opportunities in education and training. They must also have information and guidance to allow them to make sound choices as they go through school and beyond'.

The Governors at South Wigston High School gave due consideration to the advice by the Secretary of State and the result was that training days for the teaching staff became the order of the day. This involved teachers coming into school for training sessions, to explore together aspects of their curriculum, when the school was closed on mid-term breaks etcetera. Not surprisingly the Staff Training Days became known, irreverently, as 'Baker Days!'.

A change in the Deputy Headship occurred in January 1988. Mr Edward Thomas was appointed in succession to Mrs Jane Collins who had been appointed Headteacher at Welland Park Community College, Market Harborough, a position she held until 31 December 1996.

By the spring of 1988 Claire Allen 3TD had emerged as a talented and competitive cross country runner. She regularly represented the County Schools and had come third in a National Competition. She had achieved the distinction of being ranked number one on paper, for her age group in the country. The *Oadby & Wigston Mail* (18 March 1988) gave prominence to Claire's progress as a cross-country runner when it was reported in the newspaper's Athletics Section that she had been selected to run for the England Cross-Country Team against Scotland on 26 March 1988. This marked thirteen year old Claire's international debut.

Another budding writer to emerge from the school was Paula Hunt, who in June 1988, was awarded second prize in the prestigious Rotary Club Essay Competition. She was given a guided tour of the *Leicester Mercury* offices; tea at the top of the building, a *Mercury* Goodie Bag and a £10 book token.

The year 1988 marked a national milestone in educational terms with the introduction, by the

Leon's Class of 1985 Back row: Stuart Taylor, Beverley Foster, Stephen Cowell, Lee Hutchinson, Simon Lock, Leon Taylor, Katy Mellor. Second row: Steven Kaubi, Nicholas Doyle, Rachel Seneschall, Leigh Busby, Andrew Thomas, Michael Cotterill, Richard Fewkes. Third row: Michelle Bray, Nicholas Flude, Samantha Pitcher, Lorraine Patterson,Clare Hand, Michelle Weeds, Emma Icke. Front row: Claire Ellis, Suzie Foreman, Graham Holland, Mr Trevor Hansome (Music Teacher), Emma Birchenall, Mark Groves and James Calow

Department of Education and Science of a common system of examinations at sixteen-plus implemented through the establishment of the General Certificate of Secondary Education.

The conclusion of the Academic Year 1987-88 marked the completion of fifty years of South Wigston High School. During the past half century the school had experienced many changes and had met the challenges of the post war era with fortitude and vigour. Everyone past and present - staff, pupils and parents could all take pride in the school's achievements and the celebrations to acknowledge fifty golden years could now begin.

Chapter Seven
Opt Out - Cash In
(1988 - 1998)

The new intake of pupils to South Wigston High School in August 1988 quickly became aware of the rather special significance attached to their date of entry as the Golden Jubilee anniversary celebrations got underway. The school, its buildings, history and traditions were to become a focal point in the locality and beyond in the months ahead.

Wednesday 31 August 1988 marked the day when fifty years earlier the first intake of school children to the Blaby Road Schools took place. Over the next three months the Head Teacher Mr Bothamley, and his staff devoted a great deal of their time in planning the Golden Jubilee Day celebrations to be held on Friday 25 November.

A special badge to mark the occasion was designed by Mr Edward Thomas, the Deputy Head Teacher, and this became the symbol of the event which Mr Bothamley was to describe as "50 exciting years."

The Golden Jubilee Badge

Meanwhile, events were being shaped at Westminster which would have a profound effect on the future of the schools across England and Wales. The passing of the Education Reform Act 1988, by the Conservative Government, heralded a number of fundamental changes to the educational system. Kenneth Baker, the Secretary of State for Education and Science, was responsible for the framing of the legislation and ensuring that it reached the statute book.

The Act, which was passed by Parliament on 29 July 1988, was an enormous piece of legislation which had taken up to 370 hours of parliamentary time – a post-war record – and contained 283 pages.

Part I, which covered 122 pages of the Act, introduced two fundamental areas of reform. Teaching in schools was to be given a new direction by the introduction of a basic National Curriculum which was defined in terms of foundation subjects, three of which were core subjects, English, mathematics and science. The other foundation subjects were history, geography, technology, music, art and physical education plus a modern foreign language, specified by the Secretary of State, in relation to third and fourth key stages.

The Act also included a requirement for religious education to be provided within the National Curriculum.

The 1988 Act also divided the school years into four sections to be known as Key Stages:

1st	Infant Age Range	(up to 7 years)
2nd	Junior Age Range	(up to 11 years)
3rd	First 3 Years of Secondary School	
		(up to 14 years)
4th	Last 2 Years of Secondary School	
		(up to 16 years)

The Act contained a provision for the making of arrangements for testing pupils at the end of each Key Stage.

Another important aspect of the Education Reform Act 1988 was for the introduction of a new type of school, a Grant-Maintained School, whereby a Local Education Authority school could opt out of LEA control to become directly funded by the Government through the Department of Education and Science.

The Palace of Westminster was not due to feature in the school's celebrations but the radical new legislation would certainly be instrumental in paving the way ahead. The Golden Jubilee year of South Wigston High School was to be remembered in more ways than one.

As the autumn term advanced, preparations to celebrate the Golden Jubilee of the school gathered momentum. In his Newsletter to parents (number 37) dated 12 October 1988, Mr Bothamley reported that there had been an excellent start to the school year. A portion of his letter was taken up with providing information to parents of the arrangements for the celebrations:

Golden Jubilee:
These are the finalised details of this celebration:
Wednesday 23 and Thursday 24 November
School Open Evenings 6-9pm. Past pupils will be welcomed to join the present generation of parents touring the school. They will note the many changes since they were here and admire the exhibitions of work designed to illustrate life over 50 exciting years!

During these Open Evenings we shall hold Music and Drama concerts in our school hall from 7.30 - 9pm. Clearly these will appeal mainly to present parents; Wednesday being drama, choir, bells and individual or small ensemble items. Thursday when our senior choir, orchestra and band perform. However, anyone with a ticket costing £1.50 will be admitted. They will be on sale from Mr Bray or by post from the school office.

Friday 25 November Jubilee Day
The Lord Lieutenant of our County, Col. Sir Andrew Martin has kindly agreed to chair our anniversary tea party exactly 50 years to the hour that his uncle and name-sake performed a similar honour. At this meeting our distinguished guests will be Sir John Farr MP, the Mayor of Oadby and Wigston, the Chair of Blaby District Council, and our own Director of Education together in thanking God for his past goodness, and anticipating a rewarding future here serving local young people.

The time from four to six will not be all spent in sipping tea, speeches and sandwiches. Entertainment will be provided by our award winning choir, championship band, past pupils in ensemble, and the outstanding Leicester Schools' Concert Band who have used our school as their home base for the past seven years.

Saturday 26 November 8 till late - Anniversary Dance
Grown-ups only! Pupils past, and parents present will dance, jive or jig to music from the last 50 years. Our PTA are organising this social event. Accommodation is limited and tickets are bound to be at a premium so do book the day now. Included in the cost £3.00 each are light refreshments, access to our own bar, and plenty of off street parking. Mrs Baxendale in Fabrics is selling the tickets, or by post from the school office.

A disappointment for the Head Teacher was the school's inability to continue to run the Ten Plus Base in the way he had envisaged and striven to accomplish. His letter to parents contained the following explanation of why it had become necessary to end the base system:

The End of an Era
'I write of the demise of the 10+ Base as we knew it. It is necessary to explain why our system changed after it was advertised at New Parents' Evenings.

Built as a six class unit, despite my presentations, we have struggled to make it work with seven classes right since it started. Soon we shall have eight classes coming in each year. So we had anticipated that next year, or the year after, we would have a radical reorganisation anyway.

All through last year I endeavoured to plan a time-table that would keep the base structure but allow setting in maths and science for the senior pupils. It became obvious that it could not be done. If setting came in, the base would have to go.

Then one of our key Junior style teachers returned to Primary Education for a good promotion. Another signalled his intention to follow suit (and was promoted to a Primary deputy headship only yesterday). It was clear that with the national shortage of primary teachers I couldn't expect to replace them with teachers of similar calibre – but I could with good secondary subject specialists.

Lastly we realised that a large number of the intake year would need extra support in their lessons, to be taught as they had been used to in their Primaries, if they were to stand any chance of maintaining their educational progress. So we had to beef up our remedial provision in maths, science, the humanities, French and English. I could not do that and run the old base system. So, in the end, after a lot of heart ache, it went!

With plans advanced for the Golden Jubilee celebrations, an article appeared in the *Oadby and Wigston Mail* (3 November 1988) under the heading 'Calling all former pupils'. In the article, Mr Bothamley said: "Our eldest pupils will be in their late 60's and we want them to come and look round as a nostalgia trip. A terrific amount has changed since they were at the school and it will be interesting for them to come and visit their old classrooms."

Friday 25 November 1988 was the day of the Golden Jubilee tea party at the school. The celebrations were opened by the Lord Lieutenant of Leicestershire, Colonel Sir Andrew Martin who expressed his delight that so many old pupils should have wanted to return to the school for the occasion.

The oldest guest was Miss Constance Wright, aged 94 years, the former Needlework teacher and Deputy Headmistress at both the Bassett Street Girls' School and the Blaby Road Girls' School when it opened in 1938. After tea she was able to visit her old classroom and commented: "Everything is very, very different."

In an article by Cyndy Elson in the *Oadby and Wigston Mail* (1 December 1988) Miss Wright said, "Changes have hit me in the eye but it is all in the name of progress and I accept it. I think co-education is natural. It is very nice to be back at the school, this is my first visit since I retired."

Miss Wright recalled life in the classroom during the Second World War. "When the siren sounded, I said, 'Down pens girls, stand in line by the door.' Nothing was out of place, the discipline was marvellous. Then we all filed down to the recreation ground."

A number of former colleagues attending the party remembered Miss Wright's renowned reputation as a disciplinarian. She was described, doubtlessly out of earshot, as being a formidable woman in her day and regarded as such not only by pupils but by staff alike!

Miss Wright had been retired for 26 years and continued to live in South Wigston where she resided with her cousin Miss Jennette Matilda Richard, a retired Matron. They shared a house together at 32 Leopold Street.

Philosophically, Head Teacher Mr Bothamley said, "I have learned this week that it is not just the fabric of the school that former pupils come to see, they want to know about their teachers. Like them, we have today a dedicated band of teachers generating the quality of education here for generations to come."

The only occurrence to mar the great day was an

Miss Constance Wright with her cousin Miss Richard, who is pictured left in the garden of 32 Leopold Street.

Past pupils from 1938, Mrs Rita Smith, Mrs Norah Butcher and Mrs Irene Taplin hear about computing from third year pupil Jonathan Sarson at one of the school's open evenings to celebrate the Golden Jubilee Anniversary (Leicester Mercury)

incident which took place on the morning of the Golden Jubilee when four South Wigston High School pupils, travelling on a school bus, were bitten by a dog which also bit the driver. Fortunately no-one was seriously injured. The incident happened on the Eyres Monsell Estate and was the subject of a police investigation.

The Fiftieth Anniversary tea party was a great success and an event enjoyed by all who attended, young and old alike. An indication of the pleasure felt by one of the principal guests is contained in the following letter, to Mr Bothamley, from Mr Keith Wood-Allum the Director for Leicestershire.

The interest of the school generated by the Golden Jubilee celebrations continued unabated. When arrangements were made for the school's carol concert in early December 1988, some 80 parents were expected to attend. In the event 380 parents accepted the invitations to attend. The staff had to rearrange the hall which should have been laid out with tables in casual groups to a more formal setting with rows of chairs in order to enable everyone to have a seat.

In the newsletter, Mr Bothamley referred to the car park attendants who: "Stand out in all weathers to help people park." As a mark of appreciation of

Letter from the Director of Education

their work he wrote a special note of thanks to them. The Head Teacher also thanked the Performing Arts Department and the Design Department for the work they had done and the manner in which they had contributed towards the school's Golden Jubilee celebrations.

Despite all the achievements and many congratulations, South Wigston High School, like any other school, had to address the unacceptable behaviour of some pupils. Writing in his Christmas newsletter to parents, Mr Bothamley urged parents to be on their guard following a spate of shoplifting. The Head's article contained the following:-

"The spate of shoplifting was finally pointed-up by a sharp eyed and caring mother.

We parents all need to be aware how easy it is for our own children to be led astray by their friends. These are days of keen pressures. Full marks to the security staff of Lewis' who put our lads through the hoop when I returned with them and the toys they had stolen.

They were lucky they weren't caught red-handed. They could have ended up in court.

Lesson to parents: Don't give your child a chance to go to town unsupervised."

The Head Teacher also reported that a pupil who had been at the school for only a week was expelled for stealing dinner ladies' monies.

The contents of Mr Bothamley's actions and warnings were reported in the *Oadby and Wigston Mail*, 5 January 1989.

The school's orchestra had another successful year in the regional Open Music Festival which was held at Oundle Public School, Peterborough, in April 1989. Schools competed from the Leicestershire, Northamptonshire and Peterborough areas.

First places were obtained in the under 15 instrumental duet, the grade four brass solo, the grade four woodwind solo, the grade five brass solo and by the school's under-14 Wind Band, Brass Ensemble and the Senior Choir. Mr Bothamley expressed his delight that the pupils had achieved so much. He said: "Their success showed up the strength of Leicestershire's visiting music teaching system and the solid foundations laid in local primary schools that the staff have been able to build on."

The Head promised that the general public would be given the opportunity to hear the school orchestra at the South Wigston Arts Festival on 20 and 21 June in the school hall.

Another success story occurred during April when Georgina Spencer, a thirteen year old third year pupil at the school, achieved the distinction of becoming Leicestershire's Young Cook of the Year. Georgina, who lived in Glen Parva, competed against three other contestants at the East Midlands Gas Board showroom in Market Street, Leicester.

The four entrants were required to make Derby cheese fingers and mushroom and watercress soup, emphasis centred upon presentation and they had to wash all the utensils afterwards. The judges awarded first prize to Georgina and she was presented with a

Colonel Sir Andrew St George Martin,
KCVO, OBE, LL D, JP

camera and a personal stereo.

In June 1989, the booklet *South Wigston High School: The First 50 Years*, was published. The booklet was the work of two teachers Michael Booth, who taught mathematics, and Claudine Fray, an English Teacher. The foreword was written by the Lord Lieutenant of Leicestershire, Colonel Sir Andrew Martin who clearly was delighted to undertake the task as his comments illustrate:

"*It gives me particular pleasure to be connected with this booklet which I strongly commend to all past and present members of this school.*

My late uncle, Lt. Col. Sir Robert Martin, was the Chairman of the County Council when the school was officially opened and he was present at the ceremony. He was Chairman of the County Council from 1925 to 1960. I was Lord-Lieutenant of the County from 1965 to April 1989 so our two appointments spanned the first fifty years of the School's life but for a small gap of five years between my uncle's appointment ending and mine beginning. It was therefore my great pleasure for my wife and me to share with the school its 50th Birthday on 25 November 1988. My family can thus claim to be a very small part of the history of the school. It is for us a privilege so to be.

My congratulations to everyone who has had a part in providing material for this booklet and in its production. It is a remarkable chronicle of the first fifty years of the school's life. Reading the booklet has brought back many memories of events both national and local. The pages contain many names and happenings whose recording is vital to an historical record. The choice of subject matter is very interesting and will give all those who read it who have been connected with the School a great deal of pleasure and amusement.

I wish everyone who has taught or been taught at School who reads this booklet the pleasure and satisfaction it has given me."

(Signed) R.A.St G Martin, Colonel
June 1989

A concluding article in *South Wigston: The First 50 Years*, was contributed by the Head Teacher under the heading The Next 50 Years. Mr Bothamley's overall assessment together with his sage comments make fascinating reading:

The Next 50 Years
Before I anticipate the changes and challenges to come, I would first like to thank Sir Andrew, Sir John and the many others who contributed to our anniversary celebration, which conclude with this souvenir publication.

Mr Michael Booth, the editor, particularly deserves to be given this special mention!

Throughout our brief history, the ages and ranges of academic abilities of the pupils that we have been directed to serve has changed often, as has the catchment areas where these young people have lived.

Demographic instability, fancies, and political expedients will doubtless oblige us to change in much the same way again in future decades!

There has however been much consistency in 50 years' educational service. Our current emphasis on academic excellence, propagating to traditional 'high' culture, and pride in diverse recreational achievements, would be very familiar to the staff and pupils who opened these schools. They would not be surprised to learn that we find it necessary to intervene in social and domestic disputes to safeguard children's good schooling; but I think they would be proud to anticipate that through our popularity, we are now possibly the largest school of our type in this Local Education Authority.

Three generations on, those pioneers would give thanks that our nation is no longer worried about invasion and war triggered by world powers; though they might be incredulous that we seem powerless against raving despots in the Middle East and Ireland whose pleasure would be to spread anarchy in our confusion.

Then they were confidently proud of being, undoubtedly, a major European power; now they must be disappointed that our standard of living is in many ways at a lower level than that of our continental cousins, (though quite immeasurably different in style).

They could not have anticipated then that in 1989, parallel with the rest of the country, a third of our pupils, 250+, would experience their parents' relationships being restructured, nor the expansion in Leicester's racial and cultural diversity.

We have much to learn from the people who have triumphed over adversity, who are not afraid of hard work, and who are prepared to make a practice of a high moral code!

We teaching-staff are determined to enable our pupils to compete successfully in the new inter-dependent European Community, to encourage them in practising a traditional morality and to assert that they should take a pride in building their part into the continuum of our English Heritage.

We face the future with confidence, but with much humility. For though we know that there will always be a place for a school like ours, we also know that teachers cannot achieve these demanding goals trusting in their own strengths alone.

(Signed) Eric Bothamley
19 June 1989

Crime prevention against schools, particularly vandalism and arson, was considered to be a serious issue in Leicestershire schools in 1989. In the previous year a lot of vandalism at schools cost £200,000 and arson a further £1.5 million. In order to address the problem a pilot scheme 'School Watch' was promoted by the South Leicester Crime Prevention Panel and involved 54 schools in the Wigston Police sub-division. The scheme which was designed to encourage pupils to take an active interest in crime prevention at their own schools, was launched at South Wigston High School in September 1989.

The Head Teacher, Mr Bothamley, gave his views to the *Oadby and Wigston Mail* (5 October 1989) when he said: "I welcome the initiative in my school, I have recently tried to get over the crime prevention message and can already see some effects. I hope we will be able to carry this further. Damage to and loss of school property can cause both financial and educational problems for schools."

Numbers of pupils attending the school were being well-maintained as a report by the Head Teacher, to a meeting of the School Governors, showed when on 31 January 1990 Mr Bothamley confirmed that the number of pupils on the roll was 789 and the teaching staff establishment was 42.

The culinary skills acquired and developed by pupils at South Wigston High School continued to capture the headlines when, in April 1990, 14 year old Susannah Gil was awarded first prize in the Leicestershire Young Cook of the Year annual competition. Susannah, who lived in Leicester, competed against three other young pupils, all aged 14 years, who represented Leicester Grammar School, Leysland High School, Countesthorpe and Brockington College, Enderby.

The event, which was the district final of the British Gas Board's East Midlands competition took place at the Beaumont Leys showroom. Susannah earned top marks with her recipe of chicken tartlets and banana crunch slices. She won a cash prize of £50 and a wrist watch and became the second pupil from the school to win the prestigious award for cookery skills following in the footsteps of Georgina Spencer the previous year.

The many talented pupils from the school who excelled in dance and drama were given the opportunity to perform in public in June 1990 when they joined with youngsters from Judgemeadow Community College and Sir Jonathan North Community College, Leicester to perform Ample Space – a look at the freedom of the world through the medium of dance. The dance, music and performance spectacular took place at the Haymarket Theatre, Leicester on the evenings of 18 and 19 June.

One of the senior members of staff at the school with vivid memories of the early 1990s was Mrs Judith Matharu who was appointed as Deputy Head

Teacher in 1989. Warwickshire born Mrs Matharu was educated at Nuneaton High School for Girls prior to undertaking a teacher training course at Warwick University. Initially she trained as a Physical Education and English Teacher and, at the time of her appointment at South Wigston High School, she was able to work alongside a more senior, more experienced Deputy in Edward Thomas and the combination of youth and experience at this senior level was the ideal pairing that the Head Teacher, Mr Bothamley, sought as he strove to move the school forward.

Mrs Matharu spent five memorable years at the school and derived great benefit from the influence of good leadership and management. There was a good relationship between teachers, staff and pupils, thus her involvement in senior management, where one of her roles was to support teaching staff, enabled her to develop her management skills in an enjoyable working environment.

She enjoyed participating in a range of activities and recalls that the pupils were developed to high standards in music and sport. The school was a hive of activity and Mr Bothamley encouraged everyone to join in.

The minutes of the Governors Meeting (5 February 1992) recorded that Mrs Matharu had been awarded a Master's Degree by Loughborough University. She had been encouraged to read for her higher degree by Mr Bothamley and after three years of hard work she finally achieved her goal.

Having been well prepared at South Wigston, she was further encouraged by Mr Bothamley to apply for Headships. In the event she applied for and obtained the post of the Vice Principal at Sir Jonathan North Community College, Leicester. During her five years at the upper school (1994 – 1999) a new Principal was appointed – Mrs Jane Collins, the former Deputy Head Teacher at South Wigston High School, who had moved to Welland Park Community College, Market Harbrough in January 1988. Mrs Collins became the Principal of Sir Jonathan North in January 1997 and she and Mrs Matharu became professional colleagues and good friends.

Judith Matharu became Head Teacher at Hastings High School, Burbage, Leicester, in 1999 and in 2006 was appointed Her Majesty's Inspector for Secondary Schools for the whole of the East

Mrs Judith Matharu photographed on the day she took up her appointment as Deputy Head Teacher at South Wigston High School

Jeremy Herbert receiving his awards from Mr Eric Bothamley.

St Thomas' Parish Church, South Wigston

Midlands, excluding Leicestershire.

During 1990 Jeremy Herbert, whose mother Valerie (nee Mathers) sisters Gail and Jane and brother Mark had all attended South Wigston High School, was rewarded for his outstanding achievement in his French studies. Jeremy was awarded a certificate and shield for his accomplishments, which were duly presented to him by the Head Teacher, Mr Eric Bothamley.

Jeremy attended the school from 1986 to 1990 before moving on to Guthlaxton College.

At a meeting of the School Governors, on 5 February 1991, the Head Teacher reported the sad death of Mr Clive Atkins, the school's Head Caretaker, who had collapsed and died of a heart attack. Mr Atkins, aged 61 years, who lived in Bassett Street, South Wigston, had been the Head Caretaker for over twelve years, having taken up his post on 18 December 1978. Mr Bothamley, in a letter to parents, paid tribute to Mr Atkins and on the day of the funeral the school closed early to enable staff to attend and to participate in the service which was held in the nearby St Thomas' Church.

The Rugby Union traditions of South Wigston High School took on a global aspect in 1991 when Australia became the second winners of the Rugby World Cup - the Webb Ellis Trophy. A former teacher from the school played an important role in the success of the Wallabies.

John Elders, who had taught at the school from 1953 to 1955 and had enjoyed a distinguished career with Leicester Tigers before becoming the England Coach (1972 – 1975) emigrated with his wife to

Australia in 1982 and this led to him achieving further success but this time on the other side of the world. He was appointed Sports Master at Downlands College in Toowoomba, Queensland and he went on to become the coach to the Queensland County Schools XV. Two of the talented young players who he coached and developed were Tim Horan and Jason Little. They progressed to form a remarkably successful centre partnership for Australia in many international matches.

Australia triumphed in the World Cup in 1991 when they defeated England 12-6 in the final which was played at Twickenham. Upon the return of the team to Australia, Tim Horan and Jason Little made a point of visiting their old schools. One of the visits was to Downlands College where they renewed their acquaintances with their influential coach John Elders who was delighted to welcome his two former protégés now World Cup winners and to congratulate them upon their outstanding achievements.

John Elders and his wife returned to England during 1992 and he finally retired in 1995. Although still living in Newcastle Upon Tyne, he continues to follow the progress of Leicester Tigers and to take a pride in the achievements of his old club.

John Elders holding the World Cup flanked by Tim Horan left and Jason Little right at Downlands College in 1992

Mrs Marion Baker retired in 1992, having experienced, enjoyed and adapted to countless changes during her many years of teaching at South

Wigston High School which had commenced in September 1953 and, apart from a break between 1962 and 1970 to start her family, had been continuous.

With many changes in the Education system, Mrs Baker recalls that all of the teaching staff had to keep adapting as the introduction of the 4 Plus intake at the Primary stage meant that pupils in Year 6, aged 10 years, entered the High School. Mrs Baker soon found that she enjoyed teaching this age group as well as the older pupils. The school had a good orchestra with talented boys and girls. Plays were also produced revealing budding Thespians. Over the years fetes were held to raise money for books and equipment. Mrs Baker recalls that these were well supported as were the various concerts. Money was also raised, by the school, to support the work of the Family Service Unit in Leicester. Finally, Mrs Baker extends, "My thanks to so many of the girls and boys over the years for enriching my life."

In 1992, a momentous decision was taken by the parents of pupils at South Wigston High School when they voted in favour of grant maintained or GM status in accordance with the provisions of the Education Reform Act 1988. Together with the parents of children at Abington High and Bushloe High Schools, in nearby Wigston Magna, they felt that the school had been badly hit by the way the Leicestershire County Council had allocated monies to the High Schools taking 10 to 14 year old pupils. It was also the strongly held view by the Governors and Mr Bothamley, together with his staff, that application for GM status should be pursued in the best interests of the school.

By December 1992, the application to opt out was awaiting final Government approval. At that stage South Wigston High School was one of five county schools to have voted to opt out of Local Education Authority control.

At a meeting of the Leicestershire County Council on 27 January 1993, a report of the Education Committee was presented, entitled: Information on Grant-Maintained Status. The Education Department had made available for parents a leaflet covering issues concerned with grant-maintained status. The leaflet was first produced for the parents of pupils attending the Wigston Magna and South Wigston High Schools during the schools' discussions of GM status.

Extracts from the County Education Department leaflet explained the position to parents:

Grant - Maintained Schools

Some questions for parents from the Leicestershire Education Authority:-

What is grant-maintained status?

"When a school becomes grant-maintained, it leaves the local authority and is funded directly by the Government, using money that would otherwise have gone to pay for local authority schools.

The governing body takes over the buildings and employs all staff directly instead of the local authority.

The Governors of a grant-maintained school have complete responsibility for the admission and exclusion of pupils provided that they work to the same rules as the Local Education Authority. The Governors can apply to the Secretary of State for a change in the character of the school. This would enable them to select children by ability and special aptitudes for music or technology for example."

The leaflet also pointed out that once a school had achieved grant-maintained status it could not apply to go back to local authority control. It also added that although many government bodies were thinking about making an application to become grant-maintained the majority of schools had decided not to go ahead.

Although South Wigston High School and their two neighbouring High Schools were clearly in a minority in seeking to become grant-maintained schools the respective Head Teachers clearly felt that direct funding by the Government would enable them to receive extra money, some of which could be used to increase staff numbers and facilities.

The Head Teacher, Mr Bothamley, was convinced that to opt out of LEA control was the right option for the school and he was the driving force behind the bid. It was a courageous decision and South Wigston High School became a grant-maintained school on 1 April 1993. In acquiring its new status the Governors became responsible for the buildings and staff plus other services previously funded by the Leicestershire County Council, these included school meals, financial and legal services and major building repairs.

Within a short time of gaining grant-maintained status and taking over the kitchens, the school was visited by the local Health Inspector who promptly closed the kitchens down. A Government grant enabled the Governors to have the school kitchens refurbished and brought back into use. Compas Catering, a private firm of caterers, appointed by the Governors, then took over responsibility for providing the school meals.

A change in the Deputy Headship of the school occurred, when at the end of June 1993, the long-serving Edward Thomas retired. Ted, as he was affectionately known to all of his colleagues, and doubtless by many of the pupils when out of earshot, had served the school loyally for 35 years. He had commenced at the original Boys' School in 1958 and during the following three and a half decades he had acquired a wife from within the teaching staff, raised the Art Department to new levels and, through a series of promotions, had deservedly reached the position of Deputy Head Teacher.

A retirement party was organised and a buffet was enjoyed in the school hall. Mr Thomas was presented with an easel, by colleagues past and present, in order that he could continue his art work. Thus, after a career spanning a third of a century, the school said its farewells to one of its most popular teachers.

The newly appointed Deputy Head Teacher was Gary Leslie Toward, born at Dipton near to Newcastle Upon Tyne in October 1960, he had received his higher education at the City of Liverpool College of Higher Education where he received his Bachelor of Education, Design and Technology (Lancaster). He had previously taught at the Sir Frank Markham Community School, Milton Keynes, Eaton School, Norwich and St Aidans School, Sunderland where, from January 1990 to July 1993, he was the Head of Technology Faculty.

The minutes of a meeting of the School Governors, held on 21 September 1993, confirmed the appointment of Councillor Geoff L Welsh as the new Chairman of the Governors. Interestingly Councillor Welsh, who was a former pupil at the school, was now the head of the governing body at his old seat of learning.

On 25 October 1993, Kris Akubusi MBE, the former Olympic and world-renowned athlete, visited the school. Having served for nine years in the British Army's Physical Training Corps, during which time he developed his athletic career, he went on to achieve enormous success in his chosen sport. His international career commenced in 1983 and his tremendous accomplishments included the winning of medals in the Olympic Games and in World, European and Commonwealth Championships.

A successful 400 metre hurdler and a member of Great Britain's 4 x 400 metre relay squad, his greatest triumph, as an athlete, was in Tokyo in August 1991 when, as a member of the 4 x 400 metre relay team, he helped Britain to win the Gold medal when they defeated the powerful American team in the World Championships.

Visions of the hit TV series Superstars were revived as Kris put the pupils through their paces, in a sponsored event, with a series of challenging exercises including press-ups, sit-ups and bench jumps. The scheme required the children to do as many attempts at each exercise as possible in 30 seconds. They were also given first class advice on fitness by an athlete renowned for his fitness and competitiveness.

Kris Akubusi (Willowstone Photography)

Kris Akubusi, who had visited schools and universities across the country taking part in similar schemes, explained that the scheme taught children about their own capabilities and limitations. He told the pupils: "You don't have to be the best but you do

Pictured (left to right) are Daryl Ormin, Steven Walters, Natalie Tebbett, Amanda Harrison, Sarah Derringer, Robert Carter, Sean Chambers and Mark Warner (Leicester Mercury)

have to give your best. I encourage children to reach for the top but am more interested in them realising that sport can be a rewarding part of their lifestyle."

Deputy Head, Gary Toward, said, "He has been an inspiration to the kids. It is a rare chance for them to meet someone of his calibre."

The money raised on the day was divided between the Superstars Charity which assisted in the training of up and coming athletes and the school's Physical Education Department.

Kris Akubusi is now one of the country's top business motivational speakers and presenters.

As Christmas approached in 1993, all of the pupils took part in their second charity effort in order to bring festive cheer to elderly people in the Wigston area. Each class at the school made up a Christmas hamper and this followed on the pupils' efforts in the previous year when an impressive forty food parcels were assembled for distribution.

The *Leicester Mercury* (13 December 1993) featured an article describing how the kind-hearted pupils had raised hundreds of pounds to purchase food at a Christmas fair.

A picture in the *Leicester Mercury* showed some of the pupils outside the school, about to take the Christmas parcels to Age Concern, Wigston.

The giving of food parcels at Christmas continues to be an important event in the life of the school today and the teachers now contribute boxes of food items to supplement the efforts of the pupils in their

work on behalf of the wider community.

By the spring of 1994, the school had applied to the Government for a large grant, amounting to several hundred thousand pounds, for a new Science Department. The bid was unsuccessful initially but was put on a priority list for the following academic year 1994-95. Mr Bothamley remained undeterred in his belief that grant-maintained status remained the best option for the school and in an article on grant payments, to the local opt out schools, in the *Leicester Mercury* (16 March 1994) the Head said, "My only regret is not becoming grant-maintained a year earlier."

An article in the *Leicester Mercury* (28 September 1994) drew its readers' attention to the fact that evening classes were once again being taught at South Wigston High School. Five classes were on offer – computers for beginners, watercolour painting, wine making and wine appreciation, quilting and dressmaking and French for beginners. The courses were of seven weeks duration and were a great success so much so that the school planned to offer further classes in the New Year. Gary Toward, who was the tutor for the computer studies course, said the classes were intended to improve the school's service to the community.

The Deputy Head added, "The school did its own market research to find out exactly what classes people would be interested in. Many of the people who have joined the courses - particularly French and computers, are parents who want to keep up with their children."

All of the classes were taught by people well known to the school and most of the tutors were qualified teachers. The re-introduction of Evening Classes after a lapse of some 36 years was clearly fulfilling a need in the local community - as it did when Leslie Wild was responsible for the courses when they first featured in the life of the school in 1953.

Homework - a word that all pupils, past and present, associate with their school days, a challenge for some, an imposition for others, it remained an inescapable feature of school life!

In August 1994, the Deputy Head, Gary Toward, set out the school policy in relation to homework. The requirements shown below were definitive and unambiguous:

Homework

It is school policy to set homework for most lessons. Below is the weekly homework timetable. All pupils are provided with a 'Homework Diary' which should be used to record the details of homework when it is set. Form Tutors will make regular checks to ensure pupils are using these and we would encourage parents to also examine these regularly:-

HOMEWORK TIMETABLE 1994-95

	MONDAY	TUESDAY	WEDNESDAY	THURSDAY	FRIDAY
6	Maths	Humanities or English	English or Humanities	Science	French English
7	French	Maths English	Science	Humanities	English
8	Science English	Humanities	English	French	Maths
9A	Humanities Maths	Maths German	English	Science French	English
9B	German Humanities	English Science	French Maths		English

Notes

1. Pupils may have a second science and maths homework on days to be determined by the teacher of each group.

2. One English homework will be used to reinforce our spelling programme.

3. Homework will occasionally be set in other subjects and all pupils will be set one design research project which will span a six to seven week period.

4. Pupils in Years 6 and 7 are expected to spend approximately 20 minutes on each homework.

5. Pupils in Years 8 and 9 are expected to spend approximately 30 minutes on each homework.

6. French homework for year 6 will not be set until later in the autumn term.

7. All pupils are given a homework diary into which all homework should be entered when they are set.

8. Design homework will be set occasionally during the course of each 6 week project block.

Pictured from left to right are Mrs Janet Waterfield, Mrs Carole Gamble, Mrs Heather Parkinson and Mrs Dorothy Chambers, all pupils at the school between 1955 and 1959. Pupil Gary Smith demonstrates his computer skills aided by I.T. Technician Gareth Williamson (Leicester Mercury)

Hi-Tech: Edward Garnier QC MP, and pupils Paula Barratt, Danni Hough and Mark Stone examine a computer controlled milling machine (Leicester Mercury)

Many former pupils had the opportunity to make a return visit to South Wigston High School in October 1994 as the school opened its doors, on two evenings, to enable them to see the improvements in the facilities. It also allowed them to appreciate the achievements of the pupils in the last decade of the twentieth century.

This was a rather different occasion to the annual Open Day in that past pupils were able to view the many changes which had occurred over the previous eighteen months and to have a real insight into how the school worked and had reached the standards achieved by the Year 1994. Activities from all departments were featured including rehearsals for a silent movie

production in drama, performances by the orchestra and demonstrations of computer-aided design work.

Pupils who entered the school fifty six years earlier in 1938 mingled with those of later years together with the pupils of 1994. Deputy Head Teacher, Gary Toward, commented in an article in the *Leicester Mercury* (28 October 1994): "We wanted to show people that the new information and technology centre is up and running and we wanted to give them a chance to try it out for themselves."

A month later a major facility to boost skills in computer-aided design and manufacture was formally opened at the school. The classroom, which housed the equipment, included two computer controlled milling machines, a computer controlled lathe, fifteen individual computer work stations, two printers and a plotter. Pupils were enabled to use the computerised system to create designs in an updated version of old-style technical drawing. They were also able to use the computer controlled lathe, milling or embroidery machine to cut out the finished article.

The Chairman of the School Governors, Mr Geoff Welsh, said, "Parents want their children to be well versed in computers and the latest technology." The £40,000 state-of-the-art project was officially

CHEERS! School Head Eric Bothamley (left) and Chairman of the School Governors Councillor Geoff Welsh, toast the school's success. (Leicester Mercury).

opened by Mr Edward Garnier, the Member of Parliament for the Harborough Constituency who described the new technology as helping to 'demystify' science.

To conclude a year of tremendous achievement and advancement the school announced, in December 1994, the award of a Government grant of £435,000 to build a new science block. Deputy Head Gary Toward, commenting in an article in the *Leicester Mercury* (23 December 1994) said, "The Department of Education has obviously been impressed by the school's commitment to teaching technology and the staff's determination to provide their pupils with a modern, scientific curriculum. This is a vote of confidence in our achievements since going grant-maintained and will provide the facilities to achieve even more."

Kelly Holmes in her greatest moment of triumph

Friday 24 February 1995 was a red-letter day in the annals of the school's sporting history when international middle-distance runner Kelly Holmes was the celebrated guest for the day. The twenty four year old 1500 metres Commonwealth champion and European silver medallist came to put pupils through their paces during another sponsored fund-raising event as part of the National Super Schools Scheme. Having joined the British Army at the age of eighteen, Kelly was initially a lorry driver in the Women's Royal Army Corps, reaching the rank of Sergeant. She became the Army Judo Champion before becoming a full time athlete in 1997.

During the time she spent at the school, the world class athlete met dozens of children individually and had her photograph taken with as many of them as time allowed. She took part in a sponsored event, based on the old Super Stars television show in which pupils were sponsored to carry out a series of exercises. Once again the money raised was divided between the school's Physical Education Department in order to set up a fitness centre and the other half was donated to the Super Schools fund.

Kelly Holmes went on to achieve lasting fame at the 28th Olympic Games, held in Athens in 2004, when she won gold medals in the Women's 800 metres and 1500 metres finals.

She was appointed a Dame Commander of the Order of the British Empire in January 2005.

April 1995 saw the eagerly awaited commencement of the new science block. The architects chosen were Barnsley, Hewitt and Mallinson of 1 White Hart Lane, London and the building contractors were J. E B Wheatley Ltd of Coventry.

Early stages in the building works

In an article in the *Leicester Mercury*, County Councillor Alan Kind said, "The new block will be married sympathetically to the school's original 1930's structure." This was indeed reassuring, coming as it did from someone who was able to speak as a County Councillor for the area, a School Governor who chaired the Premises Committee, an architect and the son of a former Deputy Headmaster at South Wigston.

Events moved swiftly and by the end of April the rear entrance to the East Wing of the school had been demolished to accommodate a corridor and new entrance. Several courses of bricks had been laid and the anticipated completion date of December 1995 was a realistic expectation.

The tradition of hand bell ringing was maintained at the school and in June 1995 a group of 15 pupils went along to Holmes House - a residential home for elderly people, situated in Kenilworth Road, South Wigston, to entertain the residents. A selection of music associated with the Second World War was performed, the theme being the 50th anniversary of VE Day, the most popular item of the repertoire was the aptly-named 'Bells of St Mary's!'

Schoolmates Craig Thurlow and Daniel Butler both aged 13 years with 82 year old Maurice Kendall (Leicester Mercury)

The Head Teacher, Mr Eric Bothamley, was quoted as saying, "Bell ringing has become something of a tradition at South Wigston. It is a very social club." The visit to Holmes House, where the children had performed previously, marked a further link with the school as the home was named after the late County Councillor John Henry Holmes, who was a former Governor of the school.

The school's reputation as a centre of excellence in sporting terms was designed to reach new heights when, in November 1995, it was announced that the Governors were investigating the possibility of the building of a Sports Centre, at a cost of £500,000 on the school's playing fields. Planning permission for the new hall had been approved by the Oadby and Wigston Borough Council despite some objections by local residents who expressed concern that such a development would bring added noise and traffic problems in its wake. Head Teacher, Mr Eric Bothamley, met with residents and reassured them that the Governors were committed to ensuring residents should not be disturbed in any way and that the intended new facilities would be available for use by local residents and groups outside of school time.

The funding of this ambitious new project was the subject of detailed discussions with the Leicestershire County Council, Blaby District Council and Oadby and Wigston Borough Council to investigate the possibility of mounting a joint bid to the National Lottery Sports Foundation.

It was envisaged that the building of the £0.5 million sports hall would commence in the financial year 1997 - 98 and that it would cater for a range of activities with a viewing gallery, lounge area and bar, changing rooms and reception area. Facilities for disabled people and fifteen additional car parking spaces were also included in the plans.

In a letter to the Oadby and Wigston Borough Council, Mr Bothamley stated that one day a week would be set aside for use by community groups catering, for example, for locally retired people and groups with specific needs. The new sports centre would replace the one remaining gymnasium, of the two original 1938 gyms, which was considered to have become old-fashioned and inadequate in meeting the needs of pupils in the 1990s.

The additional wing of the school which housed the new science block

As the year progressed the new science block was completed. Building construction had necessitated the use of a 100ft crane which had been involved in some amazing delicate work lifting and positioning concrete slabs watched by an admiring youthful audience of onlookers. By June some of the roof tiles were in place and work had continued throughout the summer break. At last the new extension was complete and brought into use in 1995.

The school's commitment to the training and support of its staff was recognised in February 1997 when it received a prestigious award in recognition of the effort made in terms of staff development. An article in the *Oadby and Wigston Mail* (6 February 1997) under the heading, 'School's Investment in People Pays Off' announced that South Wigston High School had become one of the first schools in Leicestershire to be given the Investors in People award for the entire staff - ancillary workers, teachers and governors. The award was given to organisations around the country in recognition of their employee training and opportunities and lasted for a period of three years.

The award was officially presented to Councillor Geoff Welsh, Chairman of the school's governing body at a celebration buffet held later that month. Mr Welsh commented: "The school has been working towards this for nearly four years and it is significant that, on the way, the school has achieved major success thanks to the hard work and dedication of its staff. The Governors feel that it is very important that all staff play a role in the development of the school."

The present position, as defined by Mr Toward, is that whilst the school does not subscribe to the Investors In People package due to funding not been provided by the Local Authority, it still very much subscribes to the 'investors' ethos.

During February 1997, the Head Teacher, Mr Eric Bothamley, together with colleagues from other Wigston High Schools, travelled to London to discuss education reforms with a Government Minister. The delegation consisted of Mr Bothamley representing South Wigston High School, Mr Eric Cook, Head Teacher of Bushloe High School and the Head of Abington High School, Mr Alex Green, they were accompanied by Mr Edward Garnier, MP for the Harborough constituency.

The purpose of the visit was to meet the Under Secretary of State for Education, Robin Squire, to discuss the way forward for the three Wigston High Schools. (Robin Clifford Squire, MP the Conservative MP for Hornchurch, had become Under Secretary of State in John Major's Government and was generally known as the 'schools minister'). The agenda included such items as standards in reading and writing, student discipline, VAT on school improvements and the important issue of the appeal process for grant-maintained schools.

The Head Teachers felt that a change to the appeals process which, at the time meant that popular schools had to process hundreds of appeal forms from hopeful parents when the places requested were simply not available. Each of the three schools had a mailing list of children from within and outside of their respective catchment areas.

The minister promised to examine the various issues put forward, including the thorny question of whether the three schools, unlike Local Authority schools, should have to pay VAT on building and improvement work.

Clearly the status of a grant-maintained school did not ensure that schools were without problems and the need to reform but at least, with the support of their local MP, they were able to make their voices heard at the Palace of Westminster.

The Palace of Westminster

For the fifth consecutive year the school took part in the Super Schools Fitness Day and was visited during February 1997 by Nicola Fairbrother, the former Olympic Women's Judo silver medallist and the Olympic Gymnast Lee Harris. Nicola Fairbrother was awarded the silver medal in the judo lightweight class at the 1992 Barcelona Olympics and four years later was placed 5th in the same event at the Atlanta Olympic Games held in 1996.

The pupils once again competed in a series of testing exercises before the two athletes gave demonstrations and talked to the students of the benefit of participating in sport and demonstrated how they had reached the top levels of their respective sports.

Up to six hundred pupils took part and they raised more than £2000 in sponsorship. This sum, together with monies collected at previous Super School Fitness Days, exceeded £7000 in total. It was a very impressive effort by the pupils and once again demonstrated the school's commitment to sporting

A work of fiction at local school

Pupils dressed for their Book Week. (Leicester Mercury)

activities and the desire to assist young athletes in need of cash support and to help in the development of their own Physical Education Department.

The General election, held on 1 May 1997, heralded a huge victory for New Labour and the defeat of the Conservative administration which had come to power eighteen years earlier under Margaret Thatcher in 1970. The new Prime Minister, Tony Blair appointed David Blunkett to the all-important post of Secretary of State for Education and Science. One of the first decisions taken by the new Government was to end grant-maintained status. The worrying aspect now facing schools like South Wigston High School was what did the future hold in terms of their status as a grant-maintained school? The Governors and teaching staff could only wait, with trepidation, for New Labour to decide the future of the schools which had opted out of LEA control.

Councillor Derek Vann receiving the cheque from the pupil representatives (Leicester Mercury)

On 5 November 1997 some two hundred Year Six pupils took part in South Wigston High School's annual Book Week, which was part of a national campaign to raise literacy levels in schools. A range of activities included anagrams trails, quizzes and designing costumes. Local residents must have been slightly puzzled as they saw Dracula, Oliver Twist and the rabbit from Alice in Wonderland all arriving at school to participate in the event. They were, of course, the children dressed as many of the characters they had chosen from works of fiction.

Deputy Head Teacher, Sandra Tansley, commenting in the *Oadby and Wigston Mail* (13 November 1997) said, "We have been using computer and CD Roms as well as books to encourage reading. I think the pupils have had a super time and have been very enthusiastic."

As Christmas approached all eight hundred and twenty pupils at the school took part in a fund-raising event to raise money for the Mayor of Oadby and Wigston's chosen charity. The Mayor, Councillor Derek Vann, had decided to support Menphys and the Multiple Sclerosis Society during his Year of Office and was delighted that the

Champions: Year 9 rugby team members Mark Carers, Reece Dempsey, Kris McFedries, Michael Smith, Gareth Dakin (Leicester Mercury)

pupils, who arranged the event themselves, as part of their personal and social education class activities raised more than £850. The money collected resulted from a series of challenges, cake stalls, an auction and a skittles competition.

The following month, Councillor Vann publically thanked the school children for their 'wonderful efforts' at a meeting of the Oadby and Wigston Borough Council where he was presented with a cheque by four of the pupils - Nikki Ball, Danielle de Carle, Katherine Hoy and Chris Foster.

The rugby tradition of South Wigston High School was maintained during 1998 when the young players' achievements were featured in a report in the *Oadby and Wigston Mail* (21 May 1998). The article was headed 'Young Rugby Stars Blazed a Trail in County Competitions.' During the season, Years 7, 8 and 9 had excelled in the new county league which was divided into two sections with the winners of each section playing each other in the final.

The school's Year 9 team won all of their games to top the South area league and in a hard-fought final they defeated Long Field High School, Melton Mowbray 32-7. This success was followed by victory over Lancaster Boys School, Leicester, to win the Lutterworth Sevens Tournament. Years 7 and 8 also showed a great deal of promise, both teams played well to finish second in their area leagues.

A contributory factor in the successes achieved during 1997-98 was the involvement of players from the Leicester Tigers who had given tuition to the young pupils. Richard May, Physical Education Teacher, told the *Oadby and Wigston Mail*: "This has been an excellent year in which our teams have benefited from the extra coaching."

Cross-country running was another sporting activity in which the P.E. staff worked particularly hard to develop a number of very promising boys and girls. Extra-curricular sessions were held which resulted in some outstanding achievements in the spring of 1998. The Year 8 boys' team won the county championship and county relay competition. Year 6 girls' team won the Mid-Leicestershire championship and topped the Mid-Leicestershire League.

The top individual achievement was recorded by Rebekah Randle, aged eleven years, who became the county champion in her age group. For sixty years pupils of South Wigston High School had run through the mud and rain around the fields and the area of Crow Mills and the Grand Union Canal and had built-up a tradition in cross-country running. The remarkable series of results, achieved throughout the year, carried on the tradition forged by their predecessors.

As the 1997-98 academic year came to a conclusion, accolades for scholarly excellence, sporting and musical achievements together with work in the community were presented to one hundred and twenty Year 9 pupils and top achievers in Years 6, 7 and 8. The end of year awards ceremony was attended by the Mayor of Oadby and Wigston Borough Council, Councillor Lesley Thornton. Cups and certificates were presented and the event was featured in the *Oadby and Wigston Mail (2 July 1998)*. Deputy Head Teacher, Gary Toward, described the school's Year 9 as, "One of the best in recent years. This has been very positive in all curriculum areas and their work in the community."

Headmaster Mr Eric Bottomley with his Staff 1980s

Thus, as the 60th birthday was celebrated, the academic achievements, its sporting prowess and its involvement in the community remained the pillars of strength of South Wigston High School as it prepared to enter the new Millennium.

Army Day 2007

Black Country Museum.
2000

Bologne 2005

County Cup Winners 2002

Dad's Tie Day 2008

World Book Day 2006

The Menin Gate, Yrpres

Spooky school production!

Pupils enjoying a sponsored play session 2002

Information and Communication Technology 2008

The Prom 2007

Mandy Langdale's English class 2008

On the sports field 2008

Lincoln Cathedral 2000

Professor Peter Welton's masterclass 2008

Year 7 football

Ski Trip 2004

Spooky Sleepover 2002

The Head's Challenge, Kinder Scout

Chapter Eight
Curtains to Computers
(1998 - 2008)

The last decade of the history of South Wigston High School leads us to the new Millennium. How strange it feels to contemplate the end of a century drawing to a close. The curtain is slowly drawing on the scene encapsulating people in time but before the final close there is still a little left to peek at.

The 1998 Education Act laid down Government plans on how Special Educational Needs would develop. Increases in funding to support the development of inclusive education started to come from Central Government.

Foundation schools were set up under The Schools Standards and Framework Act of 1998 to replace grant-maintained schools. It gave guidance regarding the change of status and category of the school. Foundation schools have a degree of independence from the Local Education Authority as the school governors control admissions to the school, employ the school staff and own the school's estate.

In early March a report of a Governor visit to South Wigston High School was made by the Reverend Professor Peter Geoffrey Holmes. It read as follows:

The Monday morning enrolment was observed followed by three Mathematics classes and one Religious Education lesson.

The registration was a friendly and informative time conducted with authority and sensitivity. Children showed a sense of 'belonging' and enthusiasm.

The Mathematics classes represented three ability ranges at level 8. At one end, methods of compiling tables on paper by extrapolation without reliance on memory were tackled with enthusiasm.

The 'middle set' were receiving feedback from exam paper 2 seeing their silly mistakes and taking pre-recorded mental tests.

The Year 9 top set were applying Pythagoras to the calculation of lengths and areas. This graded National Curriculum exercise was a particularly good example of geometry without trigonometry, preparing the field for later trigonometry and co-ordinate geometry.

The Religious Education class on Moslem prayer rituals was a sensitive presentation of the ritual washing before prayer undertaken by Moslems several times a day. It was linked with a prayer mat oriented towards MECCA. The presentation was detailed and with purpose - in fact a deeply spiritual experience.

Noted in all classes was excellent discipline, good interaction between teacher and pupils and enthusiasm by the children.

On 18 June 1998 it was recorded with sadness that Mr J Harris a teacher at the school had died. At the Governor's meeting that day two minutes silence was observed. Governors play a significant role in monitoring, evaluating and reviewing the school with a number of active committees reporting to the full committee throughout each term.

During the autumn term at a meeting of Headmasters, Mr Bothamley put forward the idea that a core curriculum subject should be studied after the Year 9 SAT's examinations were over in the summer. The subject was to be prepared by teachers in the Wigston Family of Secondary Schools and would give pupils a head start with GCSE when they transferred to Upper School.

At a Governors Community Committee Meeting on 29 October Mr Bothamley informed them of discussions that were taking place within the Guthlaxton and Countesthorpe Family of Schools regarding transfer of Key Stage 3 SAT's to try to raise achievement at Key Stage 4. Recorded was the view that this would have far reaching implications for South Wigston High School in respect of organisation, timetabling and staffing. Key Stage 2 pupils could benefit by coming to the High School for a longer induction period at the end of Year 5. Although radical the committee were very supportive of the ideas.

Roger Black

In October in true sporting tradition, Roger Black the Olympic Silver Medalist visited the school. This event was in order to pass on some valuable tips to the pupils. Track students were all ears as the retired four hundred metres runner put them through their paces with a series of exercises. Years 6, 7, 8 and 9 students were sponsored for the number of sit-ups, leg drives, press ups and bench and star jumps they completed; with the cash raised going towards the school's maths department. An added incentive was also a fund towards the 'up and coming' stars of the future. This event was part of the nationwide initiative, 'Super Schools Charity'.

Shakespeare's Macbeth, 'The Scottish Play' was a highlight of an Open Evening, Mr Toward's class had edited the traditional script down into half hourly slots. The Headmaster commented that he 'saw a raft of talent on show but Siobhan Prideaux was truly outstanding'. The school regarded the study of Shakespearean plays as one of its strengths.

Congratulations were given to Mr Alan Kind, School Governor, who was awarded the MBE for his work in the community.

Andrew Ross 8JK, and Sam Smith 8CK, both members of a table tennis club after school were entered in the Woolwich League in the area. Both boys won their first match and Andrew reached the top of his league in all of his matches.

On the afternoon of 4 December a charity event took place at the school which was attended by the Chair of Blaby District Council, Guy Jackson and his wife. Funds for 'The Community Action Fund For Youth' were being raised. Councillor Dixon also attended as he was the Chairman of 'CAFY'. A total of £670.00 was raised on the stalls and games. The children were congratulated on their enthusiasm and public spiritedness.

Three days later children were decorating boxes, providing cards and collecting food to fill Christmas hampers for the elderly within the community. A total of fifty four hampers was handed over. Mr Gill from Age Concern attended an assembly to explain how the gifts would be used. He said that the school's unique contribution brought real happiness to needy and lonely people.

On 8 and 9 December the Christmas concert was held. A stylish choir performance of the 'Christmas Story' was presented in a contemporary jazz setting. A wide variety of group and individual musical items was performed. The Mayor of Oadby and Wigston Borough Council attended one evening and congratulated the pupils on their spirited performance. Councillor Geoff Welsh, Chair of Governors, explained the heavy subsidy the school put into their music teaching and assured parents of Governors' enthusiasm for this aspect of school life.

Christmas lunch on 9 and 10 December was served when turkey, beef, mince pies and Christmas pudding were demolished. The new Catering Manager, Martin Bruce produced five hundred and fifty meals besides the usual menu. Everyone enjoyed the occasion and the cracker pulling.

The Bell Ringing Group was invited to participate in the Leicestershire Women's Institute's Annual Carol Concert. They rang two selections of popular carols and then gave an impromptu concert at the end of the service. They also took part in the Glen Parva Memorial Hall Christmas Concert and arrangements had been made for them to play at the three primary schools, to a mentally and physically handicapped day centre and to the Curtis Weston Day Centre, for the elderly, in Wigston Magna.

Reported was cross country news of the pupils achievements. The Year 6 boys' and girls' teams took part in the Leicestershire Primary League and came away with the trophy. The girls' team had a close contest with Bushloe and were pipped at the post into second place but the boys' team picked up the trophy and gold medals. One hundred and fifty competitors took part.

Dean Barrett of the Leicester Riders was reported also to have visited the school. He did two coaching sessions with Year 9 basketball players.

On the last day of the school term the staff from the Humanities Department arranged a murder mystery game. It was hoped that this event would encourage pupils with a tendency to truancy on the last day to attend school. The children were required to discover the murderer of a wealthy land owner who had a few enemies. Staff dressed up as various suspects and eventually the pupils caught the landowner's son and sent him to jail.

The new term of 1999 began on 5 January. The Adult Education Programme Enrolment Evening took place two days later. Desk Top Publishing and Computers for Beginners were offered for Tuesday evenings and RSA Computer Literacy, Acoustic and Electric Guitar and Self Defence for Women on Thursdays.

Daniel Danvers 8PR, was reported to be the 'Boxing Champ'. Having won a trophy in November 1998, on 20 January this year he beat R Reddish of Derby in a competition between Leicester and Derby clubs. Daniel was a member of the Wigston Boxing Club.

Music Awards were achieved by Fiona Hickenbotham 6MM, Rebekah Randle 8CK and Briony Wilkinson, 7MF for clarinet and Amy Brittain 7NF, for violin.

Over the years music has always played an important part of South Wigston School life. In 1999 the Governors paid £8,500 for peripatetic music tuition fees. This would have amounted to £85 for each participating pupil. Fees were about to rise steeply to £4.50 a lesson for families but the many ensembles, choirs and group practices were free.

On 30 January the history class was studying the 'Stuarts'. Form 8CK were asked to write an eye witness account of the execution of King Charles 1. This was part of their 'Making of the UK' course and the three hundred and fiftieth anniversary of the event. Sarah Gamage wrote, 'The Death of Charles 1'.

On 30 January 1649 I stood outside the Palace of Whitehall staring up at the scaffolding that Charles 1 was going to be beheaded on that day. As I stood there more and more people arrived. It was a freezing day but this did not stop the crowd coming. Charles 1 was led on to the scaffolding and the crowd went silent. They removed his jewels and put his head on the block. The executioner raised the axe, I waited for the crunch and the axe went down. In one blow the head rolled from the body. The crowd groaned. The soldiers then dipped their swords in his blood and swore at his body. The people close to the scaffolding paid the soldiers to dip handkerchiefs in his blood. You could also take some bone or gristle that belonged to Charles 1. A soldier held up Charles 1 head so that everyone could see. We were then moved away by the soldiers. In all my life, I will never forget the scene I saw that day'.

Minutes of a meeting of the Governors held on 2 February 1999 at the school discussed 'the new school status'. It was resolved to reaffirm the preliminary decision to accept the indicative allocation of Foundation status for the school from 1 September 1999.

Some time later the Headmaster, Mr Eric Bothamley wrote:

'Goodbye To Grant Maintained Status And All That'.

I had thought before the elections that it was the Labour Party's intention to raise the level of funding of schools generally, up to that of the more generously treated Grant Maintained sector.

In Leicestershire at least, that has not happened. From 1 April this year we have been dropped down to the funding level we would have received if we had never been Grant Maintained. Other schools budgets has not been improved. The reduction to our annual budget is in the order of £110.000. Governors have decided to save about £30.000 from various budget headings and the rest from staffing. No one will notice a difference immediately. Gradually over the next year we shall reduce our teaching force by three.

This is regrettable for the effect it will eventually have on childrens' education. However, we do have a well maintained and well equipped building. We do have well qualified and well trained staff. We do have a belief in our vocation and a determination to serve the community. We have come a long way forwards in the last five years since we first opted out. We are not going to go backwards now despite this adversity'.

The Sunday Mirror, The Daily Mirror and Pringles Crisps joined forces to provide sporting equipment for schools. The scheme, 'Pringles Tops For Sport' requires schools to collect the tokens from the newspapers and the foil seals from the crisp tubes in exchange for free equipment.

An appeal for 'shoppers' to take note of 'Sainsbury's School Rewards 99' was made. In the past the promotion had provided wall maps, models, musical instruments and measuring equipment. Parents were urged to obtain registration forms from the school office.

Vouchers were also being collected from Asda and Tesco. The Sun, News of the World, The Times, The Sunday Times and Walkers Crisps were all producing vouchers in support of the Literacy Initiative. The first ten books from Walkers Crisp tokens had been sent for.

A warning to parents was given regarding pupil absence. This was due to a media report that two girls in the county were missing. Although the two girls were eventually found safely, parents were urged to telephone the school to give reasons why their child would be absent on any occasion. Leaving the premises at lunchtime was outlawed and was a condition highlighted on the Admissions Form. A group of pupils had been punished for flouting this rule as it existed in the interests of safety.

High expectations are required of pupils and none more so than wearing school uniform. The Governors set the school dress code and the school is happy to implement it. The Governing Body makes all the policies and ensures that the school operates them. It is responsible for all aspects of the safety and welfare of the children. Any trips taken outside of school have to be 'risk assessed' by the school and presented to the governing body for signature. The governors are equipped with a large document, *A Guide to the Law for School Governors*. A responsible and accountable task, governors are concerned with the future of the children. The Head Teacher is responsible for the day to day running of the school whilst the Governors are responsible for the strategic direction of the school and the Chair of Governors is responsible overall.

Other areas are equally strict. Rules on detention, homework and school trips were highlighted. Detention was given for failure to complete set tasks and poor behaviour. The homework policy was such that more than one evening to complete a task was given. Allocation of places on trips and visits were subject to good attendance, appropriate behaviour and general school conduct. A data bank was devised to highlight pupils who had been unsuccessful in their application because of insufficient places available for a particular visit. The school's reputation was paramount at off-site school venues and acceptable pupil behaviour was essential.

On Valentine's Day two Year 9 basketball teams were entered into the National Tournament. The 'Sunny D National 3 on 3' was held at the Granby Halls in Leicester. The teams came from all over the city both from schools and local sides. Both the A and B South Wigston teams won all of their games but only one team could progress to the national semi finals. A close match between the two teams was fought and the B team won through. The national semi finals were held at Ponds Forge International Sports Centre in Sheffield. The team narrowly lost out in three close games. Mr Clifford thanked both the A and B teams for progressing so far.

For the benefit of charity on Red Nose Day in March, pupils could pay for the privilege of wearing one item of red clothing. The sum of £100.73 pence was raised.

As 16, 17 and 18 March drew closer rehearsals were in progress for the Rocky Monster Show. Help was invited from parents for this full scale production with costumes, catering and scenery painting.

The show which was a spoof Frankenstein musical thrilled the audience which included school Governors and Councillors. The show was described as a 'slick and fast moving comedy'. Special thanks were given to Mr Paul Chivers for his splendid directing talents and to all pupils and staff involved in the production.

Meanwhile the Science Department was busy organising their annual Conker Knockout 'Conkertition'. Rikesh Mistry 6VT, finally won the day and was awarded with book tokens.

Enthusiastic and talented sportsmen and girls brought credit to the school with Year 9 rugby beating Brockington 53-12. Year 9 cross country teams competed at the championships at Melton Country Park with three boys finishing in the top ten. Shane Kiely's outstanding performance saw him become the Year 9 County Champion. At the County Cross Country Relays in Loughborough, Adam Pollard could be seen doing his lap in just one shoe which in no way hindered the success of the team which finished in second place. Rebekah Randle 8CK, represented Leicestershire in the 'All England Cross Country' at Luton.

In 1999 a report from the Disability Rights Task Force highlighted the need for the Disability Discrimination Act of 1995 to be extended to education.

It is notable to record that in April 1999 with the introduction of many new Acts and amendments to Education Acts of Parliament, that the school Governors were very much involved regarding the understanding and discussion of the changes. Mr Alan Kind, MBE and Mrs Mary Weston, two Governors of the 'Curriculum Meeting' met with Rosamund Davies, Head of Learning Support to discuss the implications of such changes.

Fun Schools attracted many pupils involvement and help from their families. Proceeds raised at the event were directed to the Learning Support Department. The Learning Support Room, sited in the new block above the science laboratories, was being upgraded with new furniture and furnishings. The department purchased its own television / video recorder and a custom built computer area was installed. A small library and teaching area was also created.

In April Tina Adams, Asthma Project Nurse, was welcomed into school to give a talk on Asthma Awareness. It has been suggested that South Wigston has a number of health issues relating to asthma and the school had a large number of students suffering from the illness. The parents of the High School and the primary schools were invited to attend.

Congratulations were given to the Chair of Governors Mr Geoff Welsh who was also a former pupil of the school, Mr Welsh was returned to Blaby District Council in the local elections.

The Headmaster and Governors were reported to have attended many Admission Committees and Appeals Tribunals to explain the fact that the school was over subscribed and therefore the necessity of turning away pupils was unavoidable.

At the end of May Miss Baker, Mrs Hickson, Mr Heritage and Mr King escorted thirty nine pupils on their annual overseas visit- destinations Germany and Belgium. Travelling through the Channel Tunnel to France then via Holland and Belgium, the party stayed at a German youth hostel at Oberwesel. The pupils visited Boppard and were able to use their well learned German language. Ascending the steep hills on the banks of the Rhine by chairlift they descended on foot in the afternoon.

On the third day of their visit the party saw the world's largest hand made cuckoo clock on the way to Koblenz where photographs were taken in front of a section of the Berlin Wall. A guided tour of picturesque Marksburg Castle and a short bus journey past the Lorelei Rock took them to the Rhineland town of Rudesheim.

The next exciting day was spent at 'Phantasialand', a German 'Disneyland'. The evening saw the party transfer to the Worriken Sports Centre in Belgium. A fun filled day was spent with a host of challenging activities which included judo, climbing, trampolining, orienteering, kayaking and canoeing. By the end of the holiday many of the pupils made friends with pupils from other school

parties and made expert use of their foreign language skills.

During May, June and July out of school trips were arranged. Year 6 were taken on a scientific zoo excursion whilst Year 6 Humanities pupils visited Stratford Upon Avon with a further visit to the Black Country Museum. This was followed by a visit to Alton Towers.

A thrilling time was had by fifty one children and five teachers at the PGL Centre near Ross on Wye, Herefordshire. An activity holiday business, named after its founder Peter Gordon Lawrence and based at Court Farm; offered various sporting activities. Abseiling, quad bikes, challenge course and archery to name just a few. Mr Toward led by example on the challenge course resulting in him being covered head-to-toe in mud. A good time was had by all!

A one day event took place in the school in early June when teachers from Guthlaxton involved in English, mathematics, science and languages visited. 'Lead Lessons' were arranged. Later in the month a two day induction of Guthlaxton taster sessions, groupings and pastoral issues were offered.

An Information and Communications Technology (ICT) course was arranged for May and June to take place on Tuesday evenings at the school. This was aimed at adults in order to familiarise parents in the subject with a view to giving a wider understanding to families.

Extending ICT to the children was helped by offering a suitable course of activity to the pupils as a summer holiday activity in August. Pupils paid £5.00 and could choose to stay with ICT or Physical Education or alternate with both subjects. The ICT was not to interfere with curriculum work.

A Numeracy Summer School was also arranged for three weeks in the summer when thirty Year 5 and Year 6 pupils from three feeder primary schools attended. The standard of teaching was checked by a Government Official. The only Year 5 project in the country, South Wigston were successful in obtaining government money. Enthusiastic support was given from Edward Garnier QC,MP, Councillor Geoff Welsh, Chair of Governors and Councillor Peter Swift, Mayor of Oadby and Wigston Borough Council.

The school was awarded a prestigious Education Extra Award for Extra Curricula Activities. £200, a certificate and the honour of adding

'DISTINCTION' to the school logo was the reward. The money was earmarked for extra out of school activities.

'Sportsmark National Award' for sporting activities was given to South Wigston High School. Only four hundred schools in the whole country were selected seven of which were in Leicestershire. Only three of the schools were High Schools.

Peer Assisted Learning Strategies, 'PALS' was trialled in 1999 with a sponsorship secured from Jacobs Bakery. Pupil mentors were selected for their maturity and empathy with their peers. Year 8 and Year 9 students mentored Year 6 and Year 7 pupils in a history project and the outcomes were considered very good in the Standard Attainment Tests, 'SATS'. South Wigston High School with the most developed project in the county gave thanks to Jacobs, Walkers, Nestle and Britvic. Thanks were also given to the National Mentoring Network for their advice and their money.

The Music Department's Summer Concert was a resounding success. A wide spectrum of musical talent was on parade for parents, teachers governors and Mayors.

Glyn Forsythe's brass solo was outstanding. The flute choir, clarinet choir, brass ensemble, orchestra, string group, bell ringing and many soloists impressed the audience throughout the evening. Songs from the shows were abundant. Eve Browning singing 'Part of your world' from 'The Little Mermaid' and James Smith's memorable 'If I were a rich man' was a highlight.

The evening ended with a lively performance of the schools pop stars, 'Crude' and the finale was a rousing patriotic orchestral performance.

New Foundation Status for the school took effect in September 1999. This was as a direct result of the Labour Government's policy. The battle won for Grant Maintained status was lost.

The Headmaster, Mr Eric Bothamley, wrote with feeling, *'Much has been made of the Prime Minister's sons' school which also used to be Grant Maintained, asking parents for a subscription of £30. a month. South Wigston and Glen Parva parents also want the very best for their children. The rich and super-rich do not have the monopoly of love and care! Since South Wigston High School lacks the private resources of the London Brompton Oratory we have had to reduce the teaching staff by three this year and spend less on decoration, resources and training. I cannot begin to tell you how much this grieves governors and teachers alike. Meanwhile the government are genuinely and actively spending more money on education. Someone in authority needs to ask some searching questions of Mr Blunkett about why this is not getting passed into schools. In the last week of the summer term I was able to spend a whole two hours with our local MP Edward Garnier QC explaining the full details of this financial blight. I also reported on the cuts at Glen Hills and Parkland, two successful and well run primary schools. They were not even Grant Maintained so why should they feel the pinch?'*

The new status eventually impacted on a new name and new constitution as the new ' Foundation School Governors' were reformatted.

At the Curriculum Meeting on 7 October the Deputy Head, Gary Toward explained the successful start to the school's mentoring scheme. One hundred and eighty students were involved as either a mentee or a mentor and fifty community /Year 11 mentors. The school had been sponsored by Nestle, Jacobs, Walkers and Britvic and had received £7,600 bursary award from the National Mentoring Association.

At the end of October sixty pupils spent the weekend at Beaumanor Hall, Woodhouse, Leicestershire built 1845-47 for the Herrick family. The Hall was requisitioned by the Government during the Second World War for military intelligence purposes. It subsequently became a resource for Leicestershire County Council.

Beaumanor Hall, Woodhouse

The children enjoyed rock climbing, canoeing and problem solving developing teamwork skills.

From the school's mentoring programme the children were a mix of mentors and mentees. The scheme built on the confidence and self esteem that the programme had already given to the mentees.

Good attendance was valued at South Wigston High School and the Autumn Term of 1999 was marked by a prize draw for those achieving this goal. Eight pupils out of one hundred and sixty seven were awarded with vouchers.

Parents were alerted to the Leicestershire Early Years Childcare Partnership, (EYDCP) with a view to joining the multi agency advisory body to the Leicestershire County Council. The body was responsible for the strategic planning for childcare. An essential part of the partnership's role was to consult with parents and to that aim a Parents Forum was planned.

Free software for schools worth £35 million was on offer. *Time Computers, The Times, The Sunday Times* and *Time Education* joined forces to offer quality equipment absolutely free to those people who collected tokens.

Christmas 1999 saw South Wigston High School in the news again when the *The Mail* reported on the pupils magnificent effort in raising £800 for the Dyslexia Association. This money was to raise awareness and help children suffering from the condition. It was reported that South Wigston pupils had sung, scored and played their way to the cash total. The annual charity afternoon held at the school had planned to raise money for the Oadby and Wigston Borough Mayor's good cause and pupils decided on the events to raise it. They ranged from fortune telling to chocolate tasting, penalty shoot outs and a basket ball challenge.

South Wigston High School Scrabble Team won through to the second round of the Scrabble Challenge Competition and were awarded a Scrabble CD-ROM for the school.

A response to parents observations on a news report was made by the Head Teacher entitled, 'League Tables'.

"Parents who read the local paper tell me that this year our Key Stage Two SAT's Results looked quite respectable. I wouldn't know. I pay no attention to Key Stage Two league tables! League tables generally tell the socio-economic grouping of a school's catchment area. Our school will never be able to compete fairly with selective schools or schools where parents are predominantly 'middle class' and 'professional'. If politicians and newspapers asked shrewd questions they would want to know how much improvement primary schools had made in pupils' performance between children starting as 4/5 year olds and the examination in Year 6. The league table of 'Added Value' would actually look very different from the league table of raw results. What we know from primary schools is that our pupils are generally not academically advantaged when they start school at 4/5 years old. Our Year 6 pupils currently arrive here as average. What we know from our own Key Stage 3 SAT's results is that Year 9 leave here markedly above average in maths and English, in fact the whole spectrum right across the ability range has been improved. That is real 'added value'. Sadly there are no league tables to show it.

Our staff here, 'whether or not they actually teach' are all committed to giving young people a first rate education. Results in Music, Sport and exam room shows our efforts are rewarded. And as vocationalists, that is the best Christmas present we can have".

The Christmas Concert was again reported as a triumph for South Wigston High School musical talent. The sixty strong choir gave a Christmas Welcome, a jazzy version of the Christmas Story, with narrations provided by Mr Eric Bothamley, Headmaster, and Mr Chris Henley. The ensembles and soloists played well and the evening was rounded off by every musician and choir member joining together to sing 'Let There Be Peace'.

The new century 2000 began for teachers on 4 January with staff training. This event preceded the return of pupils on the following day. A week later the Deputy Head reported more details of the Mentoring Scheme to which further sponsorship had been attracted. They could now add Fyffes and Fox Confectionery to the group and a Mentor's Forum had been established.

In August, South Wigston High School acquired a new Head Teacher. Mr Gary Leslie Toward firmly in post as the Deputy Head since his appointment in 1993, secured the Headship on the retirement of Mr Eric Bothamley.

Mr Toward recalls that he had to fulfil a tall order. His memories are clear as he wrote,

'I had promised that if I was appointed I would

deliver a major part of the school's improvement plan; that of building a sports centre on the school site. The plan had been on the agenda for about six years, in fact as a deputy head I had been involved in its inception, but the funding had never been found.

Knowing that I had to deliver I nagged and lobbied and finally managed to get the school to become top priority in the county's sports building programme. When in 2001 the New Opportunities Fund came along I clapped my hands as I knew the end could be in sight. However, I didn't reckon for the fact that the price of steel would shoot through the roof and that Sport England would be difficult about the nature of the building we needed. I suddenly found that we would be £250,000 short.

I am an optimist by nature and I resolved to get the money one way or another. Short of robbing banks and winning the lottery, it either had to come from the school itself or the local community. I hatched a plan to save school capital funds over a period of time and to raise a further £40,000 with the support of the school and local communities. The Head's Challenge was born when I put my heart on my sleeve and said I'd raise £2000 by completing the Three Peaks Challenge; climbing Ben Nevis, Scarfell Pike and Mount Snowdon all in twenty four hours.

So in the summer of 2002 I set off to complete the challenge supported by my seventy year old Father as driver of my Ford Galaxy and Mick Malton, an ex-colleague and rugby playing team mate. Thanks to my Dad driving like Stirling Moss, we managed to finish the task in twenty one hours despite a torrential downpour at midnight on Scarfell. £2000 in the bag.

The school and local community were brilliant and the rest of the funding was raised within a year. Our £1.5 million sports centre was opened two years ago by Gary Lineker and is now providing not only excellent school sports facilities but new opportunities for community sport in the area.

The trouble is the kids at school don't let things drop and the question was soon posed, 'What's the next Head's challenge, Sir?'

A year later I decided to involve the pupils in the next Head's challenge and took a double decker bus load to our local gym to run seven relay marathons on treadmills. Another £2000.00 was raised to support the project.

After the now expected 'What is your challenge next year Sir?' I thought it was time to step up to the mark again, this time pledging to walk Hadrian's Wall. So in 2004 accompanied by Mick Malton again three others including my Vice Chair of Governors, Geoff Welsh, who was recovering from a heart attack, I set off with my Dad once again as the drop off driver. Geoff was the real hero on that walk, as not only was it a challenge after his heart attack, he developed terrible blisters on the first day. After around one hundred and eight miles walking and taking advice from a local shepherd by lining Geoff's socks with sheep's wool from barbed wire fences, we ambled into Bowness on Solway. This time my sponsorship went to redeveloping the inside of the school.

The last three years has seen the Head's Challenge develop into a major school mentoring programme, with around fifty pupils yearly joining a scheme which not only challenges them physically but stretches them mentally too. Each pupil involved has to take on a new skill, a new experience, carry out community service, complete an expedition in the Peak District and raise funds for charity. Most of the pupils who take part (half are selected as pupils who need a boost or challenge to help them raise their game) raise their effort levels in school significantly, resulting in higher attainment and improved self esteem.

This year I again carried out a personal challenge which was to scale Mont Blanc. The pupils of the school chose two charities for me to support. The Royal British Legion, as we have very strong links to our local World War One heroes, and the Matt Hampson Trust as the school has a huge Leicester Tigers' heritage. Luckily again I was supported by a friend, Noel Melvin, another Head Teacher.

This was my biggest challenge, not least because of a fear of heights, which has haunted me for years. I have tried hard for some time to fight the problem but I knew on the Mont Blanc climb I would be really challenged and I was. The first hurdle was a climb down a three hundred foot rock face to a glacier to practice ice climbing. It seems odd now that I not only managed that feat, but also managed it without being roped on. You just had to get on with it.

The first mountain climb, a practice before the

big one, was the Aquille de Tour, 'The Needle Tower'. At 3600m it posed a decent challenge on its own. After a half day climb to an over night stay in a French mountain hut (terrible food and very sweaty) we set off at four in the morning with our guide. Most of the climb was on glacier and we had to negotiate our way over crevasses and steep inclines using our ice axes for support. Wearing crampons was a novel experience, a sort of four wheel drive on your feet.

Glaciers are dangerous beasts, and the scale of the things is incredible, with hundreds of feet of ice below your feet and crevasses, both obvious and hidden all over the place. Our guide told us that last winter one of a party had skied into a crevasse and a rope was dropped to rescue him. However, a different skier was pulled up who'd been off-piste by himself and fell in the same hole. Luck man. When the first skier was eventually rescued he said that he thought he had heard a dog barking down in the crevasse. The guide with him was lowered down and later emerged with a dog hooked by the collar with his ice axe. Apparently it had been lost for six days.

The last bit of the climb was up a rock face about three hundred feet roped together. What a view and what a sense of achievement.

When we arrived in Chamonix for the climbing we heard straight away that five people had died earlier in the week, all on Mont Blanc. Three had frozen in a storm and two had fallen as a ledge collapsed. It put my challenge into perspective. I say this because on the day we set off for Mont Blanc our guide told us that a really bad storm was due to hit the peak for the next two days. We could begin the climb, but would likely sit for two days in huts as no one in their right mind would attempt the climb in an electric storm as was predicted. We therefore diverted our big climb to Italy and took on the country's biggest peak, Gran Paradiso at 4100m lower than Mont Blanc but a big challenge nonetheless.

Again it was a half day's walk up to an Italian mountain hut, which I am pleased to say had good food and was relatively pleasant. Still we rose at four AM and set off for the top. The first three hours were in the dark over moraines, rocks and boulders left by retreating glaciers, and as the sun began to rise, we joined a steep and heavily crevassed glacier. The scale of these places is hard to visualise and what

seems like a short distance is actually miles away. From the glacier the summit looked a stone's throw away, but it took three and a half hours or more to get there. On route the weather changed and clouds set in. We'd been joined by a second guide, and he was worried about the possibility of lightning. Being on top of a mountain with an ice axe in your hand makes you a bit of a conductor so I could understand his concern. The effects of altitude hit me at about 3900m and my head spun and stomach churned. What looked to me like a half hour's walk was revealed to me as a bit further when the guide said, 'It's only another couple of hours'. It was time to get my head down, grit my teeth and meet the challenge.

Two hours passed and I can remember little of that time except focussing on my feet and where I was placing them. The sight of the summit only 400m banished the altitude problems as adrenaline kicked in. My excitement turned to fear though as when we approached the rocky summit with our crampons still on I saw the five inch ledge we had to cross to get to the top. A sheer drop of a hundred feet loomed below and I remember thinking, 'no bloody way'.

There was no time to think much more though as when you are roped to a guide you just follow and somehow I glued myself to the rock face and wobbled across the void to the summit. Noel had brought his Celtic top and I my Tigers flag and irreverently we draped the Madonna statue (a feature of most Italian peaks it seems). Call it coincidence but it was at that point that the first crack of thunder came and our guide told us to move fast. Looking back, I think we went back over that ledge without clipping on to the rock, but the fear of thousands of volts up our ice axes made us forget the drop. Back on the glacier, hail came down thick and fast and a lightning bolt struck the floor only 200m away. A party of climbers nearby hit the deck like they had been machine gunned and we scurried down hill like whippets, as fast as our spiked feet would allow us.

It took another eight hours to get to the bottom of the mountain and back to Chamonix, where the sky around Mont Blanc was being lit up by a huge electric storm and torrential rain was pounding the streets. We had indeed made the right decision not to attempt that climb.

Back safely in Leicester I look back on the challenge as my greatest ever, and despite the scares *and altitude issues, my best and most exhilarating too. With around £3000 in the charity pot was certainly worthwhile and Matt Hampson, a most inspirational young man, will benefit significantly from my adventure. Back at school, there's only one question on the lips of my pupils and staff, 'What's your next challenge?'. It's obvious though isn't it? I have still to climb Mont Blanc.*

I still have one way of supporting Matt though. I have recently published a novel under the pen name of George Taylor. '1 4 SORROW' is a thriller set in and around a school. The characters and plot are based on my many experiences in teaching over the last twenty five years and will change your vision of school life for ever. All profits of sales go to the Matt Hampson fund until Christmas.

Aquille du Tour

Returning to the new millennium more written materials was placed in every school and local education authority in England by the Government. This was in order to help support the inclusive development of mainstream schools. Through the investigation of its cultures, policies and practices the school uses a cycle of activities to help break down the barriers to learning and participation for one hundred percent of pupils

10 January was significant for Year 9 pupils as they gathered to take their mock SAT's in English, maths and science.

January was a busy month as in previous years for the South Wigston High School Governors. Various meetings were arranged for the 'Community', 'Premises', 'Personnel', 'Policy Resources' committees and on 1 February a full Governors meeting took place. The Governors play an important role in the life of the school dedicating much of their free time to important decision making.

Forty eight keen dancers and musicians from the school spent the first day of February in the West End as they were escorted to London to see a matinee performance of 'Cats'. The show was described as outstanding with the audience standing and applauding at some of the dancing and singing. After the show they all enjoyed the scenic bus tour of London viewing Saint Paul's Cathedral, The London Eye and Big Ben.

Super Schools 2000 was celebrated at school with the visit in February of the Olympic Athlete, Todd Bennett. It was arranged for Todd to speak in assemblies about the event. Money raised by the pupils' participation in events was earmarked for the Humanities Department. The purchase of computer simulations and packages and further resources to aid all pupils learning.

On 11 February, led by Mrs Wood, five hundred pupils gyrated to the sound of Madonna's 'Holiday' and 'Saturday Night' in an aerobic routine to stretch their muscles. A mystery guest turned out to be the European, Olympic and World Swimming Champion, Sharon Davies.

The SAT's examinations were getting closer each week and in early March staff were accompanying Year 9 pupils to the Haymarket Theatre in Leicester to see Shakespeare's, Romeo and Juliet. The professionalism of the actors in the main roles helped the pupils understanding of the plot.

The Allocations Department was busy sending out letters to parents of Year 9 children with advice on the school which had been selected for the transfer in September of their child. Any concerns on the choice made should be addressed with Mrs Sharpe at South Wigston High School.

An 'Extra Closure Day' during the summer term was announced by the Government. This day was to allow staff to complete training on 'Performance Thresholds'. These were new standards for all teachers to reach and performance related pay initiatives.

Congratulations were made to Sam Taylor 7GW, who was selected for his footballing prowess to be part of Nottingham Forest's Football Club's 'School of Excellence'

Congratulations also were given to Abi Favell 6VT, and Candice Gregory 6MM, who were selected to perform at de Montfort Hall as members of 'Arts in Education'.

Fourteen pupils received congratulations as poems they had composed were selected for publication in the National Young Writers Competition.

After the Easter break it was expected that pupils whose parents wished it would receive Meningitis vaccinations.

'Operation Truant', a scheme put forward by Leicester City and Leicestershire County Council was made known. Any school-aged pupil found to be out of school during school sessions would be approached by a team and questioned. It was intended to report the names of children to the schools and The Educational Welfare Service for further investigation. National statistics regarding truancy have often been highlighted by the media.

At the end of March a party of Year 8 pupils enjoyed their trip to Greenwich to see the Millennium Dome which housed a major exhibition to celebrate the third millennium.

The Millennium Dome at Greenwich, 2000

The fifth and sixth of April was not to be missed as pupils were working hard to produce their Spring Concert. This year it was to be 'The Abba Spectacular'.

New opportunities were afoot as South Wigston High School was successful in securing Government money in support of their mentoring scheme. This would enable additional after school lessons in English and mathematics for the forthcoming three years.

Advice was also given to children to set their videos for the BBC's revision programmes in all subjects for Key Stage Two and Key Stage Three. Books and CD Roms were available for purchase too.

By September parents had been informed that children taking music examinations would not be accompanied either with a pianist or a chaperone. The music department and peripatetic teachers would only be able to provide lists of suitable accompanists in order that parents could make their own arrangements.

News of changes in the Governing body of the school was being given to parents in October. The Chairman for seven years, Mr Geoff Welsh was stepping down to become the new Vice Chair whilst Mr Roy Hughes was elected as Chairman. Mr Hughes had served the school previously as a Governor and was Mayor of Oadby and Wigston Borough Council in 1986.

Mr Roy Hughes, Chairman of the Governors

County Councillor Alan Kind also stepped down as Chairman of the Premises Committee to move to 'the back benches' and was being succeeded by Mr Paul Mann. New Governors were John and Joanne Small, Jenny Nixon and Yvonne Orr.

Thanks were given to Mr Alan Kind for his continued efforts in pressurising County Hall's Property Department. This was in order to obtain the school's fair share of resources. Successfully too as news came in that the changing room roofs were to be repaired.

Mrs Knight, Mrs Griffiths and Mr Carpenter were rewarded on the night Year 6 pupils successfully performed 'The Owl And The Pussycat'. Parents in the audience sang along with the children as from practicing with them they knew the words so well.

During the Readathon Week in October Year 6 and 7 pupils were sponsored for reading a selection of books in order to raise money for Malcolm Sargent Cancer Care for Children and the Roald Dahl Foundation. A very welcome £750 was collected.

ICT was at this time on the agenda for development as the computers were in the throes of being connected to the Internet giving access to the World Wide Web. This facility was to throw open thousands of libraries to the students, data bases and bulletin boards whilst exchanging messages with other users throughout the world. The company, 'Research Machines' were to filter out and block unsuitable sites. Parents were required to give permission for their children to use the internet.

The Bitesize Travelling Theatre Company gave a gripping performance of Macbeth to Year 9 pupils in the latter part of November. Wearing impressive costumes they acted out their parts supported by atmospheric scenery. The English Department had made this special arrangement in order to help the pupils with their Stage 3 SAT's Shakespeare paper.

The Bitesize Travelling Theatre Company performing a scene from Shakespeare's Macbeth.

A call to all pupils went out for them to become involved in the Messiah Workshop and Performance in December. Guthlaxton College with their own musicians and singers, in conjunction with Broom Leys Choir and local orchestra invited all colleagues, parents and pupils to come forward.

Once again in December the children were invited to perform at the Glen Parva Memorial Hall Concert. This was a fund raising event in support of the Hall. The Bell Ringers held the audience spellbound as they played carols. Jessica Lee 7CP

and Sadie Addison 7JK transfixed them with instrument playing and dancing and Ross Brown 7CP brought the house down with his line dancing. He had to perform an encore by popular demand.

The South Wigston High School Supporters' Association was complimented on the organisation of their Christmas Quiz. A magnificent hamper was won by the Weston family, Cain, 6RB. Second prize was won by the 'redoubtable' kitchen staff and £120 profit was raised. Amy Tilley. 6VT won the lucky number prize.

In 2001 a report from the Department of Education and Employment called for a radical and inclusive approach to school building design. This impacted on the wider discussion of the effect of the built environment on inclusion and exclusion of children. Special Educational Needs and the Disability Act, (SENDA) strengthened the right to mainstream schools for disabled children.

The 2001 Act stated that special educational needs of children will normally be met in mainstream schools. This has seen the numbers of children taught in special schools decline as Local Education Authorities attempt to adhere to this principle.

On the return to business in January Mr Toward, Head Teacher, sent an invitation to parents to discuss the Standard Attainment Tests. Year 6 and Year 9 pupils would be working hard to achieve good grades at Easter. Mr Toward addressed pupils with low effort grades to improve, those cruising, to try harder and for those already working at full steam, to keep it up. For himself and the staff he saw the need to be looking at themselves to see how they could do things better. Nine new members of staff were welcomed into the school.

Missing coats appeared to be a talking point as sixty six had been left behind at Christmas. Advice was given to 'see' the caretaker to inspect his collection in bin liners before they were donated to the charity shops. Other coats lost since Christmas could be inspected in the Year Head's office. An appeal to 'name tag' garments was made.

It was made very clear that the outlawing of body piercings had arrived. One pupil had had an accident when her navel piercing caught on a desk. The rule of no jewellery at school prevailed with the exception of 'sleepers' for pierced ears and tram line hair 'do's' were definitely not acceptable either.

Beating the Bullies was explained in the school's

anti bullying policy. *'Bullying could be considered to be a combination of one or any anti social behaviours directed towards a pupil or pupils. Racial abuse may be considered as an identifiable strand of bullying'*. Parents were invited to contact the relevant Year Head if they had concerns. The school does not tolerate bullies and the message to potential bullies is, 'Don't do it'.

'Walkers Crisps' were obviously very popular in more ways than one. *'The Sun'* and *'The News of the World'* were again joining forces with *'Walkers'* in the 'Free Books For Schools' initiative. As a result over five million books had already been given to schools. For the new scheme language books had been added in readiness for the European Year of Languages. South Wigston was obviously keen to be included and appealed to parents and children, relatives, neighbours and friends to save the tokens.

Box Tops for Education was another scheme taken up by the Nestle Company. Shreddies, Cheerios, Golden Grahams were all devoured in order to obtain the tokens.

Pupils, parents and teachers tantalisingly solved quiz sheets in order to raise money for the South Wigston War Memorial Restoration Fund. £45 was raised.

The Super Schools star visitor in February was Darren Campbell the Olympic Silver Medallist. Ben Challenger, Loughborough born High Jumper and son of Romeo Challenger; the drummer of Showaddywaddy; visited too. Mrs Wood, Mr Kent, Mr Clifford and Mr Toward went through various exercise routines with the pupils which was followed by a question and answer session with Ben and Darren.

Ben Challenger, Teacher Ron Atkinson and Darren Campbell 2001

Pauline Wells from 'Rainbows' was a welcome visitor to the school in February when she addressed the children in assembly to thank them for their fund raising ability. The grand total of £990.92 for the childrens charity had been raised.

Girl footballers were keen to show their skill after practicing hard after school. A team of Year 8 pupils was entered into the U13 Adidas Predator six a side competition. A tough competition was fought between seven schools with South Wigston finishing in joint third place.

On the day that Monsieur Dan Ro Ro, a French street artist came to school; Year 7 pupils were delighted with his ventriloquism, juggling tricks, his unicycle performance and his songs.

Dan Ro Ro 2001

Memories were vivid of a past pupil who had left the school in 1995. Louis Deacon was described as an 'Ex-pupil with the eye of a tiger'. Reminiscences of Louis learning his sport on the school playing field were clear as news flooded in of him playing first class rugby for Leicester Tigers and filling the position of Captain. Previously Louis had represented England at youth level.

Reported was the news that Doctors at Leicester University were carrying out research into the Genetics of Asthma. Parents were invited to contact Lisa Pidgeon, a research nurse at the Childrens' Asthma Centre if they would like their family to participate.

In June Estelle Morris became the Secretary of State for Education and Skills, remaining in the post until October 2002 when Charles Clarke took over the reins.

Key Stage 1, 2 and 3, identify with a child's age and Standard Attainment Tests, (SAT's) taken by children at the end of key stages are nationally set. (National Curriculum Tests, NCT.)

At the end of Key Stage One, age seven, children

are assessed by their teachers. At KS2, aged eleven, pupils take nationally set tests and at the age of fourteen, KS3, results are used to judge school performances. The Value Added Measure shows how well the school helps its pupils to progress by comparing the development of similar children across the country. Comparing progress from Key Stage One to Key Stage Two measures how well the school has improved their performance. Other factors may be taken into consideration outside of the school for example, gender, movement between schools, family circumstances and Special Educational Needs.

Subjects at KS1 are, reading, writing, speaking and listening with arithmetic and science.

At KS2 subjects are reading, writing and spelling with maths, mental arithmetic and science. The National Curriculum requires that by the end of Key Stage Two pupils should all be able to swim.

At KS3 English, reading, writing, studying a Shakespeare play, maths and science are listed. Teachers assess the pupils skills in history, geography, modern foreign languages, design and technology, art and design, music, physical education, citizenship and religious education.

During the term the Humanities Department arranged for one hundred and eighty children to visit Lincoln Cathedral, Castle and Cadbury's World.

The afternoon of 7 December was a fund raising event when all the proceeds from the main charity event and 'own clothes day' went to the Leicester Royal Infirmary Childrens Hospital. Listed so far for charities was Children in Need, £508, Readathon, £956, Non Uniform Day, £11, Remembrance Day Poppies, £84, LRI Childrens Hospital £818. In addition to this wonderful work was fifty two Christmas hampers to be donated to Age Concern.

The popular Christmas Concert took the audience by storm being greeted by the swirl of bagpipes, warm mince pies and punch. Entertainment consisted of multi cultural music, keyboards, choir and band. Flute duets and a Clarinet Choir showed their skill and the dancing group moved to effect. Mr Humpherson of Guthlaxton College was given a particular 'thank you' for his support.

The Education Act of 2002 ruled that schools with innovative ideas to improve education could seek exemption from any existing laws which prevented them from carrying this out.

In the same year South Wigston High School twinned with the Dujiangyan Foreign Language Experimental School in Sichuan Province, China. Mr Zhang Quing, the school's Head Teacher made a visit to South Wigston but unfortunately Mr Toward's return Easter visit sponsored by the British Council to develop the links; was cancelled due to Severe Acute Respiratory Syndrome, (SARS) hitting China.

Mr Zhang Quing and Leadership Team 2002

Musicians sadly suffered from the lack of theory lessons at the beginning of 2002. Instrumentalists were told that lessons hopefully would be available later in the year in September.

Hair styles were once again in focus as pupils were instructed, 'no hair braids, no wraps, no jewellery, no tramlines, no outrageous colours, no logos and no beads, feathers and sequins'.

The annual Super Schools Event welcomed the British and the AAA's 400 metre champion, Mark Richardson into school. Mark achieved a silver medal in the Summer Olympics 1996 Atlanta and a silver medal in the 1997 World Championships in Athens competing with the British relay teams.

Energetic rounds of sit ups, press ups and aerobics kept pupils and staff at South Wigston in shape. Money raised on this occasion was for the school library as well as aiding the Super Schools Organisation in turn to help budding young athletes.

Jemma Perry 8PHK was congratulated for securing the role of Snow White at the YMCA Theatre's production. This was to be performed the last week in March. Jemma was also chosen with a number of singers to perform at the Royal Albert Hall in London.

More acclaim for Stevie Hardy, 9GW one of seven Leicestershire girls to be selected for England

Soccer Trials.

Omar Kalik 6MH, was voted Athlete of the Month when he participated in the Sportshall Athletics Tournament. Also the Long Jump County Champion, Omar was set to compete in the regional finals in Grantham and the National finals in Birmingham.

Mr Toward made it known that he was keen to develop the use of the school's sports facilities. Clubs owners were invited to consider the benefits of making South Wigston their home venue or training ground.

The First Class Day Nursery situated on the South Wigston High School site passed its first OFSTED report with flying colours. It was especially geared for children with special needs and had good disabled access. Staff were competent in British Sign Language and had completed other courses in addition.

The mixed voice choir of the Leicester Phoenix Youth Chorale could be found every Tuesday evening during term time singing a wide variety of music from the shows to pop and gospel. Members from different schools and colleges in South Leicestershire used the school. Trips were arranged to theatres and concerts also to sing with other choirs out of Leicestershire. Mrs Shirley Baxendale was available to speak by telephone to any South Wigston High School pupils who would be keen to join the group.

More honours were heaped upon a South Wigston High School sports enthusiast. Jonathan Morgan 9GW, was to represent Leicestershire and Rutland Cross Country Championships, whilst Chrissie Orr, an ex pupil attending Guthlaxton College had reached the regional finals of the Rotary Young Chef of the Year Competition. Twelve other contestants from the East Midlands were to compete. Chrissie's ambition was to become a Food Technology Teacher at South Wigston High School.

Staff escorted Year 9 pupils to Paris for a week's holiday in early June. The First World War battlefield of Vimy Ridge was visited during the week where they all paid homage to the fallen. The children observed a solemn moment looking at the Leicestershire Regiment graves bearing the insignia of the Bengal Tiger.

The party visited the Louvre, the Pompidou Centre and ended their trip enjoying the fun of Disneyland.

On 19 June, Year 6 pupils were enjoying a day in the historic town of Stratford Upon Avon. Walking in the footsteps of William Shakespeare they visited his birthplace on Henley Street. Moving on to Cox's Yard they learned about the development of the town.

A few days later children were delighting their audiences with their spectacular production of 'The Wizard of Oz'. A cast of seventy pupils had worked for three months even giving up their lunch times and evenings to perfect their art. The orchestra was praised for their skill in drawing the show together over two evenings.

The Wizard of Oz, 2002

The Year 9 Presentation Evening on 3 July was the annual event which made parents proud. Trophies were presented for academic success, effort, enthusiasm and approach to school life. Children were called on to the stage to be presented with their award from a range of dignitaries and on this occasion staff awards were made also. The PE Department were awarded their 'Sportsmark Gold' and Mr Michael Booth was thanked for his service to South Wigston High School of twenty five years so far. Music during the evening was provided by George Norman on tuba, Natasha Allen on flute and Nathan Hall sang 'Evergreen'.

During the summer holidays the first stage of the sports hall development took place. The redevelopment of the car park featuring a one way system was carried out.

The new autumn term saw the launch of the school website, www.southwigston.leics.sch.uk. It was the school's first attempt at publishing on the net. The aim was to create an educational site for pupils' learning. The Maths Trail, quizzes and links to other sites were available.

A grand auction was held in September in the school hall. Some very tempting lots went under the hammer. Tickets to Leicester City's Christmas Game, meals in Leicester's top restaurants, designer clothing, one year's membership of Leicestershire County Cricket Club, child's room to be decorated with cartoons, dance lessons and beauty treatment were just a few.

A popular fund raising event was staged to raise money for the impending new sports hall. The England and Nigeria football match was shown in the school hall. The next game was played by England and Brazil also screened in the hall. Pupils paid fifty pence a time to boost the fund and unsurprisingly attendance figures on those days was excellent.

After much planning in the autumn the completion of the music block extension into the school hall was finally opened at a cost of £25,000. 'Alf Wright Construction' was engaged to carry out the work. This new facility was long awaited and was achieved by closing the gap between the music room and the hall. This was of great benefit to the children who needed to change costumes between scenes for the many productions which were performed.

Ben West, 7RN, received many congratulations for his success in fencing. On his first attempt he had become the Leicestershire and Rutland 12-14 years Foil (Fencing) champion.

Ninety Year 9 pupils were accompanied by seven staff to Cadbury World in November. Pupils learned about the history of chocolate making in Britain and saw the manufacturing process and the final wrapping of the bars. Miss Harding felt very proud of the pupils as they were commended on their excellent behaviour. This was especially noticeable as two other visiting schools were so unruly.

Mr Roy Hughes, Chair of Governors and Mr Toward made a presentation to Oadby and Wigston Borough Council regarding the benefits of the sports development for the community. The Council agreed to add £7000 to the fund which boosted the total to £29,000. Grateful thanks was sent to all of the sponsors and in particular to Dunton Bassett Parochial Church Council for their kind donation. Parents had also given cheques to the fund.

6 December was another fund raising day made special by the visit of Mr Edward Garnier QC,MP. Mr Garnier joined in the fun also presenting Year 7 pupils with Ordnance Survey Maps. This was an initiative sponsored by Ordnance Survey. The event raised £700 which boosted the year's total to over £22,000. The money over 2002 was earmarked for the new sports development.

Edward Garnier QC MP presenting Ordnance Survey Maps to two of the pupils

'Investors in People' assessors were scrutinising the school systems, speaking to staff to discover if the organisation still met the criteria for the award. Having 'IIP' recognition twice in the past for demonstrating that they worked well as a team, everyone was delighted to receive it again for the third year running.

New security systems were put in place at the front door on St Thomas Road. The entrance was controlled by a buzzer, intercom and security camera system. Much of the system was supplied free of charge and greatly reduced the chance of unwanted visitors. New ramps for disabled users were put in place and the installation of a lift was in progress.

A newcomer to the staff was ex pupil Mandy Bradbury, nee Atton. Her first entry into the school had been in 1978 where her education lasted until 1981. Her memories of her form teacher, Beverley Fisher were clear but on her return as a staff member she was surprised to find Mr Norton her science teacher and Mr Booth who taught her maths still there. Mandy now works as a Learning Support Assistant.

Pupils in the Learning Support Department learning English have access to the computer programme, Successmaker for reading and spelling.

Mandy Bradbury. Learning Support Assistant

Also Successmaker Earlybird is a useful tool. One measure of pupils improvement is when they can return to the mainstream teaching programme.

Learning Support is not a curriculum target base therefore Key Stage 2 and Key Stage 3 targets are not set. Teachers plan the work around the curriculum.

A bitterly cold snowy day was reported in the December 2002 issue of 'News Update'. The fight was on to win the 'Coca Cola Under 13 CUP'. South Wigston Year 8 team travelled to South Charnwood High School having won their rounds against New College High, Stonehill High and Judgemeadow. The game began on time despite the hard conditions under foot and the first half proved a hard fought encounter. The game ended with a dreaded penalty shoot out and South Wigston were the winners. The report states that the team was magnificent. Two members from 8TD were Joe Mattock and Lee Cox.

Christmas Concert 2002

The Christmas Concert was a musical success held over two evenings. Large numbers of pupils participated displaying their talent with flute, clarinet, oboe, euphonium, a string group, xylophone duet, singing group as well as vocal artistes and solo performances. A musical extravagansa was enjoyed by all.

As the new term of January 2003 opened Mr Toward's news for parents was to remind them of the discrepancy of league table analysis by the Government in their calculation of Key Stage Three progress. Credit was never given but to date the report showed that South Wigston was in the top three percent of all secondary schools in the country. Past frustration was lifted with the news.

However In 2003 some members of the National Teaching Union attempted to boycott tests fearing that there was a danger of teaching to tests in order to score well on school league tables. The debate continued with various bodies theorising on the effect of over testing children and many studies condemned 'SAT's.

It was reported that new ICT network had been upgraded with new servers and faster switching. Broadband and the Internet were now available throughout the school.

Concerns about the school's allocated budget was voiced by Mr Toward. Leicestershire had become the worst funded county in the country. Despite running costs being similar in most schools and staff pay being on a national pay scale, it made little difference to the fact that other counties received more money. Mr Toward had written to the Government and was still urging parents to write to Mr Charles Clarke, Secretary of State for Education and Skills on the matter. Representation from the Leicestershire County Council had sent a delegation to Westminster to protest.

Katharine Merry with pupils 2003

The February Super Schools special celebrity guest was Katharine Merry who at the age of thirteen was representing Great Britain holding national titles in nine events. Katharine gained a bronze medal in the final of the 400 metres at the 2000 Olympics in Sydney.

Ben Challenger was once again visiting the school. Pupils participating were allowed to wear sports gear for the day and all money raised was earmarked for the Sports Development Fund.

The visit was termed, 'An Olympic Success'. The PE Department and the catering staff all joined in the energetic exercise programme.

The South Wigston High School Supporters' Association, dubbed, 'Your Parent Power Group' attained status as a registered charity. They worked hard for the pupils and had fun at the same time. Meeting twice a term they planned activities for the benefit of the pupils. In March their topics for discussion were, The South Wigston High School Golf Open, Talent Show, Disco and Fundraising Applications.

The sports hall update was met with enthusiasm as it reached an important step nearer to reality. All the documentation had been given the green light in draft form by Sport England. The County Council architects and planners were working to finalise the design of the building and its exact location. The community fund had grown to £36,000 with many more events to come to reach the £40,000 school target.

Cash was needed to renew the school railings but to obtain the £20,000 needed it was suggested by the Governors that 'a painting party' may be set up. It was decided to ask for willing adult volunteers to come armed with their paint brushes to give the railings a 'make over'.

Science week in 2003 was 10 to 14 March. Much fun was had at the school as they competed in a science quiz, named famous scientists, made paper aeroplanes fly in all directions and for those on the Van de Graaff generator charging several thousand volts, a hair raising experience. Animal Man arrived to cheer Year 6 and 7 enthusiasts with frogs, snakes, owls and Holly the Hedgehog.

Ninety year 9 pupils visited Guthlaxton College to see their production of Victor Hugo's 'Les Miserables'. Everyone enjoyed the excellent performance.

The Minister for Education, Mr Stephen Twigg, MP made a tour of the school in June. Accompanied by Mr Toward and the Chair of Governors, Mr Roy Hughes, he was very impressed with what he saw. Specialist status for High Schools and consequently Leicestershire schools missing out on many initiatives were topics for discussion.

The summer concert was a resounding success with traditional music and excerpts from the hit musical, 'Grease'. A few days later the pupils participated in the Summer Prom at Guthlaxton combined with Bushloe and Abington schools.

A very energetic Friday was spent at the end of June at the Enderby Leisure Centre. Mr Toward, members of staff and seventy five pupils worked in relays on treadmills to complete marathons. The money raised for their own sports development had reached £40,000.

A party of Year 8 pupils were escorted to London for a weekend. On arrival they visited Hyde Park for lunch followed by a visit to the National History Museum. The mammal room and the earthquake exhibit was much appreciated. The evening spent at the theatre to see Chitty Chitty Bang Bang ended the first day. A visit to Madame Tussauds was enjoyed on the following day before returning home.

The autumn term of September 2003 began without its Head Teacher, Mr Gary Toward. He was absent 'with leave' in order to assist for two terms at the William Bradford Community College in Earl Shilton, Leicestershire. In his absence Mrs Jane Corrall took over the role as Acting Head Teacher.

Mrs Corrall reported that the first few weeks of the term had been exciting and vowed that in her role as Acting Head Teacher she was determined to uphold the good name of South Wigston High School for well motivated, hard working, well behaved pupils and dedicated and creative staff.

Mr C Richards, the Principal Adviser for the County had visited the school. He had admired the school, commented on the purposeful working atmosphere, cheerful classroom displays and well turned out pupils.

Leicestershire County Council were seeking views regarding the School Term Patterns in 2005/2006 and beyond. The possibility of introducing a six term year in schools was to be discussed. The consultation documentation was available on the County Hall website for anyone to see and express their opinions.

The annual book week took place in October and was made memorable in school by the many competitions to participate in. A costume competition, a family quiz and an anagram trail kept people busy. Videos of famous books were shown at every lunch time, a bookmark competition and many more activities. Teachers and Support Staff's favourite poems to celebrate National Poetry Day were also displayed.

In October the previously cancelled visit to Dujiangyan in the Sichuan province of China took place. Mr Gary Toward, accompanied by Mr Cambers, Vice Principal of Guthlaxton School, visited Mr Zhang Quing and the Foreign Language Experimental School. The Chinese school had five thousand pupils on its roll. During the week Mr Toward and Mr Cambers taught lessons, led assemblies, played sports with pupils and met many officials and ministers. Mr Toward related a superb experience on his return and hoped to develop teaching and learning and promote a greater cultural understanding and linking of pupils across the world.

Annie

Annie

Annie Christmas 2003

Mr Gary Toward, Mr Zhang Quing and Mr Cambers in the school dining hall in October 2003

On the afternoon of 5 December Russell Brickett, Fundraising Manager for 'Wishes 4 Kids' attended the school as the charity had been chosen for the year for their support. He was overwhelmed 'by the enthusiastic youngsters, the whole atmosphere was amazing, so many young people raising money in such a fun way'. Pupils raised £895.75 with many stalls, games and activities. Staff and pupils enjoyed Crazy Golf, Penalty Shoot Outs, Splat The Rat and Treasure Island.

Packed audiences on two nights in December applauded the production 'Annie'. The Chairman of Blaby District Council attended and said that he was

Pupils decorating the Christmas tree

honoured to be invited to such a super production and that it was one of the highlights of his Christmas. The talented children's good acting, lively singing and slick dancing thoroughly enjoyed entertaining supported by the school band.

An unusual appeal was made for plastic bottle tops to be saved over the Christmas period. One wheelchair had been purchased as a result of this activity already.

The new year of 2004 began with Mrs Corrall still at the helm. Reporting on her visit to Guthlaxton College to see their production of 'West Side Story' she wrote that it was a real privilege to be in the audience. Many of South Wigston's past pupils were taking part in the excellent musical production good enough to rival the West End.

In February the New Opportunities Fund received the business plans, development plans and other paperwork for their final approval to release the money for the building of the new Sports Centre. Planning permission had been given and the new build would be situated behind the huts close to the netball and tennis courts. It was sad to think that so many children over the past three years who had helped to raise funds for the centre had now moved on but it was hoped that a celebration day would be arranged on completion when all past pupils would receive an invitation.

The February Super Schools star visitor to be invited was the British Athlete and BBC Superstars Champion, Du'aine Ladejo. This promised to be another successful event.

Du'aine Ladejo with pupils 2004

Two Valentine discos were arranged by the South Wigston High School Supporters Association when five hundred children enjoyed the events.

In March South Wigston High School was host to a 'Musical Master Class' when talented pupils spent time with professional musicians. The following evening they attended a concert by the London Philarmonic Orchestra at de Montfort Hall. Mrs Oakland and the pupils were received in style with reserved seats, drinks in the interval and the opportunity to meet members of the orchestra.

Jo Jackson 9PH, won acclaim in the British Karate Championships in Manchester. She came first in the KATA category and representing England later in September she secured fifth place. Jo was sponsored by the school.

Mary Gee from the School Inspectorate spent a day at the school. As part of a Government initiative she was looking in particular at Personal Social and Health Education (PSHE) and Pastoral Care. Impressed by what she saw she commented on the 'breadth of opportunities, dedication of the staff and enthusiasm of the pupils'.

At the end of March eleven staff and eighty eight pupils excitedly left South Wigston with a plan to storm Warwick Castle. On arrival they explored the dungeons and learned about mediaeval life. Five hundred and thirty steps led up to the motte, an exhausting climb for some but worth the effort to see the view from the ramparts.

The first day of April was spent at Glencroft Church by Year 6 pupils. This visit was part of their religious studies. They watched how Jesus changed some people's lives and sample life in Biblical Rome. They enjoyed dressing up and eating food of the times also watching earlier Christians being flogged.

On 2 April the long awaited ski trip to Valmeinier in the French Alps began. Thirty six pupils were in high spirits as they were transported up the winding roads towards their destination. After supper at the restaurant the assent was to begin the following morning. The party was kitted out for the slopes and their first Apres Ski Event. By the end of the week the pupils were very able skiers. During the week they enjoyed ten pin bowling, karaoke, ice skating and disco. At the end of the week all the pupils received a certificate to show how well they had performed.

The Easter break over, the Head Teacher, Mr Gary Toward returned and Mrs Corrall reverted to her role as Deputy Head. Mr Toward wrote that as he walked into school it was like coming home. He recorded that Mrs Corrall and the staff had done a superb job in his absence.

Later in April eighty six Year 6 pupils were taken to Boulogne by seventeen members of staff. Arriving at Folkestone at 7am they took the shuttle to Calais. Stopping at a patisserie the pupils were keen to practice their French by ordering croissants or a pain au chocolat. The morning was spent in the lower town exploring the shops and market later meeting at the castle for a picnic.

The afternoon was enjoyed walking along the old wall looking at the historic part of Boulogne and visiting cafes. Leaving Boulogne they made for the Cite Europe, a large shopping centre before returning home.

In 2004 the Director of Education for Leicestershire Jackie Strong retired and in December Gareth Williams, Deputy Director of Wigan Education Department was appointed to succeed. He took up the post in April 2005 and one year later was confirmed as Director of Children's Services. Mr Williams long career in education began in 1977 and during his time as a Head Teacher his school was used as a model of good practice in teaching and learning.

The Children Act 2004 defines and supports the 'Every Child Matters' statement. Five basic principles are listed. They are; 'Be Healthy', 'Stay Safe', 'Enjoy and Achieve', 'Make A Positive Contribution' and 'Achieve Economic Well Being'. The Act aims to ensure that effective schools put the needs of children and their families at the forefront.

At school advice on revision for the SAT's exams was given. Useful tips on how not to do it such as, in front of the television but recommending the BBC, Schools Revision Website.

The chosen charity for the year which was decided by the School Council was 'Rainbows'. Dana Simmons from the Childrens' Hospice, which is located on the edge of Charnwood Forest, Loughborough, gave a talk to the pupils about the work of Rainbows. The charity which serves the East Midlands and South Yorkshire gives support to families with children with life limiting illness. South Wigston High School raised £926.92 in one afternoon which would be an enormous help towards the running costs.

£213.58 was raised for Children In Need. A Pudsey Bear Poster Competition was arranged to boost the funds.

During the summer holidays a Youth Inclusion Programme took place at Leicester University. Amy Morgan 6PH received an award for her attendance, attitude and motivation whilst on her course.

The new autumn term began and Mr Toward was excited as he looked ahead to forthcoming events. The Sports Centre was ready to be built and phase one of the new centre of the school coming later in the year. Mr Toward reported that the Governors were very keen to improve the school and this was reflected in their many meetings which he described as positive and upbeat.

The Head's Challenge soon took place and the long march was on towards Hadrian's Wall. From the banks of the River Tyne at Wallsend under the New Millennium Bridge and the Old Tyne Bridge, over the rolling crags and hills to the Plain of the River Eden and Carlisle before reaching Barrow on Solway.

£361.25 was raised in sponsorship which was to be used for refurbishing the centre of the school.

Hadrian's Wall 2004

Five days in October were arranged for parents and pupils to look to the future. An Opportunities Evening for 14+ students at Guthlaxton College, Countesthorpe College Open Evening, Careers Forum for Year 9's at Guthlaxton and Year 6 Meet The Tutor Evening were all advertised.

A huge attraction was staged at South Wigston High School for the half term. The Mick Duffy Soccer School in association with the school was offering a soccer course for the full five days. Mick Duffy was an ex Leicester City player and all pupils aged seven to fourteen were invited to register for their place. The emphasis being on fun they were advised that all coaches were qualified. Proceeds from the course were intended for developing the community opportunities for sport at the school.

At last new railings and gates were to be erected. In keeping with the 1930s style and design qualities of the building, it had taken a year to gather the funds together.

Wednesday and Thursday evenings 8 and 9 of December saw pupils performing to a packed house at their Christmas Concert. Staff and pupils and a 'cast of thousands' put on a 'top draw' event to end the year.

Christmas shoppers were invited to view a compilation of Art, Design and Technology in the Customer Services Section of Marks and Spencer at Fosse Park. Staff and pupils were thanked for their fantastic display.

The term ended on Friday 17 December but on Monday 20 the teachers were back for another training day.

As the winter term had ended so the new year began with a teacher training day. The pupils returned on 5 January 2005.

The first round of the talent show took place on the thirteenth and the second round followed two weeks later.

The month was busy with the Year 9 Information Evening for Guthlaxton and a Year 6 Parents Evening. A few days later a Year 7 Parents Evening took place, a School Council Meeting and a Governors' Premises Meeting.

In February, as part of 'Super Schools' the Manchester born Darren Campbell MBE, Olympic Gold Medallist visited the school. Four years had passed since his first visit to South Wigston and in that time his achievements had reached gold. Darren, described as Britain's best 100 metre sprinter dug the first turf for the new Sports Academy assisted by Jack Shepherd, 8AH. Jack won the honour for his significant effort made at school since September in a bid to 'dig the ceremonial turf of the Sports Centre foundation'. This was a special day since ten years

of work on the project was nearer to fulfilment. Pupils were delighted to have their photographs taken with such a celebrity after which they took part in an aerobic session with their PE teachers. Having spent an excellent morning pupils and parents were then busy collecting in sponsorship money. The grand total raised was £7.500. After 'Super Schools' were paid the remaining money was intended to be used for a new Public Address System and Data Projectors for the Mathematics Department. 'Super Schools' recognised the fund raising efforts of the pupils and awarded prizes of, sweat bands, wallets, boot bags and Tee Shirts. In addition the school introduced a prize draw for those raising over £10, £15, £20 and £40. A host of pupils received awards and for a magnificent total of raising £140, Emer Buck received £10 and a certificate signed by Darren Campbell himself. The fourth of February would be remembered for a very long time.

World Book Day was designated for 3 March and to mark the occasion many of the teachers and other staff dressed up as characters from some well known literature. This was hoped to celebrate and encourage reading. Characters portrayed were Roald Dahl's Miss Trunchbull, Sherlock Holmes, Cruella de Vil, Captain Hook, Miss Marple and many more. Miss Rossa was thanked for organising the event.

In each issue of the school's 'News Update' it is interesting to note the many 'Book Reviews'. 'Private Peaceful' by Michael Morpurgo in the April Issue was described by Mrs Langdale, Head of English, as 'a stunning read, full of vivid description and detail'. The story relates the childhood memories of a World War One soldier.

The disappearance of the boys' gymnasium was welcomed as three new classrooms and a corridor was built in its place. The old huts at the back of the school were earmarked for demolition therefore the new classrooms were a necessary addition.

The decision was taken for the school to run their own catering service. Surveys, research, feedback and much discussion had been carried out and with the same kitchen staff the school management went into action.

New meals were on the agenda after Easter in a bid to eat healthily. Some pupils obviously missed their daily dose of chips but the School Council were on hand to advise and mediate. New saver cards were issued advising pupils to buy nine main meals

Darren Campbell with Jack Shepherd 8AH cutting the first turf with guests and pupils. Others identified are the Chairman of Leicestershire County Council, Peter Winckless, Councillor Bill Boulter, the Revd. Professor Peter Holmes and Alan Kind MBE.

and a pudding and get the tenth one free. Health and Safety issues meant that no hot water could be poured on to pot noodles in the future.

Funding for Schools was high profile again in 2005 as the Leicestershire Education Authority was believed to be the lowest funded in the country. Despite the protests of 2003 the same situation was in evidence. The Government's policy of 'Every Child Matters' was disputed in Leicestershire and parents were urged to write to the Secretary of State for Education and Skills, Ruth Kelly. Also it was suggested that parents should write to their local Member of Parliament and the Prime Minister.

'That's Show Business' was the title of the summer concert. A wide range of song and drama styles brought together by Mrs Griffin was applauded. The show was described as 'two superb nights of performance'.

The mid June Sports Day was greatly assisted by the new more powerful public address system which the PE staff were able to purchase. This had been made possible by the money which had been raised by Super Schools.

All parents were invited to the 'Wigston Family of Schools Art Exhibition' in July. This was to be held at Guthlaxton College and the aim was to develop the childrens' understanding of the value of art in their lives whilst bringing together all of the schools in Wigston.

A regular feature in the *News Update* issues was 'Sports Development'. The Governors had announced that 'Competition Line' had been chosen as the partner to oversee the management and development of community sport. The building was ready for internal works to begin and colour schemes, fixtures and fittings were about to be selected. The sports hall plan had been based on a design model by Sport England and had been passed by County Council architects. The building contractors were N E L Construction.

The special day had arrived, 13 October. Just eight months after the digging of the first turf the ceremonial opening day dawned. The new Sports Academy was officially opened by Leicester's own Gary Lineker. The £1.5 million sports facility where money was raised by the community, staff and parents was now a reality.

Winter Sports Day was a resounding success with inter-form competitions. Every pupil was involved in some way throughout the day. Football, hockey, rugby and bridge building were all enjoyed and everyone showed their competitive spirit.

An appeal was made for more girls to join the football team. The existing team had won all of their

Gary Lineker cutting the tape

The Sports Academy

group matches in the County Cup and were only pipped in the Semi Final by Thomas Estley School, Broughton Astley, in a penalty shoot out.

One pupil to be praised was Declan Lonergan, 8JJ who in November won silver and bronze Karate medals at the French Open in Paris. The silver medal was for Kata - movements and set pieces and the bronze for weapons - traditional.

Ellis Goodwin 7MB who also won medals at the Great Britain Competition and Declan Lonergan were both to be sponsored by the school to represent Great Britain in Mexico.

In the Autumn of 2005 an HMI inspection took place in the school. The Physical Education and Health Education was judged to be 'outstanding' and for the second year running the PE Department was awarded 'Sports Mark Gold'. The school was assessed as teaching above the national average for PE.

Karate kids, Charlie Smith, 7TM, and Ellis Goodwin, 8MB, showed off their medals brought back from Paris in November. Ellis won a silver and Charlie a bronze in semi contact points fighting.

In early December the Design Department made an exciting visit to the Clothes Show at the National Exhibition Centre in Birmingham. The pupils were enchanted by the dazzling lights, pouting models and the College Catwalk. The latest fashions were paraded for an hour before everyone set off to view the clothing retailers stalls. Sellers gathered from all over England to show their goods ranging from 'Punky Fish' to the designs of Betty Jackson.

A new experience for ten pupils was enjoyed when they visited de Montfort University in Leicester. They were conducted on a tour of the university grounds before being led into the virtual reality suite to learn about the concept of three dimensional televisions. The pupils thoroughly enjoyed the peculiar sensation of floating through doughnuts and a lecture which included a robotic dog.

A spectacular 'Festival of Light' concert was given on two evenings when pupils performed to packed houses.

This year a very special role was played for the year's chosen charity, the Oncology Ward at the Leicester Royal Infirmary. Mr Toward delivered chocolates to the pupils dressed as Father Christmas.

January 2006 was celebrated with Mr Toward, Head Teacher, conveying good news to parents; He wrote,

'Happy New Year' and what a start! We have now received data that tells us we sit in the top 1% for Key Stage 3 learning. That's a fantastic achievement for our past Year 9 pupils, the school staff and Governors and not least parents for the support we get at home. It is a difficult task, but hopefully our current Year 9 will also be trying to push themselves to fulfill their own potential. The countdown to the SATs has started for both Year 6 and 9'.

Monitoring performance and standards and setting challenges is explained in *'News Update'*. Although OFSTED (Office For Standards In Education) is the external judge, South Wigston have developed a system over ten years which they have used to inspect themselves. Lessons are observed and feedback given to teachers both by the Head Teacher and Head of Department. Each Head of Department produces an in depth analysis of all aspects of their department's performance. In a similar way, there is an in depth analysis cutting across the curriculum and also for premises personnel and community dimensions of the school. Governors received these reports at a presentation by Heads of Departments. Targets for future years are set three years in advance and modified each year if new data group performance suggests a different picture.

On top of this at an individual level teachers, support staff and pupils all have specific targets that apply to them and are monitored by different line managers (or teachers).

'All in all we feel that we have a pretty robust system on track'.

Later in January the Royal Navy and Royal Marines visited the school. A presentation was given to Year 8 and Year 9 pupils who gained a great insight into the lives of the men and the particularly gruelling training for the Royal Marines. They were told that a nuclear submarine patrolled the waters every day of the year and sometimes not surfacing for weeks. This meant that often the men on board had no communication with the outside and had no idea where in the world they were.

On 22 February three members of the Royal Marines visited Year 9 pupils who were interested in taking the GCSE PE Examination. Roseanne Billany 9RAC, reported in 'News Update' 'we were set a scenario which was that we were stranded on an island with just three wooden poles, rope and a flag. We had to work as a team to put together a high flag pole with a flag that moved up and down to create an 'SOS' signal.'

At the end the pupils put on helmets and lifted the pole in the hope that it did not fall down. The event concluded with a game when they had to get the whole team across a mine field using only three tyres.

Science Week in school usually coincides with National Science Week when a number of activities provide stimulation and fun. David Pearson alias 'Animal Man' was the highlight this year. From the Natural History Lecture Service, David trains the owls for the Harry Potter films. On his visit to South Wigston the pupils were treated to the guests he brought with him, Katie, the kinkajou, BBC, the Boa Constrictor and Fluffy the hairy Tarantula. Mrs Coles the science Learning Support Assistant has been reported as 'not being the same since' Fluffy got upset, leapt into the air and landed on her knee. The pupils were highly amused at her piercing shriek.

The reward scheme at South Wigston took on a new dimension in March when pupils earned points to give their parents a treat. The Cafe Bruxelles in Leicester offered a ten percent discount for two adult diners and how proud the parents must have been to know that their child had made the greatest 'effort' of all to win it for them.

The importance of 'Success for All' at South Wigston has been envisioned as 'widening horizons and raising aspirations'. The hope is to encourage pupils to look beyond their own sphere of knowledge and to see the vast array of opportunities that will be open to them when they complete their time at South Wigston. To this end a programme of college visits was carried out. Eight pupils in Year 9 followed a six week alternative curriculum course on Thursday mornings in the spring term at South Leicestershire College. They met with pupils from eight other High Schools. At the end of the summer term thirty pupils attended a chosen vocational course.

Eight pupils from Year 8 and 9 enjoyed links with Leicester University throughout the spring term and students from the University visited South Wigston to mentor the group also. A day visit to the University of Leicester was the culmination of the Support Programme.

Seventy two pupils also visited to participate in 'taster' courses. These were vocational but aimed at more academically inclined pupils.

Science pupils from Year 9 visited the Genetics Department at Leicester University. A lecture was given and a tour of the facilities was enjoyed.

The Humanities Department and forty three pupils visited the historic castle at Warwick in early May. Pupils learned how the castle was built to defend itself and the weaponry used by the soldiers. They tried on the helmets, wore chain mail and handled the shields. Displays by the bowmen and falconry were enjoyed but four men pulling a trebuchet, (a siege engine used to smash masonry walls) was the highlight. A five ton boulder was launched two hundred metres across a field. The afternoon was spent trekking across the castle ramparts to view the magnificent sites of Warwick and the castle.

In partnership with the Beachamp and Guthlaxton families of schools, South Wigston, Abington, Bushloe, Gartree and Manor High presented an evening of dance on 24 May. One hundred and eighty dancers and spectators gathered at Guthlaxton Community College for the inaugural Partnership Dance Festival. The purpose of the event was to showcase some of the best dance talent and included all styles of dance. The competition categories included, best sense of timing, most original dance, best musical interpretation and best choreography. There was also an award for the winner of the best expressive performance.

The judging panel was made up of dance experts, Sally Ann Read, Charlotte Anderson, Maria Bilson and Michelle Lloyd.

Staff and student helpers from Guthlaxton and South Wigston High School were on hand to assist with stage lighting, music playing, curtain pulling, organisation of acts and front of house duties.

As the judges deliberated South Wigston pupils entertained the audience. When the results were announced South Wigston had won two of the categories.

July was an exciting month as pupils looked forward to the visit of Ross Brewer to their sports academy. Ross is the English and British Men's Gymnastics Champion and Commonwealth Games Medalist. During the day at school he gave a demonstration of his skills and conducted a coaching master class. Prizes were awarded during the afternoon.

International Peace Day was celebrated on 21 September when one hundred and fifty pupils made pinwheels with their views and ideas of how a peaceful world should be. The pinwheels were then laid out in the quad spelling the word, 'PEACE'.

Pupils, staff and visitors also signed the 'South Wigston High School Peace Pledge'. This was hoped to promote a more peaceful society in our world.

Inspired by the poor quality of school meals nationally, Jamie Oliver, well known television chef, spearheaded a campaign for change. After a long battle, Prime Minister, Tony Blair agreed to pour £280 million into schools for the improvement of better ingredients for school dinners. At South Wigston High School their own innovative teacher of Food Technology, Mr C Vallabh, had his own ideas and had already introduced some very tempting and healthy options to school menus. Recorded in the 'South Wigston High School Newsletters' Mr Vallabh's recipes and helpful tips are regular features.

Food Technology has taken on a new dimension in South Wigston with many cosmopolitan dishes to tempt the pupils. A far cry from the simple cheese potato and onion pies which came steaming in huge dishes from the school kitchen in times gone by. In cookery lessons too some basic recipes which still delight the discerning connoisseur can be found in Beverley Whiting nee Allen's, 3BK, little saved recipe book. Jam or treacle sponge, coffee kisses, toad in the hole, scones, Irish stew, brown stew, rock buns and gingerbread and many more. Beverley is now Mr Toward's Secretary.

The fourth day of October was designated as 'World Animal Day'. As part of their Citizenship Curriculum, Year 6 pupils listened to Susannah Peat, a voluntary worker from Animal Aid, talk to them about the care of animals. This was in addition to a video followed by fun activities in the lunch time period when they also raised £78.71 for Animal Aid.

October was the time for the school's 'Spooky Sleepover'. On the evening of Friday the thirteenth, sixty Year 7 pupils gathered to be 'scared out of their skins'. It began with a scary film in the hall followed by a hot dog and a drink. Pupils then split into five groups and were led on a torchlight procession of the school. They encountered spooks, monsters and witches. Fortified by cake and hot chocolate at midnight everyone settled down to sleep in classrooms and the gym. Thanks were duly given to the South Wigston Supporters Association, staff and family members.

13 October was also 'Wear Your Trainers' day. This was a fund raising event to help two fishermen in Sri Lanka to purchase fishing boats and nets. The men had lost their houses in the tsunami and they could not be rebuilt due to the proximity of the sea. The men with their families were living in a tsunami camp with forty other families sharing only four showers and eight toilets.

Three hundred pounds was needed for each man to buy boats and nets. Donations of fifty pence to one pound was asked for if children wore their trainers. The grand total of £663. was raised.

In November The Education and Inspection Act 2006 stated that, 'every child in every school in every community gets the education they need to fulfil their potential'. Two of the provisions of the

Bugsy Malone 2006

Act were to appoint School Improvement Partners (SIP) and new nutritional standards for food and drink for maintained schools.

'Sums 4 Mums' was set up in November. This was an evening set up for parents in order to demonstrate current approaches to maths teaching and hints on how to help with homework. '*Pearson Maths* material had been invaluable'. These books are published in a wide range of mathematical subjects.

After ten weeks of rehearsals pupils put on their very successful production of 'Bugsy Malone' to entertain their Christmas audiences. Standing ovations were given at their evening performances and matinees despite the audiences being treated to the effects of 'splurge guns'

In 2007 under the leadership of Gordon Brown the Department for Children, Schools and Families was created with its own Secretary of State. A second Secretary of State was appointed for Innovation, Universities and Skills. The Department for Children, Schools and Families complies with the Cabinet Office Code of Practice on consultation by adhering to six criteria.

In January Eco School Assessors were busy at the school to interview pupils from 'The Active Citizen Today Group'. They toured the school for two and a half hours accompanied by Mrs J Small, School Governor, on their inspection. Comment was passed by one of the judges that South Wigston was the best school that they had ever seen applying for an award. The certificate and green flag were duly awarded.

The active Citizenship Group encourages pupils

to become involved in all aspects of community life. The game, 'Getting to Know You' has proved popular using 'Smarties'. Lunch hours were given up to weigh used Christmas cards for re-cycling whilst plans were under discussion to acquire a wind turbine in the school grounds, re-vamping the pond and nature area and cleaning out the 'Ford' close to Glen Parva Manor.

New close circuit television, (CCTV) monitoring was installed in the school in January also.

The 'Aim Higher' road show visited the school on 22 January for the day when seventy five Year 9 pupils attended a workshop on the 'Aim Higher' bus. This was followed by a 'question and answer' session with the help of students from de Montfort University.

A party of Year 7 and 8 pupils enjoyed a residential visit to London where they enjoyed the production of 'The Lion King' and a visit to the Globe Theatre.

The Art and Design and Food Technology Department ran a Junior Master Chef competition after school for the more able Year 8 and 9 cooks. This ran for twelve weeks.

Talented musicians took part in a community activity to visit the elderly. They also visited the feeder primary schools with a view to inspire young musicians who will eventually attend South Wigston High School.

There is much liaison with the 'family' of schools. Sharing good practice and bridging projects are discussed and the transition of pupils between the schools is of great importance. Having knowledge of each other's systems and the capabilities of the pupils are used to plan the way forward in achieving National Curriculum standards.

Besides 'in house' training, training days for staff are often held at Beaumanor Hall, Woodhouse. Many aspects of the curriculum are discussed, sharing ideas, marking systems, setting, testing and assessing, computer updates and ways forward are explored.

The South Wigston High School Family Years 3 and 4 Gifted and Talented Sporting Activities was staged at the beginning of February. Two Sports Specialists, pupils from Parklands, Fairfield and Glen Hills Primary Schools experienced a range of sports in the South Wigston Sports Academy.

The pupils were split into mixed teams which allowed them to meet new friends. They participated in a number of different activities including Boccia, New Age Kurling, Table Cricket and Table Tennis. They were supported by coaches and three Sports Leaders Students from Guthlaxton College. Parents and teachers became involved competing with the pupils in a mini Boccia tournament.

February was an exciting month with the visit of the International Judo Champion, Kate Howie. This was described as a morning of fun and active learning. Working with PE teachers, Kate put the pupils through short aerobic exercises and posed for photographs. Pupils were required to raise a minimum of £1.00 in sponsorship and were allowed to wear their own 'sporty' clothes on the day. Money raised was for the Design Technology and Art Department.

Later in February Year 6 pupils were taken to the de Montfort Hall in Leicester to see 'The Awful Egyptians'. The audience was treated to some of the most gory and gruesome parts of the ancient Egyptian civilisation, writes Mrs K Smith. They watched brains being pulled through the nose, body parts being removed as mummification was being demonstrated coupled with the building of the pyramids and to view how tombs were made. With their 3D Bogglevision glasses they experienced the weighing of the heart ceremony in the afterlife.

George Hart, a pupil from 6PS unlocked the secret tomb. 'I am glad that I joined my friends at 'The Horrible Histories' show yesterday because it was so funny. I was surprised when my name went on to the screen in English and Egyptian with the serpent next to it. I was scared because when I put the 3D glasses on objects came flying at me. It was awesome!'.

Mrs Smith concluded that it was a fantastic adaptation of the Horrible Histories Series as they laughed, sang, booed and cheered. She also thanked Mr Schalkwyk and Mrs Terry for joining the party.

At South Wigston pupils were enjoying raising funds for Comic Relief with dance, car washing and mini quizzes.

Science week which commenced on 12 March was notable with paper aeroplane competitions, junior petunia competitions, family quizzes and The Brainiac Quiz.

The £250,000 Resource Centre was opened on 25 April by the celebrated author, playwright and past

Gary Toward, Rosamund Davies and Sue Townsend at the opening of The Rosamund Davies Resource Centre 2007

Paris 2007

pupil, Sue Townsend. The centre was named in honour of the very first leader of the Learning Support Department Rosamund Davies. Rosamund worked for fourteen years and set up a team and systems envied country wide. She was the Special Educational Needs Co-ordinator and the news of her death later that year saddened everyone in school.

During Careers Week in May pupils visited Rutland Water to engage in canoeing, kayaking and raft building. The purpose of the trip was to encourage team building, co-operation, problem solving, communication skills and leadership.

A major learning event took place as pupils visited Paris and Ypres. Following a course on the events of the First World War ninety children and staff visited the Menin Gate on which men who lost their lives in the war and have no known graves are listed. Having named their school houses in memory of seven local men pupils were anxious to find their names and pay homage to their memory. Laying wreaths and the Act of Remembrance was carried out by the children. Mr Gary Toward read the citation to 'The Glorious Dead'.

The House Names commemorate, Trooper James Spencer Potter, Private Thomas Chapman, Corporal Thomas Henry Foster, Rifleman Frederick Arthur Mynard, Private George Edward Boulter, Private Bernard Corbett and Sapper George Whyatt.

Kathryn Smith, Head of the Humanities Department remembers;

'The first time we went to Belgium. The pupils wrote their poems and laid them on the graves of the soldiers at Tyne Cot Cemetery. It was a very moving experience. Also finding the graves/names of our House Heroes brought something we talk about at school a lot to life'.

On 'Super Schools' Sports Day energetic events such as aerobics body combat, long skipping, Chinese skipping, basket ball shots and an assault course was listed.

World Maths Day was notable as Josh Linnett won a trophy. In stark contrast to the pupils of 1938 children benefit from computer software lessons with such programmes as Mymaths, Rainforest Maths, Sam Learning and many others. One aspect of school life which has never changed is that plenty of homework is given out.

The modern pupil sets out their objectives on target cards and once achieved set the next target. These are accompanied by feedback sheets ultimately being transferred to target sheets in their individual exercise books.

June was memorable for forty five pupils and six staff as they visited the Army Barracks at Bassingbourn in Hertfordshire. This trip was a

Annual Awards Evening 2007

reward for Year 9 pupils who had been involved in the Peer Mentoring Programme.

Beginning with a parachute jump by the Red Devils and followed by motor cycle display teams and infantry display unit demonstrations there were other various activities in the main area. The Army assault course, bridge building exercises and sport challenges proved very popular with the pupils.

The Annual SIP (School Improvement Partners) report by Cath Powell was presented to the Governors in June. The content covered Achievement and Standards, Personal Development and Well Being, Quality of Provision, Leadership and Management, Overall Effectiveness, Local Authority Support and Actions.

The appointment of Mr Edward Michael Balls, the new Secretary of State for the Department of Children, Schools and Families made news in June. One of his aims was that children should attain the highest standards of achievement.

On 5 July the school Awards Evening took place with various invited guests to present the trophies. The happy prize winners were photographed outside the school all looking very proud.

The first ever School Prom was an exciting event in July known as the Year 9 Leavers Prom. Pupils dressed in their finery arrived by various modes of transport to the red carpet in their numbers. The school hall was transformed to entertain over one hundred pupils. A two course meal was catered for by Mrs Downes and staff from the school kitchen and was served by the very smartly dressed waiters and waitresses (school staff).

After the meal pupils made hay with the chocolate fountains and danced to the disco music and thoroughly enjoyed the Soul Band.

More triumphs and medals for five talented pupils were recorded in the *South Wigston High School Newsletter*. Annie Napier, 6KS, competed in a National Ice Skating competition in Essex. She won first place in the beginner category of her age group in the open championship in Chelmsford and has also taken second and third place in other competitions. Annie trained at the Nottingham National Ice Centre and was selected to skate in an exhibition for Jane Torvill in November.

Mollie Walden, Joe Storton and Charlie Smith went to the World Championships in Italy for World Stage of Karate. Mollie returned with two silver and one bronze medal, Joe won silver and bronze and Charlie won one silver and two bronze.

Alex Mickowski, 7SO achieved first place in a skate boarding competition.

Healthy Lifestyles Day took place in mid October when all pupils abandoned the normal timetable. External speakers were invited into school including representatives from the St. John Ambulance Brigade. Issues discussed and explored were,

The Royal Albert Hall. November 2007

Anatomy of a Cigarette, Smoking Health Issues, Personal Hygiene, Dental Health, Physical Fitness and Burning A Hole In Your Pocket. Added to that was Making a Healthy Snack, Diet and Exercise, Accidents at Home, Water Safety, Life Saving, Minor Injuries, Teenage Pregnancy and Contraception.

Pupils accompanied by Mrs Oakland and Mrs King made a memorable visit to the Royal Albert Hall in London in November. The pupils took part in the five hundred strong massed choir performing a piece of music entitled, 'Food with Attitude'. The composer of the music, Alan Simmons attended commenting that he could not have asked for a better performance of his work. 'Land of Hope and Glory' was traditionally sung at the end of the concert with balloons and confetti descending from the galleries.

The following evening in the school hall, staff, Governors, parents and friends arrived to bid for generously donated items by companies for the 'Auction of Promises' event. Arranged by the South Wigston High School Supporters' Association one hot bid was for Mr Henley to wear a dress for a day. This caused quite a stir and much hilarity when a week later Mr Henley sportingly attended school attired in a little mauve dress. The grand total raised for the funds was a magnificent £1,669,82p.

During December the Chairman of Leicestershire County Council, Councillor Mike Jones and Mrs Jones visited the school. Assemblies and lessons were taken in during the morning and Mr Jones was most impressed with the experience.

Mr Edward Garnier QC,MP also visited the school presenting them once again with a set of maps from the Ordnance Survey. Mr Garnier was most impressed with the new Rosamund Davies Resource Centre.

The musical production 'Joseph And The Technicolour Dreamcoat' was a sell out in January 2008. The show was performed on three nights and superb portrayals by the cast was applauded. The choir and the musicians contributed to a top quality show and a standing ovation on the last evening was led by the Mayor.

Drama at South Wigston has always been held in high regard with many professional standard productions to delight their audiences. New ways have been used in the interpretation in order to aid understanding of the subject as in the enactment of 'Beowulf'. Year 7 pupils portrayed the scene at Hygelac's Great Hall when the sea captain arrived with the terrifying tale of the sea monster. A 'News at Ten' style report of Beowulf's arrival on Danish shores brought the scene to life.

Not to be outdone, Year 8 pupils chose the play, ' Liquorice Bootlaces'. Recreating the scene at Mrs Pratchet's shop the work was developed from a radio play to a scene which they acted out. The pupils

Year 7 '5' A Side Football National Champions 2008

concentrated on elementary drama skills, facing the audience loud and clear with a clean start and finish.

Year 9 pupils concentrated on Richard 111 attempting to unravel the intricacies of the tangled web of the Plantagenet Dynasty.

South Wigston High School Year 7 boys Five A Side Football Team emerged from the East Midlands Finals at Pride Park in Derby as champions. South Wigston qualified for the finals by winning the South Leicestershire Finals by beating Kibworth, Heathfield and Lutterworth at the beginning of January.

The final was against Netherthorpe in Chesterfield and the perfect start was made from a penalty by Eliot Putman. It was a very close game with South Wigston controlling the tempo. Despite efforts by Rob Morgan and Mylan Charles, South Wigston was unlucky not to increase the lead. The defence led by Joe Doyle-Charles comfortably eased out the game leaving South Wigston crowned East Midlands Champions.

Mr Glover and Mr Clifford were full of admiration for the team congratulating them on their discipline and flair.

Geoff Glover, PE Teacher recalled his most significant memory as very recent. In March 2008, Year 7, Five a Side Football Team had qualified to play in the ESFA National finals at the JJB Soccerdome in Derby. 'The whole day was fantastic and was capped by the boys winning a tight final 1-0 and thus being crowned National Champions. That feeling will stay within me forever and that would be my defining moment so far'.

The Leicester Mercury, 19 March 2008 ran the headlines, 'Super South Wigston land national crown'. More than four thousand schools entered the national competition and South Wigston came out on top by beating Shenfield of Essex 1- 0 in a tense final. The team who won fifteen games and drew four in the entire competition were coached by PE teachers, Jeff Glover and Richard Clifford. Mr Clifford was quoted as saying 'this is a major achievement for a small school'. Having battled their way through local and regional competitions South Wigston earned the right to represent the region alongside seven other regional winners. They topped their qualifying group by beating Clere, (Andover, Hants) and Shenfield and drawing with Grange Grammar, (Cheshire). A 1-0 win in the semi final over Staffordshire side, Walton Primary, courtesy of a goal from Mylan Charles, ensured their place in the final. In a close game there were some splendid performances, not least from Joe Doyle-Charles, goalkeeper, Justin Peace and Eliot Putman

Samantha Palmer surrounded by admiring pupils

who is with Leicester City. Rob Morgan who is with Notts Forest scored the winner with three minutes left. He said, 'I hit it as hard as I could. I didn't see it hit the net but I heard the cheers. I can't describe the feeling'.

The School Council consisting of pupils debated which charities they would like to support in 2008. After much discussion and consultation with fellow pupils they chose 'The Premature Baby Unit' at the Leicester Royal Infirmary and the 'Faraja Orphanage and Nursery' in Tanzania.

In February 2008 issue of 'South Wigston High School News' 'Christmas comes twice in February' catches the eye. It reads that:

'South Wigston High School has received two major awards in the last month. We've been working towards becoming a specialist Art College for a number of years and the Government have now agreed our application. This means that we will be able to provide and develop a wider range of learning opportunities.

Also our feeder primary schools, Glen Hills, Fairfield and Parkland will benefit and we have also linked further afield with a two way mutual arrangement with Gartree High School. Our partners in this venture are Guthlaxton College and Bushloe and Abington High Schools.

The second award arrived and added another pot of money to our Arts funding.

We've been awarded a Heritage Fund Grant to help us develop pupils' and community learning. The project is mostly about developing a Living History website where pupils who have been trained up will record videos of former pupils' memories of the school and local community'.

In the last week of February as part of Super Schools 2008 Samantha Palmer visited the school. Samantha is known as the Women's Tumbling Champion, gold medallist in the World Cup Final and the European Champion.

Pupils were put through sponsored aerobics routines after which Samantha demonstrated her tumbling techniques. This was followed by a question and answer session.

An historic occasion in March when the school once again changed its name as it became a Specialist College of Arts with English, art and design and music subjects taking the lead on development. This meant additional funding to support school development right across the curriculum and into the community. The new title of 'South Wigston High School and Arts College' goes forward in the twenty first century.

During the first week of April the talent show was

Katharine Ardley

Mariah Braithwaite at an etiquette lesson

described as 'A Star Studded Night'. After three auditions and fifty acts, twenty six pupils got through to the final comprising singers, dancers and musicians. The overall winner for 'an amazing flute medley' was Katharine Ardley from Year 7.

A catalogue of events was experienced on 'Learning to Learn' day in April when over eight hundred pupils took part. The action packed day was aimed at delivering new personal and thinking skills. From good manners and table etiquette at Year 6, to Year 9 pupils understanding the consequences of split second actions was led by the Police Armed Response Unit.

Children learned about the work of the Royal Society of Protection of Birds whilst the Leicestershire Fire and Rescue Service instructed from their 'pod' about hazards in the home. African drumming, playing Giant Jenga and Kubb proved very popular. South Leicestershire College staff helped pupils to relax the holistic way and learn about Indian Head Massage. Jason from Jinz Gym helped to raise awareness on how fitness levels can impact upon learning. The local Ju Jitsu group promoted self discipline and basic self defence techniques. Local Police Officers checked students bicycles, gave out helmets and made sure that pupils understood how to ride safely. The 2nd Battalion, The Royal Anglian Regiment spent the day also providing a taster for their planned visit in May.

Over seventy visitors attended the school that day all having complimentary things to say.

Celebrating England's patron Saint George on his day, 23 April, was not only a lesson in legend but a

Learning to Learn Day 2008

grand feast day. The catering staff cooked traditional roast beef and Yorkshire pudding, sausage and mash, jam pudding and custard and cream scones.

Karen Downes, In House Catering Manager ensures that the school's healthy eating policy which was formed with the help of the pupils' School Council is maintained. A wide range of options are available in the canteen daily.

Taking place in May for the third year running was 'Army Week'. The 2nd Battalion, The Royal Anglian Regiment known as 'The Poachers' joined forces with one hundred Year 9 pupils to give them a taste of army life. Lorry loads of equipment and a huge climbing frame was erected by the team whilst everyone else was kitted out in their combat uniforms to erect the tents.

Sergeant Gage's programme of events included paintball target practice, climbing wall, foot drill, circuit training and trim tail. The theme for the week was teamwork. Physical Training Instructor, Lance Corporal Ross Milton watched pupils progress at press ups and at night pupils slept under canvas. Learning to cook army rations, lessons in camouflage and concealment and first aid were on the agenda. At dusk the lantern stalk caused much excitement.

After retiring to rest recruits were awakened for fire watch shifts. At the end of the week parents and pupils enjoyed their proudest moments on their passing out parade. Sergeant Al Gage and Head Teacher Gary Toward carried out the inspection.

One section led by Private Jackson won the trophy for the best section and receiving a camera each for best female and male was Amy Morgan and Reece Johnson.

Julie Lee-Shield, Cover Supervisor/Learning Support Assistant, writes, 'I have been in my position for nearly two years. I have watched Army week come and go twice. The memory that sticks in my mind is when the Year 9s turn the corner on parade. This makes you feel proud you are part of

Pupils on the march 2008

the South Wigston High School Team. A tear forms in my eye and it brings a lump to my throat. How grown up they have all become and our team has been part of that process'.

The Paris Trip was once again a resounding success with a very full itinerary. Visiting Sacre Ceur to view its splendour, the Pompidou Centre, the grandeur of the Louvre, the steel and glass modernity of the Defense and the magic of Disney made such a memorable holiday. Visiting the war graves in the cemeteries at Belgium and the ceremony at the Menin Gate was a solemn occasion.

The Homeless Sleepover took place in May as part of the Citizenship Curriculum. Forty two Year 9 pupils and six members of staff took part. Pupils were required to build their shelters out of cardboard boxes progressing on to various learning techniques on how people become homeless. Pupils spent a damp and drizzly night before returning home at 7am.

The Egg Baby Project is designed to teach children the responsibilities of parenthood. Over two hundred Year 8 pupils 'cared' for their babies, some twins and others with triplets. Eggs are carefully nurtured and supervised making sure that no harm befalls them.

Environment month was begun with a blue bag collection followed by an assembly with the theme focussing on what could be done in small ways to save the environment. Pupils were asked to think about ways of securing the land for future generations to enjoy. Saving water and electricity were two topics for discussion.

Fair Trade food and products was hoped to be introduced into school life. Fun activities were introduced at lunch times in order to help students understand why the issue is important.

One World Day extended the pupil's knowledge with a series of workshops. Listed in the May/June newsletter students learned to distinguish Italian food from Greek, how to play a digeridoo, to learn what a Jain Temple looked like and the interesting subject of deforestation.

Twycross Zoo Visit 2008

Two very worthwhile causes were the subject of fund raising for Charity Day. Pupils set up a wide variety of stalls raising £990.94 to be added to a fund totalling £2039.00 for The Faraja Orphanage in Tanzania and the Leicester Royal Infirmary Premature Baby Unit.

Special visitors to the school were Matt Hampson when pupils handed over a cheque for £2000. for his Trust. Mr Toward had previously climbed in the Alps to raise funds. Matt was a Tigers' Under 21 player when he suffered a dislocation of his neck which trapped his spinal cord, paralysing him from the neck down.

Matt was joined at school by Brett Deacon, the Leicester Tigers' star and former pupil of the school.

In June ninety Year 8 pupils were taken to the Black Country Museum to experience a nineteenth century day. Two highlights of the day was a Victorian school lesson when pupils were required to sit with their hands behind their backs and to write on slate with chalk. They were also taken on a visit down a coal mine. The children visited the cottages to see how people lived and learned about industrial life.

One hundred and eighty eight Year 7 pupils were accompanied by staff to Twycross Zoo. The primates were particularly entertaining. An educational and fun day out gave pupils the opportunity to see how animals have adapted to their environment.

The school field was transformed in mid June with a Music Prom. The event represented the great partnership between the school and the feeder primary schools. Hoards of spectators gathered with their picnics to watch pupils perform.

Congratulations were extended to the South Wigston High School Table Tennis Team who had been promoted to the Premier League of the Leicestershire Table Tennis League.

Proms on the Park 2008

Saffron Lane Sports Centre 2008

Eight pupils participated in a golf competition at Oadby Golf Course. The course included six skills challenges and South Wigston pupils were declared the winners. Six schools took part.

In the one hundred metres Girls U13 race in the Mid-Leicestershire Final congratulations were given to Shakira Fraser who came first. Following up her success she gained second place in the County Championships.

On the last day of June children were able to experience the facilities of the Saffron Lane Sports Centre as part of their annual Sports Day. This was recorded as a great success with outstanding performances from South Wigston pupils.

On 9 July as part of Oadby and Wigston Borough Council's 'Pride of the Borough' and Britain in Bloom competition, South Wigston High School and Arts College was awarded 'Silver Gilt' in the category, 'Best School Garden'. The judges were Mr Rupert Atkinson, B.Sc. and F D Hart formerly of Nottingham City Council. The sections to be judged were;

• Usefulness in Education and Curriculum,
• Value to wild life,
• Contribution to healthy eating and food awareness
• Quality of care and maintenance.

Shakira Fraser 7GW

The school's comprehensive re-cycling policy, accessible wild life area, the signing up to BBC Breathing Spaces, climate change initiatives, bird boxes, crop rotation and home grown produce which is used in the school canteen all helped in the process. The active Citizenship group which meets after school and the pupils involvement in making their own hanging baskets, the comprehensive compost system are all part of the Eco School.

The term ended on Friday 11 July.

Looking back over seventy years it is fascinating to note the changes that have taken place in the life of the school. To observe how new Acts of Parliament and amendments to Educational Law have taken effect and how the differing styles of teaching have coloured the views of onlookers fuelling many a controversial argument.

From Bassett Street to South Wigston's Intermediate system (SWIS), the Secondary Modern Schools for Boys' and Girls'; to High School and High School and Arts College status: it has been a journey of revelation.

Strict discipline meted out by teachers could be described as brutal over the years. Thrashings appeared commonplace and accurate missile throwing a regular daily occurrence rarely missing targets. Even this did not deter some pranksters as we have seen. The debate goes on. 'Spare the rod, spoil the child'?

Control by the 'House System' attempted to publicly shame wrongdoers by reading out their names at assemblies. The house system still exists and is still competitive. House marks and order marks in the 1950s moved on to merit marks in the 1980s and no pupil wants 'yellows' in 2008. Today the emphasis is focussed on rewards, praise, commendations and consequences. Other changes mark the difference in the society in which we now live. There is no Act of Worship in assembly today or the sound of children's voices singing hymns floating through the open windows. Typewriting students have no need for 'Tipex' as the modern computers with correction keys and 'cut and paste' facilities erase their mistakes at the touch of a button.

The 1940s pupils were mindful of wearing their wartime gas masks for fear of sniffing nerve gas in an attack from the enemy. School drills to the Anderson shelters in the hope of avoiding a bomb strike, learning how to operate stirrup pumps in the event of fire and hiding their white shirts and blouses from enemy planes was a more common practice.

Our ancestors would be filled with amazement to hear of 'Army Week' taking place in their school. Would they ever dream that the pupils today would be visiting war graves in 'a foreign field' to pay their last respects to their much mourned family members? They would be so proud. Many a past pupil was little more than a boy himself when going to war.

To appear in school improperly dressed with as much as one item of uniform missing was once a punishable offence with pupils being sent home immediately to change. Today non uniform days are a prize for good work and good behaviour but they are also a means of South Wigston's magnificent fund raising abilities. As explained by Jack Bradley, 9GG, pupils are required to earn fifteen commendations and 'no yellows' throughout the term to qualify for one of these days. With twenty eight forms divided into seven houses and the highest effort from an achieving boy and girl also tasked, the 'House' can be awarded the second non uniform day and finally £1.00 or fifty pence is requested from all pupils for the school funds on the last day of term for the privilege.

The simplicity of the form titles. A, B, C, and D and A, G, C, and P have been replaced by a confusing language to the untrained eye. 7GW, 2CK, 3MB and so on was explained expertly by Billy Brinkley, 7GW. This method identifies the teacher and the forms and demonstrates that today's children are not baffled by this combination of letters and abbreviations.

Megan Footman 8CV was involved in helping with the induction of Year 5 pupils and Tommy Ginns, 7GW, ran his own 'War Hammer Club'!

Jessica Newland. 8RAC. writes that, 'In the school I take part in the school choir and in the Rhythmic Gym Team. The school dinners are very different each day. We have to line up for about ten minutes. You can get a drink, main meal and a cake for £1.95. It is very loud and crowded in the dining hall. I have just done a challenge called the Head's Challenge'.

The school holidays was a subject for debate amongst staff at South Wigston and their family member, Guthlaxton in the year 2000. The Local Education Authority set term dates and on occasion the length of term is said to be either too short or too long. Various school Heads joined the millennium debate and it is interesting to see in September 2008 the *Leicester Mercury* reporting on the same issues. The County Council having already set their dates is now causing concern as the City Council plan to adjust theirs. This is currently seen as conflicting and disruptive as the dichotomous situation which the two authorities are currently in predicts chaos in county and city schools.

Annual Awards Evening 2008

The Head's Challenge continues to inspire pupils. Reported to have the most deprived school roll of any Leicestershire High School the scheme is helping to motivate and raise the aspirations of the children. Participants have to complete five challenges; community, skill, new experience, expedition and fund raising. Depending on how far the pupils stretch themselves they can be rewarded with bronze, silver and gold awards.

The Community Challenge involves some collective community work and a personal 'community work experience'. This typically involves pupils walking dogs for disabled neighbours, helping out at the nursing home where Mum works or possibly gardening for an elderly neighbour. In order to complete the Skill Challenge pupils must learn a new skill. This has ranged from cake decorating to plumbing. Pupils are also required to join one of the school's fifty seven clubs or an external one. To gain Gold Level pupils must also join an Arts based club or group in school.

A recent challenge was accomplished by sixty children with Mr Toward, Head Teacher, on their ascent of Kinder Scout in the Peak District. Oozing with pride at the summit one hairy incident was recalled when one pupil's boot was sucked into a peat bog. He had accidentally stepped into it but fortunately the boot was retrieved.

The expedition which is supported by two training walks, takes in an eight mile circular walk from Edale.

With sponsorship from previous occasions the school has a stock of walking boots and waterproofs. All pupils are given a mentor who meets with them every three to four weeks to check on progress, give advice and provide support.

Super Schools is an annual event to look forward to with the thrill of meeting such renowned celebrities and the added value of fund raising. The vast sums raised in school over the years with so many events to improve and enhance school life is commendable. How could so much be achieved without this added revenue?

All successes are celebrated and certificates and house points awarded publicly. The Annual Awards Evening is a night when parents beam with pride to see their offspring collect their trophies and perform. Trophies presented by staff and visitors to the school is prestigious. In 2008 one of the presenters was Professor Peter Welton, the celebrated artist and water colourist.

Other sources of inspiration exist within the School Hall of Fame. The corridor walls are filling at a rapid pace with past pupil achievers in their chosen fields. Faces from 1938 onwards look out from their frames encouraging children to achieve.

One past pupil of whom the school can be extremely proud is Sue Townsend the internationally known writer. So many literary masters have loved her series of 'Adrian Mole' diaries. Together the five Mole diaries have sold over eight million copies. Also the author of several stage and radio plays, Sue was the best selling novelist of the 1980s.

From the back cover of 'The Secret Diary of Adrian Mole, aged 13 and 3/4, are quotes from Jilly Cooper, 'set fair to become as much a cult book as *Catcher in the Rye* and Tom Sharpe who 'not only wept but howled and hooted' before he could carry on reading and from the *New Statesman*, 'a wit to touch the hearts of three generations'.

An article in *The Independent* recently quotes Sue Townsend as she recalls her school days at Glen Hills Primary. She says that the 'good English teachers are eccentric and the brilliant ones slightly mad'. Mr Moles who taught her to love English comic writing read from the *'Wind in the Willows'* and *'Winnie the Pooh'* and made himself cry big tears of laughter and slide down his desk laughing. Sue says, '*I didn't learn to read until I was eight and a half in three weeks when I was away from school with mumps. I learnt from some 'Just William' books'. In the interview she continues, 'South Wigston Girls' High School had been the equivalent of a grammar school but at the time was for eleven plus failures. I mostly enjoyed the lessons. Miss Morris loved William Blake, Shakespeare, Milton, Oscar Wilde and Peter Ustinov. We had to learn a poem a week and write two essays, 'compositions'. Miss Morris took us to the Netherlands with a school passion play. I played Jesus. I was the tallest in our drama group and hung from a cross for twenty minutes with my arms up. it was agony*',

Sue left South Wigston High School at the age of fourteen. In 2007 she became a Doctor of Letters at Loughborough University in recognition of her contribution to literature and laughter.

In July 2008 Sue Townsend received a Distinguished Honorary Fellowship from the University of Leicester, the highest accolade the University can bestow.

So what has changed so dramatically?

The old HORSA Huts have gone and with them the stigma and isolation of the D Form pupils. From the beginning of the history of our school it is quite illuminating to note the gradual changes in terminology and the approach in which Special Educational Needs are tackled. Learning Support, a vital part of school life today; has slowly by legislative means improved the lives of children with difficulties helping them to succeed. Recognising disability and catering for special needs has been hard fought and the hope that today's children will not feel the pain of segregation or misplacement as some did in the past is ongoing. Mrs Fawlds and the team of Learning Support Assistants work hard to promote movement back into mainstream education wherever possible.

Others situated in the HORSA Huts may have enjoyed a little more freedom from being 'under the Head's eye' helping the disadvantaged children to succeed and reach their potential but today the huts have been replaced by a brand new sports hall which has seen many a celebrity pass through its doors. A time capsule buried deep on the school field was constructed by Mr Small, one of the school Governors. A variety of memorabilia and documents were hidden in the capsule by everyone for future generations to discover.

The new assembly hall, music block and later the new science laboratory built in keeping with the 1930s existing buildings add extra dimensions to the school. The joining of the former Boys' and Girls' Schools enables students to freely walk from one side to the other. This is a major development which would have been unheard of in the early life of the school. An offence outlawed even to the staff in the late 1930s and onwards until the co-educational model was introduced.

The school's great rugby tradition is as much

Brett Deacon (Leicester Tigers)

Louis Deacon

Louis Deacon (Leicester Tigers)

alive today as it ever was with brothers Brett and Louis Deacon playing for the Tigers. In May Louis was voted the club's Players' Player of the Year. Louis skippered the Tigers during Martin Corry's World Cup absence and has made one hundred and eighty seven appearances for the club since his debut in 2000.

Joe Mattock (Leicester City F.C.)

Footballing professionals are Lee Cox playing for Leicester City and ace Joe Mattock. Joe has rocked the footballing world with his skill and is expected to make history for his fans. South Wigston High School and Arts College has cause to be proud of

this foursome of sporting heroes.

The Five A Side Football National Champions have also brought fame to the school. The triumphant team of under twelves were, Justin Peace, Mylan Charles, Rob Morgan, Joe Doyle-Charles, Ben Fisher, Callum Blockley, George Parker and Eliot Putman. Four thousand schools entered the competition and this ferocious squad won the title. Watch out for these 'Aces' in the future.

The new arts status will greatly enhance the provision of English, art and design and music. Music it seems has always been so much in need of more finance. Looking back instruments were begged and borrowed in order to build such successful productions. From a mere £25. in the early 1950s Miss Avis Fawcitt built up such a wonderful orchestral group. Today six peripatetic teachers assist the teaching of music yet the subject which gives so much pleasure to musicians and their audiences sadly has lacked the funds it so much deserves.

Education Acts will continue to change and amend as each new government makes its mark on school policies. Leicestershire is renowned for being at the forefront of new ideas too. It was reported in the *Leicester Mercury*, 2008, that teachers and education bosses have backed plans to make Britain's involvement in slavery a mandatory part of the history curriculum for secondary school pupils. The announcement made by the Qualification and Curriculum Authority, QCA, means that from September 2008 reformers such as William Wilberforce and former slave turned campaigner, Olaudah Equiano will be taught to pupils aged eleven to fourteen. This has particular significance for Leicestershire as in 1807 in Rothley, William Wilberforce and Thomas Babington drafted the bill which later led to the abolition of slavery.

The 1920s green curtain exists no more to divide the sexes or the subjects. Musty folds have been slowly drawn and thrown open wide encompassing the world wide web of 'computer land'. Limited floor capacity replaced by cyberspace and with it a window on the universe. A relic from the 1970's, the Mentor, a forerunner to the calculator, was demonstrated by Mr Michael Booth, Assistant Head Teacher. This heavy piece of equipment, now redundant is replaced by pocket size inventions and computer programmes. Schools Maths Project, (SMP) and other Information Technology systems.

Power Point presentations assist use of 'Mult-e-Maths' toolbox and 'Abacus2' learning. Pupils enjoy the maths website which encompasses games and activities with a mathematical content. 'The Maths Trail' is very popular. These aids to teaching provide demonstrations and explanations of a range of maths concepts such as angles, metric units and fractions. Other programmes include 'Sudoku', 'Kakuro' and 'Nubble Express' which aims to provide improvement to numbering skills.

Computer technology is not just confined to maths pupils as other disciplines take full advantage of appropriate programmes. Design and technology, art and science modules and in the music room computer language all helps to enhance teaching and learning. The 'Electro Metro' aid to learning French, 'Smart Board' and 'Task Magic', 'Successmaker' for improving reading and spelling, 'Miracle Maker' DVD's, Visualisers and digital cameras are just a few invaluable tools.

How did our forbears manage without such technological inventions? Each generation professes to be better taught than the last. Argument regarding the standards of examinations or whether children should be tested at all refuses to evaporate. One thing we can all be grateful for in Leicestershire is our extreme good fortune to have had the most eminent, enthusiastic and dedicated Directors of Education to steer policies which they truly believed in, forward.

Since 1949 Professor Pedley lectured in England and abroad on comprehensive education, his ideas in many areas being adopted but there were also many teachers with misgivings. The plan was not universally welcomed by all.

Walking down St. Thomas Road our school looks the same. The fabric remains. One could almost imagine the scene inside but it is deceiving. Its quiet exterior hides the buzz within yet whatever the decade, the purpose is constant. To make of oneself what one can, have social skills and be a valued citizen.

What next can pupils achieve when even the Moon has been conquered? Where will they go from here?

From its inception this must be a question that has passed the lips of many. Alan Blackhurst, (Bushloe High School, Wigston Magna) in the 1978 issue of *'The Leicestershire Plan Today' A journal of ideas and practices in Leicestershire High and Upper Schools'*, was asking the same question then.

'Where do we go from here?' He wrote that since he joined the teaching profession thirty years ago, (1948) *'that some changes in schools have come as products of a changed social and economic structure; others have resulted from, or have been stimulated by, various educational developments such as comprehensive reorganisation, the raising of the school leaving age, the introduction of Nuffield schemes and so on'. He goes on to say that, 'if changes in schools are to be really effective and are to permanently benefit our pupils, they must increasingly originate in the schools themselves and develop from the professional collaboration of 'extraordinary' teachers. Changes or innovations are in the control of teachers in a way that social or economic are not. This is particularly so in a liberal education authority such as Leicestershire where the freedom entrusted to schools enables and encourages teachers to initiate and develop new approaches to teaching and learning'.*

Thirty years on we can look back at the history of South Wigston High School and trace the way in which this philosophy has worked. The people who have been 'extraordinary' the 'innovations' and the 'innovators' which have shaped the lives of many, the battles fought, won and lost again, yet ready to fight the next. Most of all the dedication of staff to the job, the increasing numbers of pupils looking out from the Hall of Fame and today the confident children emerging from its doors. The key word is 'EFFORT'. They are told that they don't have to be the best, they have to do their best. Looking back to Miss C M Wright's words of wisdom in chapter two, 'well rounded, well balanced, confident individuals', this philosophy is not so very different after all.

For all of the children who have not personally been named in this book, look back at those words and **'Be the best that you can be'**.

In fifty years time all of you will recall and relate your school memories. What will you say? What will you write? What new technology will astonish you and your children?

From curtains to computers! What will follow?

The South Wigston High School and Arts College together with it's family of schools marches on with banner flying, It reads,

SUCCESS FOR ALL

'Bon Voyage'.

Head Teachers

South Wigston Secondary Modern Schools with Intermediate Departments 1938 - 1946

South Wigston Secondary Modern Schools 1947 - 1956

South Wigston High School 1957 - 2008

South Wigston High School And Arts College 2008

Boys' School	**Girl's School**
Howard Kenneth Harrison 1938 - 1952	Emma Gertrude Smith 1938 - 1943
Mark Rutherford 1953 - 1963	Edna Walker 1943 - 1963

Coeducational School from January 1964

Mark Rutherford	1964 - 1973
Graham Bowen Norris	1974 - 1981
Eric Duncan Bothamley	1981 - 2000
Gary Leslie Toward	2000 -

Appendix B
Chairmen of Managers and Governors

Arthur William Holmes	1938 - 1957
Curtis Weston	1957 - 1983
Primrose Wray	1983 - 1985
Tim Swift	1985 - 1990
Revd. Ray Gifford	1990 - 1992
Lynn Smith	1992 - 1993
Geoff L Welsh	1993 - 2000
Roy Hughes	2000 -

Curtis Weston and his wife Gertie photographed before leaving for a Buckingham Palace garden party

Appendix C
Governors

Roy Hughes   *Chairman*

Derek Ogden   *Clerk*

Phil Augustus

Linda Brittain

Ann Haughton

Chris Henley

The Revd. Professor
Peter Holmes

Georgina Keene

Pat Long

Mary Machin

Diane Neale

Jenny Nixon

Diane Rushton

Joanne Small

John Small

Shirley Spence

Chris Stokes

Sue Toon

Geoff Welsh

Professor Peter Welton

Mark Wood

Appendix D
Staff

School Manager	Christopher Marsland
Senior Finance Officer	Barbara Sills
Finance Officer	Susan Read
Estate Manager	Mo Orr
Premises Staff	Colin Everington, Martin Orr, Kevin Taylor, John Grady
Partnership Development Manager	Suzanne Woods
Pastoral Tutor	Yvonne Orr
Attendance Officer	Amanda Salmon
Reception Staff	Stephanie Ashby, Caroline Ross
Secretaries	Amanda Salmon, Jenny Nixon, Beverley Whiting

Teaching Staff

Head Teacher	Gary Leslie Toward
Deputy Head Teacher	Shaun Caldwell
Deputy Head Teacher	Jane Corrall
Assistant Head Teacher	Ron Anderson
Assistant Head Teacher	Michael Booth
Head of ICT	Tina Arora
Head of Design, Technology & Art	Phil Augustus
Learning Support	Stephanie Ashby
Languages	Dawn Baker
Science	Lucy Barker
English	Martin Barsby
ICT Technician	Dipan Bhagalia
Mathematics	Claire Bibby
Learning Support Assistant	Mandy Bradbury
Allotment Manager	Ron Bridges
Learning Support	Dave Burbidge
Design Technician/Learning Support	Debra Butteriss
English	Sirina Chaudhury
Physical Education	Richard Clifford
Humanities	Stuart Collison
Library Technician	Jo Delves
Mathematics	Tim Dennington
Mathematics	Stuart Dunford
Head of Modern Foreign Languages	Katia Dunie
Science	Andrew Ferdinando
Learning Support Assistant	Tess Fletcher
Learning Support Teacher	Margaret Fawlds
Physical Education	Jeff Glover
Head of Science	Barrie Gooch
Science	Zoe Hampson
Learning Support Assistant	Jane Hassall
Arts Co-ordinator	Chris Henley
Languages	Peter Heritage
English	Marie Hill
SS/CO Physical Education	Anna Ife
Teacher of Learning Support	Cathy Jones
Learning Support Assistant	Helen King

Art and Design	Chrissie Knight
Head of English and Literacy Co-ordinator	Amanda Langdale
Learning Support Assistant/ Reprographics Assistant	Louise Longton
Learning Support Assistant	Julie Lee-Shield
Learning Support Assistant/ Reprographics Assistant	Alison Love
Reprographics Technician	Lisa Marsden
Library Assistant	Sarah McMahon
Learning Support Assistant	Alisa Meredith
English	Emma Milward
Design/Computer Aided Design	Janine Morris
Physical Education	Tina Morris
Head of Mathematics	Richard Newby
Learning Support Assistant	David Nicholson
Learning Support Assistant	Karen Nicholson
Music	Julian Oakland
Head of Music	Sally Oakland
Learning Support Teacher	Pat Oaten
Learning Support Teacher	Judi Oglesby
Learning Support Assistant	Sandra Robinson
English	Michyla Rossa
Art	Natalie Scully
Humanities	Debbie Sharpe
Learning Support Assistant	Lisa Sheppards
Head of Humanities	Kathryn Smith
Modern Foreign Languages	Nadine Smith
Science Technician	Sandra Smith
Head of Learning Support	Nikki Squires
Design (Textiles)	Claire Stewart
Learning Support Assistant	Rebecca Stokes
Humanities	Norma Terry
Humanities	Robert Utting
Design (Food Technology)	Chetan Vallabh
Science	Charlotte Von Anrep
Learning Support Assistant	Kerrie Walker
ICT Technician	Gareth Williamson
Head of Physical Education	Gail Wood
Cleaning Staff	Ann Allen, Caroline Taylor, Jane Hassall, Angela Woolman Joanne Smith, Jeanette Williams Irene Colver, Robert Colver, Dhankorben de Gouveia, Jack Nixon, Craig Warner Dawn Pawley, Linda Doyle
Kitchen Staff	Karen Downes, Christine Aldred, Tina Jefford, Susan Rowley, Lynda Leatherland, Cynthia Mills, Elizabeth Newman, Mandy McNulty Katherine Darkins, Susan Connolly Tracey Dillon

Appendix E
Hall Of Fame

Camilla Bevans	1996 - 2000	Jeff Kenney	1952 - 1956
Sharon Coe	1975 - 1977	Adele Ladkin	1978 - 1981
Jack Cooper	1932 - 1936	Daniel Lowry	1996 - 2000
Lee Cox	2000 - 2004	Joe Mattock	2000 - 2004
Lance Davis	1940 - 1944	Margaret Nobbs	1944 - 1948
Lorraine Davis	1979 - 1983	Jonathan Norman	1996 - 2000
Keith Davis	1938 - 1940	Alan Norman	1970 - 1974
Roy Davis	1938 - 1939	Kelly Pratt	1992 - 1996
Elsie Dawson	1939 - 1943	Peter Reeves	1945 - 1949
Brett Deacon	1993 - 1997	Arthur Schofield	1936 - 1940
Louis Deacon	1991 - 1995	Derek Seaton	1942 - 1946
David Dryden	1950 - 1953	Cliff Shephard	1946 - 1950
Keith Dunckley	1948 - 1951	Geoffrey Smith	1943 - 1946
Joel Etoe	1990 - 1994	Laura Swann	1927 - 1929
Donald Green	1936 - 1939	John Tipper	1935 - 1939
Jack Green	1943 - 1947	Sue Townsend	1956 - 1960
Alan Gregory	1949 - 1953	Pamela Ward	1953 - 1957
Trevor Hall	1955 - 1959	Geoff Welsh	1966 - 1970
David Hillsdon	1947 - 1951	Tom Welsh	1990 - 1994
Janet Hughes	1948 - 1952	Les Wilson	1940 - 1943
Patrick Hunt	1945 - 1949	Brian Worth	1952 - 1957
Jo Jackson	2000 - 2004		

Bibliography

Baker Denis, Clamp Colin Duckworth Steve, for the Coalville 150 Group	*Coalville*	Stroud	1998
Booth, Michael & Fray, Claudine	*South Wigston High School: The First 50 Years*	South Wigston	1989
Boynton, Helen & Pitches, Grant	*Desirable Locations: Leicester's Middle Class Suburbs 1880 - 1920*	Leicester	1996
Broughton, Gerry	*People in Wigston Magna Portraits of a Community*	Wigston Magna	2000
Campbell, John	*Margaret Thatcher Volume Two: The Iron Lady*	London	2003
Craig, F.W.S.	*British Parliamentary Election Results 1918-1949*	Chichester	1983
Farmer, Stuart & Hands, David	*The Tigers Tale: The Official History of Leicester Football Club 1880-1993*	Leicester	1993
Follows, Stuart & Mastin, Peter	*The Way We Were 111 Years of South Wigston 1883-1994*	South Wigston	1995
Harris, Kenneth Holmes	*A Wartime Diary*	Lutterworth	2001
Higgins, Walter	*Well Wunted: A Leicestershire Lifetime*	Great Glen	1984
Jones, Donald	*Stewart Mason: The Art of Education*	London	1988
Kelly, A.V.	*The Curriculum: Theory and Practice*	London	2005
Lucas, Duncan, Berry, Tricia & Mastin, Peter	*Wigston Magna and South*	Stroud	1997
Mastin, Peter	*South Wigston: The Early Years 1883-1913*	Wigston Magna	1997
Mastin, Peter	*South Wigston: Between the Wars 1914-1945*	Wigston Magna	1997
Pedley, Robin	*The Comprehensive School*	Middlesex	1963
Pinkett, Eric	*A Time To Remember*		1969
Simon, Brian	*Education in Leicestershire*	Leicester	1968
Ward, Pamela	*Wigston At War*	South Wigston	2004

Bibliography - Other Sources

School Records:

Head Teachers' Log Books

The Magazine of the South Wigston Modern School for Girls

The Viking

The Wasp

South Wigston High School News

Acts of Parliament:

Children Act 2004

Elementary Education Act 1880

Education Act 1902

Education Act 1918

Education Act 1970

Education Act 1980

Education Reform Act 1988

Education Act 2002

Education and Inspection Act 2006

Schools Standards and Framework Act 1998

Special Educational Needs and Disability Act 2001

H.M. Inspectors' Reports

The Company History of J. C. Kellett and Son Limited by Lynne Kellett

Kelly's Directories of Leicester 1885, 1904, 1938, 1951

Kelly's Directories of Leicestershire and Rutland 1904, 1925, 1928, 1932, 1941

Leicester Evening Mail

Leicester Mercury

The Advertiser

Illustrated Leicester Chronicle

Oadby & Wigston Advertiser

Oadby & Wigston Mail

Oadby & Wigston News

Leicestershire County Council: Minutes of the County Council and the County Education Committee

Leicestershire Archaeological & Historical Society Transactions

Index